Forays
in France

ALSO BY IRVINA LEW

You Can't Do It All: Ideas That Work for Mothers Who Work

Moms' Survival Guide

In and Around New York

Forays
in France

A FLAVORFUL MEMOIR

— ◆ —

Irvina Lew

PENATAQUIT PRESS

NEW YORK

FIRST EDITION

Designed by Alison Bloomer
Photographs ©ManusiaIkan/adobe.stock.com (page xx),
©Guenter/adobe.stock.com (page 74),
©Richard Semik/adobe.stock.com (page 188)

Library of Congress Cataloging-in-Publication Data has been applied for.
ISBN 979-8-9911416-2-8

2025 2026 2027 2028/10 9 8 7 6 5 4 3 2 1

I AM MOST GRATEFUL TO MY POSSE:

ALISON, SHARON, JENIFER, EMMA, AND SAGE

Contents

foreword
by Marion Fourestier

———◆◆———

Bonjour,

I am the former and recently retired Director of Communications USA of Atout France, aka the France Tourism Development Agency, the sole national organization responsible for the development and promotion of tourism to France with outreach to our French travel industry partners—in this case, Americans.

A French national, I was raised in the United States from the time I was a twenty-month-old, and during a nine-year stint in France, I spent six years in Paris. Most of my career has been in New York, and since 1983, at the French National Tourist Office (FNTO), where for the last twenty years I served as the director of communications.

During that time, I informed Americans working in every sector of the travel industry, and especially the press, about the latest travel developments in France via newsletters, events, and familiarization trips. For me, working at the FNTO was a perfect way to foster a better understanding and appreciation between the two countries I love.

As you have probably surmised, Irvina and I go way back. Irvina is someone who knows what she's talking about and has always done so with gusto. It has been a privilege and joy to work with her and with the travel press in general.

Her newest book, *Forays in France: A Flavorful Memoir*, is an entertaining, in-depth, informative, and very personal travel and food memoir. Irvina's love of France jumps out at you—even as she recounts difficult moments.

Having lived in Paris for six years, her experiences in the city resonate with me. Much like Irvina, I am enthralled by Paris. I remember thinking almost every day about what a beautiful city Paris is, with little surprises and unexpected sights at every turn. Like Irvina, I studied at the Sorbonne near the great Boulevard Saint-Michel and also lived in the neighborhood enjoying its great monuments, like the Panthéon, and mouthwatering market streets such as the rue Mouffetard. I loved her descriptions of all those distinctive Parisian neighborhoods.

I recommend going to Lyon, which she features, and not only because it's a bastion of French cuisine—home of Paul Bocuse and native city of New York's top chef Daniel Boulud—but also because it's one of France's most ancient and beautiful cities, where two powerful rivers meet: the Saône and the Rhône.

Along with Marseille, which also appears in this culinary travelogue, I was very moved by the chapter about Bordeaux and its wine region. My father's side of the family is from the nearby Lot-et-Garonne, and my grandmother is from Bordeaux. As a child, my parents and I would visit my grandparents every one or two years. When I was about six—and I must say, to my dismay—my grandmother proudly brought me to Bordeaux, which was quite a gloomy regional capital back then. As Irvina shares, it has been transformed into a glorious and lively city—one that I now enjoy visiting.

Countless tourists, travel writers, and travel agents learned about these cities and their regions from the Atout France website, france. fr, which shares news about France with consumers and travel professionals: the latest high-speed rail lines and newest hotels, its architectural heritage, agricultural innovations, lesser-known French destinations, and food and wine trails.

For the past twelve years, I particularly enjoyed producing video presentations for the travel press to announce the news of the upcoming year and highlight unfamiliar areas of France. The latest, shown in the fall of 2023, was the "Top Reasons to Visit France in 2024"—also shown to the travel trade and to American consumers.

On that note, the personal vignettes in *Forays in France* go beyond the "news" and give the prospective traveler—or armchair reader—the author's sense of passion about the people, foods, and places.

Our agency's efforts were also aimed at trying to clarify some of the misunderstandings and preconceptions resulting from the cultural differences between France and the United States, both warmly related Western countries. It is with great relief and pleasure that I can say that these issues are a thing of the past and have been for quite some time now.

As I reflect on my career, I'm very proud of certain contributions and innovations. The U.S. bureau of Atout France was the first to introduce social media and, in the 1990s, to create a comprehensive website for American travelers to further inform consumers and the travel trade. I influenced writers like Irvina to become more knowledgeable about France and develop an affection that she shares with readers. Irvina and I are not alone in that affection.

France has been the world's number one travel destination for more than twenty years and has the ambition of becoming the world's number one sustainable travel destination by 2030.

I invite you to enjoy Irvina's France and hope that her memoir will encourage you to discover—or return to—France, so that we can warmly welcome you—our American friends—and say "Bienvenue."

un premier mot
(a first word)

MY LATEST FORAY IN FRANCE TOOK PLACE IN MAY 2025 and reaffirmed a truth discovered young: France is my happy place. This certainty has been the case since I was a nineteen-year-old student at the Sorbonne and continues still.

I was a Francophile before I knew the word, listened to Yves Montand, or read Antoine de Saint-Exupéry's *The Little Prince*. Mademoiselle Julie Franchi, my high school French teacher, introduced me to France in ninth grade and to world history in tenth, with a curriculum that undoubtedly included dates, wars, and revolutions, though my takeaways were art, architecture, faraway places, and extraordinary people.

As a freshman at the College of William & Mary in Williamsburg, Virginia, where Thomas Jefferson is a "living" legend, I learned that the Founding Father loved France and French wine, information that influenced my decision to major in French, study in Paris, and teach French. The language played a central role in college, during a thirty-three-year teaching career, on visits to France, and at restaurants, as a freelance food writer. Let me tell you how that happened.

I started teaching at twenty, about a month after graduating college in three years and three summers and just six weeks after my husband, Bob Lew, and I welcomed our first child. By the time I was thirty, Alison was ten, Sharon seven, and Jenifer two, all redheads like their father and me. When my colleagues started having babies and needed advice, my girls were thriving as teens.

The tips that I shared with my coworkers helped them through that busy time, changed my focus, and initiated a book designed for working moms. Years later, while being interviewed by a prospective literary agent, he questioned: "Have you ever been published?" I said "No," but realized that published clips would help. I immediately started pitching article ideas to editors about what I knew best: boating, feminism, food, mothering, and teens. I submitted op-ed pages to *Newsday* and the *New York Times* and soon contributed to various magazines, including *New York Nightlife*, where, as dining editor, I featured five restaurants a month and four spas a year for the next five years.

In 1986, MacMillan published *You Can't Do It All: Ideas That Work for Mothers Who Work* and organized an eight-city book tour; Berkley published the paperback. Someone on the Moms' Campaign team for Ziploc Storage Bags noticed an excerpt in *Ladies' Home Journal* and asked me to be their national spokesperson. I did three annual Back to School and Mother's Day media tours, for which I took personal days from school. It felt natural to talk on radio or TV shows about how Ziploc storage bags help organize children's swim, scout, or baseball gear, because I always used them to keep clothes dry on sailing trips.

Later, Contadina Pasta Ready hired me as their spokesperson and trained me to say: "The tomatoes are picked and packed within minutes," a phrase that came in handy during a cooking demonstration on the Food Network. Donna Hanover treated me graciously, but when her cohost, David Rosengarten, questioned using "canned" tomatoes for sauce, I spouted it to assure their freshness.

With that exception, every minute of those tours was a thrill. The experience also triggered a strategy to retire from teaching as soon as I could secure my pension and health benefits and become a full-time freelancer writing about what I loved: food, spas, and travel.

That peripatetic freelance life started when I retired in February 1994 and lasted until the pandemic shutdown in March 2020. I absolutely adored the research, the travel, and seeing my articles in print. The teen who found her happy place in Paris, blossomed as a woman, wife, mother, teacher, author, spokesperson, and freelancer.

During those years, I often traveled to France—and elsewhere— without Bob, who had a business to operate. It was a choice that garnered criticism way back when. Having moved from home to college to married life before twenty, I was almost fifty when I first experienced the joys of solitude. And whenever I traveled with others, I made it a habit to add two nights alone to do what I liked best: sip, sup, stay, spa. Some claim it's "gutsy" to travel solo. Perhaps, but it's doable and satisfying.

Some of my best trips were with Bob; each of our daughters; granddaughter Emma; and oldest grandniece, Lyndsey. I also vacationed with friends, most often with my childhood pal, Val.

I've toured France by car, plane, and van; on one riverboat and three uber-slow, four-mile-per-hour barge cruises; three-week-long Mediterranean cruises; and by ferry from Cannes to Saint-Tropez. I can't count the number of high-speed trips I've taken on the *Trains à Grande Vitesse* (TGV); they travel at about 185 miles per hour and are my favorite way to get from Paris to other destinations. My most unforgettable rail excursion was the slow journey on the over-the-top Venice Simplon-Orient-Express from Venice to London, with an overnight in Monte Carlo and a pause for passengers—and provisions—in Paris.

The school calendar determined my travel schedule for three decades. Once free of the academic routine, I booked midweek flights in off-peak seasons with mileage award points. I jam-packed activities on weeklong jaunts, staying in different hotels every, or every other, night, because I was determined to discover the next magical village, the most charming inn, the newest "best" chef before I rushed back to Bob.

After fifty years of marriage, I was widowed in 2008, which was bizarre, abnormal, appalling, and altogether new. I couldn't say three words without crying about the man who had been the center of my universe; the loss was life-changing. One challenge was to keep grief from smothering joy.

For as long as I can remember, I had resolved to live "to the max" and in the moment. Even fifteen years earlier, I was musing out loud about making the most of my post-teaching career. I asked the principal, Steve Howland, "What will they write on my gravestone?" He quipped, "Here's Irvina, she knew how to live!"

I embraced the credo: "Make lemonade from lemons!" In France, I often enjoyed *citron pressé*, a lemonade made by juicing lemons, adding water and, perhaps, some sugar. That act of juicing reminded me of the Spanish word *disfrutar*, which translated means "to enjoy." Yet, the spirit of the word connotes the far more proactive motion of squeezing every bit of juice—not just from fruit but from life. To me, *disfrutar* is the essence of *joie de vivre*. It's how I choose to live. So the goal of my recovery after Bob passed was to feel elation again.

I started the search for my smile, which spontaneously reemerges in France, where I linger, now that there's no reason to hurry home. In 2018, I discovered the comfort of a three-week apartment rental in Juan-les-Pins; the following year, Val suggested renting in Cannes, which was so nice that we scouted for another rental for May 2020.

Travel stopped in mid-March and they canceled due to Covid.

My online calendar still lists the flight to Nice and emails log the reminders, though none were necessary. The Covid shutdown provoked conflicting feelings and fears, confusion, worry, and sorrow. I also felt grateful for three children living nearby, good health, a secure retirement income, and living in a home with easy—and safe—access to the outdoors. And I felt guilty, because my disappointment about a canceled trip was totally out of proportion to the overwhelming global tragedy.

After travel came to a complete halt, I truly wondered if I would ever write about it again. For years, I hadn't been home in May to see white irises bloom; in 2020, when they emerged, Van Gogh and Arles came to mind. That summer's Fourth of July fireworks evoked memories of 14 Juillet (Fête Nationale) in Paris. When golden sunflowers crowned deep plastic pails at the farmers market, my memories meandered through Provence. As September approached, I recalled a Labor Day flight, and an inimitable 2018 harvest in Burgundy.

I've heard about "muscle memory" and wonder if something similar exists for the mind.

While housebound, I "organized" and combed through cardboard cartons that survived Superstorm Sandy in October 2012. I retrieved notes recorded in more than fifty 5-by-7-inch spiral notebooks, emptied dozens of white cardboard magazine holders filed by destination on my office shelves, and found my 1958 trip diary, as well as itineraries, brochures, maps, and cookbooks that I had collected. I opened a large plastic storage box on my closet floor, which contained a collection of oversize menus, many signed and dated by Michelin-star chefs. I also found a paper carton stuffed with hundreds of clips from the pre-PDF era, and picked through to find the ones about France, which jogged my memory; some evoked a clearly defined image.

With forty-thousand images in my Mac photo library, I would input a date certain to find *marchés*, *cafés*, *pique-niques* in France and images of desserts. There were portraits, too, in a garden with my youngest, at the table with a friend, or posing with a chef. I spent hours studying our old passports, deciphering dates on faded entry stamps to learn where I went when; I used the data to create an Excel sheet of travel dates.

Each new piece of information motivated me to begin the long-postponed travel memoir that I had promised myself to write, if/when I stayed home for an extended period. Who could have guessed that the pandemic that grounded us all, gifted me with time to remember an unlimited number of France-inspired memories and to write?

Whatever the weather, I stayed at my desk, writing about walks rather than taking them, thinking about a towpath, a riverside quay, a narrow cobblestone street. Words grew into vignettes; interactions with remarkable people turned into anecdotes that accumulated into chapters, parts, a book.

The stories describe contact with people whom I could never have hoped to meet without venturing from home; most reveal a budget that has always been more limited than what I'd prefer, which is why I depend on award mileage for flights and I book rooms in sweet two-star lodgings, at the "little place next door" and, rarely, at five-star hotels. At home, I eat out sparingly; in France, I splurge on the occasional fine-dining lunch, because for me, gastronomy is as much about the cultural immersion, artistic creativity, and a theatrical energy as it is about eating. My spending habits mimic how I eat: healthfully 90 percent of the time; indulging 10 percent of the time.

Thanks to some lucky writing assignments and serendipitous invitations, I've also been privy to a few extraordinary experiences. I will introduce you to people whom I've met in magnificent venues: some are chefs, who have moved on or passed away, and some of the places may no longer exist, but the majority that I remember glowingly still are superb.

Traveling alone or with a friend is particularly interesting now, as an octogenarian, because I've repeatedly met younger women who say variations of this: "I hope to live it up like you when I'm your age!" It's happened at a fashionable cabaret in Paris, on a bench in Cannes, and even on train trips, and it makes me wonder. Do younger women fear losing out on fun late in life? I believe they do and think that they need to see more role models of happy women living big.

On another note, I've added a few extras in the text to enhance your next trips:

- *un peu plus* (a little extra): brief descriptions of special people and places or historical factoids
- *chez moi* (at my house): my interpretations of some favorite French dishes
- *mes bonnes idées* (my good ideas): a chapter filled with my practical and personal "if you go" travel tips

My forays in France have enhanced my life and I wish the same for you, whatever your age or your travel preferences.

Salut!
Irvina

PARIS

———◆•◆———

"Paris is always a good idea," said Audrey Hepburn in the movie *Sabrina*. I agree. Paris conjures up notions of gastronomy, glamour, grandeur—words that evoke splendid visions of this cultural capital. They entice folks who, like me, are drawn to beauty and are enthralled by the city's imposing historical monuments, architecturally significant buildings, world-class art museums, illustrious dining establishments, one-of-a-kind art boutiques, glorious gardens, impressive rooftop terraces, over-the-top nightclubs, and yachts on the Seine.

Women, especially, appreciate these emblematic venues and the City of Light's reputation as a center for fashion and romance. Not so long ago, research indicated that 61 percent of Americans who visit Paris are women. I'm proud to be one of them. I'll never be a local or an insider, but it's good enough to be a tourist, a repeat visitor, a flâneuse (one who strolls languidly and observes).

The pandemic gave me time to process countless visits to Paris, where I feel so completely comfortable.

On one long-ago trip, Val and I breakfasted at the same café each day on busy rue Saint-Honoré, a distinctly chic street on the Right Bank lined with boutiques. On Day 1, we ordered coffee and croissants and were treated courteously. Day 2, the server smiled when he brought the order. Day 3, the server noticed us at the door, readied our usual request, and greeted us warmly when he delivered it to the table.

That experience reminds me of an ancient Pakistani adage, in which a Tibetan explained: "The first time you share tea with a Balti, you are a stranger. The second time you take tea, you are an honored guest. The third time you share a cup of tea, you become family."

That's how I feel in the capital. With its tree-lined boulevards, medieval to Haussmann-style architecture, and majestic riverside charms, I find an intensity of loveliness beyond any other place. For me, the city is like a gift waiting to be unwrapped, with every street offering its own special surprise: a secret garden, a pedestrian passageway, a courtyard.

Post-Pandemic Paris

———◆•◆———

FROM THE START OF THE COVID SHUTDOWN—WHICH LEFT an absolute void where a social life should have been—I called my nearest and dearest during "cocktail hour." The French call the predinner drink hour *apéro*, and relax with *les aperitifs*, as did I. At five, I stopped writing, left my office, poured myself a glass of white wine, sat on my comfy sofa with glass in hand, and dialed.

I often chatted with my most frequent travel partner, Val—friends since we were ten years old. At the beginning of the pandemic, our conversations focused on whether we'd be willing to travel to Cannes that May for our second apartment rental, but it was a wasted effort. Almost immediately, in mid-March 2020, the landlord returned our deposit and canceled "due to Covid."

We never asked, where to? or what next?; instead, we questioned: When?

Spring 2020 passed, as did summer, fall, and winter. A year later, we realized that we would not see summer in Cannes; instead, we'd head to Paris as soon as American travelers were welcome in France. We hoped that mid-October 2021 would be safe—thankfully it was—and planned a three-week trip mostly in Paris, with

3

three nights in Champagne, an overnight in Versailles, and the final night at the airport.

We searched online while talking on the phone together trying to find hotels in our favorite walkable neighborhoods: the historic 1st arrondissement; the lively 6th in Saint-Germain-des-Prés; and the sophisticated 8th near the Champs-Élysées. We found, booked, changed, canceled, and rebooked reservations.

In the end, we added a couple of far more beautiful hotels than we first imagined: the grand Prince de Galles, a Luxury Collection Hotel, on Avenue George V in the 8th (where the concierge arranged our dinner reservations and recommended the pharmacy where Val got tested to obtain the required QR code).

Post-Covid fears persisted that fall, but the restrictions in France were reassuring because they guaranteed that everyone had been vaccinated. It didn't seem to bother anyone to show QR-code proof of vaccinations everywhere, or wear masks, and we sat outdoors whenever possible.

Having visited Paris together and separately for decades, we each had our own preferences about what we would do once there. Two mutual priorities were to tour the Palais Garnier Opera House and visit the Fondation Louis Vuitton, where she'd never been. Val wanted to return to the Louvre; I always visit the Orangérie, to pay homage to Monet's *Water Lilies*; and we both wanted to return to Musée d'Orsay. Val had never been to the Rodin Museum, where I once sat and read in the garden; because I hadn't been there since it reopened in 2015, after a four-year closure for its $17.4 million renovation, we decided to add it to our list.

When we visited the museum, a light-filled urban villa, with its parquet flooring and ornate ceilings, we stared at the emphatically erotic *The Kiss* and admired some of the sculptor's three hundred

4

works, including *Clasped Hands*, and lingered in the room dedicated to sculptor Camille Claudel, with whom he had a long relationship. In the outside garden, *Le Penseur*—an intense monsieur in bronze—is deep in thought. The stark pain in the faces of the six condemned *Burghers of Calais* is uncomfortable to witness.

un peu plus: MUSÉE RODIN

The Rodin Museum villa sits amid gardens and was constructed between 1727 and 1732 and named for the owner, Peyrenc de Moras. In the 1880s, it became Hôtel Biron. Early in the 1900s, artists were allowed to use the space until a new owner bought it, and writer Jean Cocteau, artist Henri Matisse, dancer Isadora Duncan, and others had studios there. So did sculptor Clara Westhoff, who informed Rodin about the property. Only Rodin was permitted to live and work there after the estate was officially sold to the French government in 1911, and the artist was so eager to spend the rest of his life working there that he negotiated with the government.

"I give the State all my works in plaster, marble, bronze, and stone, and my drawings, as well as the collection of antiquities that I had such pleasure in assembling for the education and training of artists and workers. And I ask the State to keep all these collections in the Hôtel Biron, which will be the Musée Rodin, reserving the right to reside there all my life."

A year before he died, in 1916, officials voted to create the Rodin Museum, although the building wasn't in good shape. With seven hundred thousand annual museumgoers, it deteriorated substantially over the next century, which made the multimillion-dollar renovation necessary.

Whether sculpture—or gardens—excite you or not, the serenity of the location, with close-up views of the Eiffel Tower and the golden dome of Les Invalides (where I had sketched the head of Napoleon in my diary in 1958), is worth the visit.

As for meals, we usually breakfast at our hotels and lunch at whatever convenient café, bistro, brasserie, or *boulangerie* (bakery) is appealing. After about eighteen months homebound, we were ready to splurge on eating out.

We both tried online from home but couldn't access a reservation for the Cheval Blanc hotel's newly launched, panoramic seventh-floor restaurant, Le Tout-Paris, which overlooks the Seine river from Nôtre-Dame to the Eiffel Tower. I sent an email to the concierge at our first hotel, who arranged that table and one for CoCo, where the late-night cabaret takes place within a striking room inside the Palais Garnier Opera House. (The host offered us—*dames d'un certain age*—a table under a staircase in the back and outside the main dining room. Not acceptable! Once we were seated at an appropriate table, we had a great evening.) Val also had her heart set on going back to the trendy Girafe, where she had dined on the terrace viewing the Eiffel Tower. (It was still glamorous in November, even with the terrace closed.)

We ate at two gastronomic restaurants: L'Écrin at Hôtel de Crillon, a little jewel of a Michelin one-star inside one of my favorite hotels, and at Le Gabriel at La Réserve.

LE GABRIEL

At Le Gabriel, where executive chef Jérôme Banctel has since earned a third Michelin star, we dined in a quietly posh room with parquet floor, monochromatic leather-wrapped columns and dividers, and walls embossed in a floral pattern, and at a table set with Lalique water glasses and embossed linen napkins monogrammed with the owner's elephant-R logo. Our five-course meal—a seasonal culinary journey through Brittany—featured the chef's favorite producers, and wine pairings with the owner's wines, including *Michel Reybier Champagne Brut Premier Cru, Cos d'Estournel 2017*. (In 2024, the four-course Escale lunch was priced at 98€; many others were double.)

LE RELAIS DE L'ENTRECÔTE

While we were staying at Hotel Bel Ami, in Saint-Germain-des-Prés, I noticed long lines across the street every noon and early evening, with patrons waiting to enter Le Relais de l'Entrecôte. It was not among the concierge's recommendations when I was staying alone there in 2018, and I usually try to avoid lines anyway, so I didn't bother to try it. In 2021, my curiosity prevailed when one late afternoon there were only a handful of people waiting for the doors to open. Val and I decided to join them, just to see what made the place so popular.

It became obvious before the meal's end: the fixed price *formule* dates to 1959. The meal included a walnut-studded salad; tender sliced steak with a mustardy cream sauce; hot matchstick fries; a choice of desserts; complimentary second and third portions of anything; plus, a very pleasing, owner-produced Château de Saurs wine. If you don't mind feeling a bit *pressé* (rushed), it's a good value for about 40€ at the six Paris locations.

Planning that 2021 itinerary jump-started a zillion memories dating from my first summer in Paris in 1958.

6 rue Gay-Lussac

———◆•◆———

LOCATION, LOCATION, LOCATION. THAT WAS THE BEST thing about 6 rue Gay-Lussac. I was one of only two French majors at Adelphi University who decided to study at the Sorbonne during the summer; my classmate Linda was the other. We opted for a rooming house just three short blocks from the University of Paris in the Student Quarter on the bustling *Rive Gauche* (Left Bank), in the 5th arrondissement. There are twenty numbered districts in Paris and the number indicates its age and proximity to the 1st (premier) arrondissement, which is the oldest *quartier* (neighborhood).

Before finding my 1958 trip diary during the pandemic, I mused-from-memory about the room we shared in a 2008 article about Paris that I found in a box salvaged after Superstorm Sandy flooded my office in 2012. Only the first paragraph of the piece in *The Charlotte Observer's SouthPark* magazine was legible: "My tiny room on the Left Bank at 6 rue Gay-Lussac had a sink and a bidet, but the 'toilette-in-a-closet' was down the hall. The tub was in a large room on the second floor, the *premièr étage*. To bathe, I had to make a formal reservation with Madame, the landlady, and carry my toiletries and towels down the steep spiral staircase."

Madame

Our landlady lived on the ground floor with her cat, and dressed entirely in black, in a long housedress that reached the tops of her sensible shoes. Her thick cotton stockings showed only when she bent down to pick up the dustpan or scrub brush. She scoured the front hallway floors on her hands and knees and swept the sidewalk daily, and had red and wrinkled hands from her labors. Madame locked the outside door by 10:30 p.m., just as the housemothers had done in my all-girls' dormitory at William & Mary. Twice, when Linda and I came home late and had to ring the entry bell, the little lady scuffled to the door in slippers mumbling words that weren't part of my limited vocabulary.

We called her "Madame," with the respect she deserved, but I never bothered to learn her name or ask about the poignant stories that I'm sure she could have told. In retrospect, I'm certain that she had suffered wartime hardships because, once, she stopped me to ask a question. "Mademoiselle, *est-ce que vous avez du savon eeevohree?*" (do you have Ivory soap). I wasn't familiar with the word *savon*, but I did recognize what *eeevohree* was and gave her whatever soap bars I had brought from home. Madame still considered American soap a treasure, years after Paris was liberated (August 1944) and the war ended (September 1945).

That summer of 1958 took place during *Les Trente Glorieuses* (1945–1975), and wartime losses—and shortages—were still fresh in people's memories. The thirty glorious years referred to an era of economic recovery, but I am convinced that the lack of goods that she had experienced had become ingrained in Madame's consciousness. It probably even influenced her rates. Although the room was certainly affordable by American standards, she charged half that amount to use the tub in the one bathroom that had one. I never

9

saw anyone else use that bathroom during the months that I was there; either the cost was exorbitant or bathing just wasn't a "thing." I assumed the latter.

The American shower-a-day routine didn't seem to me to be part of the local lifestyle, because most young people had long, greasy hair and almost every French girl had unshaven legs and armpits. I clearly recall the pervasive mélange of body odor and over-applied cheap cologne. I recognized one perfumed scent on the hot summer streets; it was the same Jean Naté eau de toilette that Joyce, one of my suitemates at William & Mary, lavishly sprayed on herself when she didn't bother taking a shower before dressing for dinner. When she was ready to leave for the dining hall, she gaily shouted: "We can go now, I've had my 'whore's bath'!"

When I found my original trip diary during the Covid cleanup, the posts revived memories. Tiny is always the first word that comes to mind to describe that corner bedroom, yet this entry in my diary, dated July 3, 1958, reads: "We sent our friends Marty and Mike and two others down to buy wine, cheese, and bread for a little pre–July Fourth party." I don't remember any of them, but obviously the room was big enough for the six of us.

My notes about the pension "Hotel d'Athènes—we call it home . . ." reveal that "we bought a hot plate and the neatest little fridge," plus some "big things," including "extra appliances: 1,625 francs." (I can't verify the francs-to-dollars exchange, but it vastly favored Americans.)

Another long-ago article described the view from our balcony: "The best part of my room was the black wrought-iron balcony, which wrapped around the entire floor and, from which—*if* I leaned over the rail and looked down the street and beyond the Luxembourg Gardens—I could view la Tour Eiffel . . . in the distance."

What I wrote about the view, contemporaneously at age nineteen, was a bit more dramatic: "There was the Eiffel Tower in full view standing in the sunset—we can see it so clearly from our room— and it is so beautiful. It stands there now, all lit up, and I feel as if my eyes looking at it are touching a dream come true. I've become sentimental again, tonight. I've been studying the Parisians, the language—everywhere I go—and I'm in love with the music of their tongue, with Bob, and with my parents, whom I long to tell how much all this means to me . . ." Perhaps a little wine was involved?

Summer at the Sorbonne

My roomie's uncle had an influential position at General Motors and had arranged VIP treatment for his darling niece: a driver met us at the train and delivered us to our front door in a huge new automobile. That evening, Gaby, a second chauffeur and the one I remember best, toured us around the city in a Cadillac Biarritz convertible with the top down. It was amazing. Then, he took us to dinner in a small storefront bistro where the large plastic-covered menu had a bright sun on the front and these words in bold, colorful letters: *un jour sans vin, c'est un jour sans soleil* (a day without wine is a day without sunshine).

I didn't recognize most of the items offered on that menu, but, when I spotted coq au vin, I relaxed. Chicken in wine sauce was a familiar dish, one that I recalled having eaten at Maude Chez Elle, in Manhattan, when my French teacher, who was also the high school yearbook advisor, treated me to lunch to celebrate my work as 1956 editor-in-chief. It was my first French restaurant meal but I remember the drive as vividly; my mentor made a hard-right turn north, going uptown on Broadway, and I stared, terrified, into an onslaught of traffic headed one way south, going downtown. My heart raced, but she recovered without incident, parked, and when we were seated, pointedly shared information about one former, unidentified editor who had ordered a burger with ketchup. A near-miss accident didn't impact her message: I was clearly expected to eat à la française!

Back in Paris, the coq au vin was fine, but food wasn't what made the night unforgettable: it was the wine. I was not a drinker and had never drunk wine with dinner. Gaby ordered a bottle of red wine and refilled my glass; he ordered a second bottle and poured more. I tried to make pleasant conversation in imperfect French, but even before dessert, I started giggling and couldn't stop. Back in the room, I was so homesick that I cried myself to sleep and slept so soundly that I barely heard the alarm the next morning, when we had to register for class.

Though the school was only a five-minute walk away, Linda's uncle had arranged for yet another chauffeur to take us to register, and he was waiting for us at the front door in a boat-length, ultra-luxe Buick. As thrilling as it had been the previous night to see the sights with the top down, this felt uncomfortable. As he drove on the narrow, medieval streets next to diminutive Peugeots and Renaults, the vehicle was glaringly oversize and from the back seat, we were clearly noticeable to students perched on *motocyclettes*. We became even more self-conscious when he stopped and we had to step out of the elongated, space-age, fin-adorned automobile directly into a crowd of kids our age. In retrospect, they were gawking at the show-stopping car and so captivated that they probably didn't even notice us, because in those days the French admired everything American, particularly from General Motors, which was then the preeminent American corporation.

Rive Gauche (Left Bank)

Our classes took place in a large rectangular building near the domed Sorbonne, which opened in the thirteenth century as the University of Paris and includes a seventeenth-century church. En route there and back, we could see an even more significant landmark: the stunning, column-studded, dome-topped Panthéon, which was built in the 1700s by architect Jacques-Germain Soufflot, who is buried there along with many notable national figures, including philosophers François-Marie Arouet (Voltaire) and Jean-Jacques Rousseau; blind inventor Louis Braille; authors Victor Hugo and Émile Zola; the political figure Jean Jaurès; World War II French Resistance leader Jean Moulin; and, finally, in 1995, the first female, Marie Curie, the physicist/chemist.

That short walk "home" from school to our building's squared-off, narrow tip, which was on one of six little corners where three cross streets met, was my favorite until I arrived inside the entry hall, where I avoided the old-fashioned, glass-sided, two-person mini-elevator. I had once been stuck in a Manhattan elevator and was already claustrophobic, so I usually walked up the spiral staircase to my room on the *quatrième étage* (fifth floor). (I still avoid being inside a little box with a folding metal door.)

From our room, I could hear people gather twice a week, whenever a white minivan would pull up on rue Royer-Collard, the side street below one window. The vendor—a farmer with a ruddy face topped with a dark beret—would open the back and side doors and the van instantly transformed into a mini mobile market. Whenever it arrived, I ran down the stairs, because if I didn't hurry, he'd be gone within minutes. The man was pleasant but *pressé*, and he took as little time as possible with each shopper so he could slam shut the openings and move on to the next stop. That farmer/vendor introduced me to the best farm-fresh produce, and I purchased anything I recognized that I could eat raw and, usually, with my fingers: ripe berries, perfect peaches, yummy pears, and crisp *haricots verts*. While waiting for my turn to pay, I imagined him happier at home in his fields and envisioned him munching on a baguette slathered with sweet butter and topped with thinly sliced baby radishes.

A major high point that summer was having my first dream in French. I woke up grinning, as if I had achieved some colossal access to fluency. Speaking French was just one part of the cultural immersion. The program also provided guided tours of the Louvre by day, and a private *visite* after dark. There was also a trip by boat to the Sèvres porcelain factory, where I was mesmerized by the artisans at work, diminutive brushes in hand, deftly painting on chinaware; on another occasion, we took a bus to a Renault factory outside the city, where the assembly lines so intrigued me that I've since gone out of my way—in Detroit and elsewhere—to tour automobile factories.

Excursions were great, but walking—as everyone does in Paris— put me face-to-face with neighboring historic landmarks that I learned about in high school, not only the Sorbonne and the Pantheon but also the Cluny Museum and Notre-Dame.

Our prime location smack in the center of the student quarter was also just a short half-block from its major north-south artery, Boulevard Saint-Michel, where my city adventures started. And, because the school session ended at lunchtime, we had hours to wander through long afternoons and late-night sunsets. Boul'Mich, as the street is known, was teeming with bookstores, mom-and-pop shops, low-cost café terraces, a cafeteria where they displayed food, and a teeny street-level shop with a window that opened onto the sidewalk, where I remember buying sugar-topped crèpes. These days, you'll notice international brand names—Sephora, Gap, Starbucks, and Burger King—along with the mom-and-pop stores.

I often headed toward the Pont Saint-Michel, the bridge that crosses the Seine to Île de la Cité, one of two islands in the Seine, where Paris began as the Roman outpost of Lutetia in 52 BCE and from which the city expanded to the left and right banks. I always passed the Cluny Museum, which was built on the remnants of third-century Roman baths and houses a collection of medieval art, including the famous Lady of the Unicorn tapestries, which were reinterpreted at Relais Bernard Loiseau.

ÎLE DE LA CITÉ

Once that summer, on a walk to Île de la Cité, I viewed the fifteen fabulous mid-thirteenth-century stained-glass windows and the fifteenth-century rose window in Sainte-Chapelle, the little Gothic chapel. More often, though, I visited the most important monument in the neighborhood, the Cathédral of Nôtre-Dame, for which construction started in 1163. I used to make a small donation, light a candle, and sit in a pew staring as the sunlight streamed in through the rose windows; I never climbed to the tower. Nôtre-Dame's architecture, history, and beauty always impressed me from inside or out, whether staring at the façade from the square or the spires and flying buttresses from a *peniche* (barge) or, recently, from a restaurant terrace at Cheval Blanc. The cathedral was in daily use from the time of its completion, c. 1345, and during historic occasions, such as Napoleon's memorable coronation on December 2, 1804, when he took the crown out of the pope's hand and placed it upon his own head, until the devastating fire in 2019. It reopened in December 2024, and I joyfully attended the first organ concert in January 2025.

un peu plus: MEMORIAL DES MARTYRS DE LA DÉPORTATION

I was first informed about The Memorial to the Martyrs of the Deportation, dedicated to the 200,000 deportees during World War II, by journalist Linda Gould, whom I met in Bordeaux in 2007. During lunch, she told me that just behind the cathedral, in the minuscule garden right on the teeny tip of the island, there's a lesser-known, emotionally moving monument, which she had researched for a 1972 feature in the *New York Times.* It reads: "a monument to the men, women and children—principally Jewish—who were arrested and herded into cattle cars to be interned in Nazi concentration camps during the German occupation of France between 1940 and 1945."

Linda's sincere concern for the martyrs, the fact that she had been published in the *New York Times,* and that she was traveling on her eightieth birthday shortly after a knee replacement impressed and inspired me. My reaction was substantially different from the other, younger journalists we were with at lunch who ignored her and the aged *patron* (owner); he had earlier shared stories about what had taken place during his Resistance-era childhood. Their ageist disdain reminded me of what my feminist activist friend once warned: "Sexism? You haven't seen anything until you deal with ageism." But I digress. Be assured, I paid my respects at the memorial the next time I visited Paris.

Rive Droite (Right Bank)

In 1958, I often ventured beyond the second bridge across the Seine from *Île de la Cité* to the Right Bank and the centerpiece of the 1st arrondissement: the twelfth-century fortress that became a palace for King Louis XIV and the famous Louvre Museum. And I learned the bus and metro routes to get to other places on the Rive Droite, such as the belle époque l'Opéra, where I climbed the graceful staircase and saw a performance of *La Traviata*. We also climbed the stairs of l'Arc de Triomphe at the *Étoile,* the star-shaped circle, to admire the sweeping views of the twelve avenues that radiate from it and the mile-plus-long Champs-Élysées.

On 14 juillet (July 14), the legal name of the national holiday, which can be called Fête Nationale but not Bastille Day, we watched the parade on the Champs-Élysées commemorating the fall of the Bastille prison in 1789. We mingled with crowds at the Champ-de-Mars, the green space that extends for blocks under la Tour Eiffel. Crowds didn't bother me a bit back then; now, I'm claustrophobic in crowds, even when outdoors.

And I admired the amazingly gorgeous shop windows, where I appreciate beauty but rarely care about owning what's on display. The most notable exception occurred in 1958, when I was browsing on my own and stopped and stared open-mouthed at a certain shop window. I saw a "must-have" elongated, oval-shaped turquoise leather bag, plus a pair of matching gloves draped over it. I also gasped and ogled at an olive-green suede belt presented alongside a thin matching suede tie. I returned again and again and coveted them; finally, I got up the nerve to enter the store and ask to see them. I left the store with a simple "Merci, Madame. Au revoir, Madame" and having already described the goodies in a letter to my parents, I had the *chutzpah* to call home long-distance (a costly rarity), and ask my folks to send money enough for all four items. That Yiddish word is the best one I know to express how nervy I was, and I still can't believe I asked and that they sent it! The boutique was called Hermès. I had never heard the name, and my mom would certainly not have recognized it.

I still treasure that precious bag almost sixty-five years later, and I am convinced that first child, Alison, feels the same about the matching gloves I gave her. (Used Hermès gloves are listed online at $300; who knows what the price is for a vintage bag.) As for their father's olive-green suede tie, one daughter (I have my suspicions) cut a patch out of it for some project, and he outgrew the belt, which he probably gave away. (I didn't buy another Hermès accessory until my sixtieth birthday, in Lyon, which I'll get to later.)

Culture Shock

At age nineteen, boys were the biggest nuisance to me. Young men routinely called out "Marry me!" on the street. I doubt that my beauty made me such an object of desire, but from the number of "proposals," it felt as if every Parisian wanted US citizenship via marriage. Maybe they recognized us as American by our clothes, accessories, or by listening to us speak; they just knew. I tried to look younger by wearing bobby socks and less voluptuous in big, baggy tops. In retrospect, my efforts may have backfired because I probably looked more American than before. In any case, they never stopped staring at my breasts, and some guys continued to move in out of nowhere and pinch my butt, which made me furious.

This bothersome behavior began even before getting to Paris, when I boarded the SS *Liberté* in New York Harbor, six weeks before the summer semester started, to sail to Liverpool. I had to follow a steward to my lower-level stateroom. He walked down long corridors, opened each heavy fire door, stepped aside so I could pass, and grabbed my tush each time. I yelled "STOP!" He just grinned!

In Italy, where Linda and I spent two weeks before classes, I had been pinched on the street so often that I was ready to clobber anyone who dared touch me. In Rome, the *pensione* owner's son—and supposed helper—barged into our bathroom, unexpectedly, while I was showering. For the next four days, one of us stood guard at the bathroom door, holding a towel in front of its frosted-glass window, while the other showered and dressed. In Milan, two guys followed and disturbed us as we were walking back to our hotel; after we entered, they lingered outside and shouted up to us. Once in our room, I filled a vase with hot water and dumped it out the window on their heads!

As confirmed in that 1958 diary, I borrowed Linda's umbrella to take on walks as protection. I'd had enough. I didn't know about sexual harassment then, and felt more resentful than afraid, but I sure wasn't comfortable. Before the shocking #MeToo reports of recent years, I assumed that "pinching women's derrières" was a relic of the past. In truth, unprovoked offers plagued me until my sixties, I guess when I became invisible.

French food was another complete culture shock, especially because I ate all meals out. At nineteen, my palate was as finicky as when I slathered mashed potatoes and ketchup on white bread at Girl Scout camp, where I often ate those improvised "sandwiches" at lunch and at dinner. I avoided lamb, pork, veal, and fish, and rejected offal altogether (animal organs were and still are prevalent on French menus), so my options were limited. I certainly would have shunned *escargots* (snails), foie gras (which I learned to love), and *grenouilles* (frog's legs), had they been on any menus.

At the time, I even rejected milk, my preferred beverage, because it wasn't homogenized; the little floating fat globules of cream that collected in the neck of the milk bottle troubled me. I didn't dare order a hamburger, either, because someone told me they were made with horsemeat, and I had no way to verify or dispute that information. When I saw my all-time favorite meal—hamburger and homogenized milk—on the menu that August at the US Pavilion at Expo 58, the Brussels World's Fair, I was overjoyed. It was my best meal of the summer!

un peu plus: LES HALLES

The cab driver who drove us to the Gare du Nord for our day trip to the Brussels World's Fair (it's about a ninety-minute train ride to the Belgian capital) passed Les Halles, the original marketplace in the 1st arrondissement that supplied food to the entire city. Even at dawn, we could see workers carrying baskets of fish and huge carcasses of beef. I'd heard that there were cafés inside where workers met to eat in the early morning when their workday was done and mused about going just to feel the excitement, movement, and energy. But we never did. By the time I returned to Paris in 1976, the original Les Halles had been demolished. What Émile Zola called the "belly of Paris . . ." was gone. Carpe diem. I should have seized the day; now, it's a modern shopping complex.

Even though I had dieted throughout high school and college and had even given up sugar and milk in my coffee to save calories, I lived primarily on carbs that summer: baguettes, crêpes, and croissants. Occasionally, I ordered a *jambon et fromage* sandwich and discarded or gave away the ham and ate just the bread and cheese, with the sweetest butter ever. If restaurants served *steak frites* (steak with fries) or *steak aux poivres* (steak with peppercorns), I chose that or *poulet* (chicken) in any style. Of course, it was a no brainer if *coq au vin* was on the menu.

That summer I missed Bob, resented boys, ignored calories, ate chicken, and fell in love with Paris!

chez moi: COQ AU VIN

Bob and I eloped two months after my return, and I prepared coq au vin for our first dinner guests, our parents, who seemed to appreciate the dish, even with all the canned ingredients I used: Del Monte baby potatoes, Green Giant button mushrooms, and Le Sueur baby peas (as well as frozen pearl onions). I *was* savvy enough to use red, not "cooking," wine! These days, this is what I do: Marinate halved chicken thighs in red Burgundy, pat dry, season with kosher salt and freshly ground black pepper, and dust with flour. Sauté lardons (pancetta or bacon) in olive oil, then add the chicken and cook until browned. Remove the chicken and lardons to a platter. In the same pan, caramelize cubed potatoes, bias-cut carrots, and mushroom halves, then stir in tomato paste, thyme sprigs, and grated garlic. Cook for a minute or two before returning the chicken and lardons to the pan, then add red wine, chicken stock, and a splash of cognac. Cover, and when it's simmering add pearl onions and a roux to thicken the sauce. The dish is done when the chicken is 165°F.

Solo, and
So Nice

———◆•◆———

LIKE MANY WOMEN OF MY GENERATION, I MOVED FROM
home to college to marriage without ever living on my own.
I can't speak for others, but when I had the opportunity to
travel alone decades later, I enjoyed the independence. It was so lib-
erating to make last-minute plans, or change them, and not need to
negotiate what to do, where to go, when to eat. I treasured it.

On one of those trips, in July 1989, I went to Paris on a mission
to see Giverny.

My Francophile Friend, Louise Smith

I met Louise Smith—her name printed at an angle in large, bold,
bright red letters on her yellow legal pad stationery—in a French
Literature class at New York University during the summer of 1961,
and we became longtime friends. "Come to my apartment," she said,
"I think you'll find it amusing." "Amusing" wasn't the first word that
came to mind when we entered her foyer. Gobsmacked was more
accurate.

Her apartment was a mini house-museum filled with works by great artists: a Picasso portrait of artist Françoise Gilot (the mother of Claude and Paloma) near the entry and a painted bronze, *The Absinthe Glass*, prominently placed on a coffee table in the light-filled living room (positioned next to the bowl of pecans purchased mail-order from her native Texas, which she always set out for Bob, who loved them). A third added interest to her guest bathroom, where you can be sure it was the first time I was within touching distance of a Picasso! A large Renoir oil painting graced the fireplace, in the corner next to windows that overlooked Central Park. In the hallway to her bedroom, where Giacometti's larger-than-life-size *Walking Man* stood tall at the foot of her bed, there was a long console where she displayed her pre-Columbian gold collection and above it an impressive series of paintings by Fauve artists: Derain, Dufy, Matisse, Kandinsky, and Vlaminck.

The pièce de résistance was the Monet *Nymphéas*, hanging on the wall adjacent to a round dining table, where we sat once to do homework together. I found it hard to concentrate while I was musing: What if someone splashed spaghetti sauce on the canvas? Silly me. Louise never ate dinner at home, and I imagine that when she did choose to eat pasta, it was in an authentic *ristorante*.

Although most of her collection was donated to the Museum of Modern Art, she gave her Braque and the Monet—considered one of the best in her collection—to New York's Metropolitan Museum of Art, where I always stop by to say hello to the painting and read the adjacent little plaque: "Gift of Louise Reinhardt Smith."

In summer 1963, Louise lent her collection to the Metropolitan Museum of Art for a show called *Paintings from Private Collections: Summer Loan Exhibition*. I had a severely broken ankle that summer and was in a cast up to my hip, so Bob pushed me through the Met in a wheelchair. As we moved from painting to painting, I shared some of what Louise had told me: "When Françoise Gilot visited me . . . When I was in M. Braque's studio . . ." and, before long, a small parade of museumgoers was following my chair, listening.

Louise very much impressed and influenced me, and she taught me some significant life lessons. The most meaningful became more relevant after Bob passed, nearly fifty years later. It was something that she shared the first time she invited me to her home. "A few years ago, my home in Westchester burned to the ground, my husband died, and my only son was killed in an automobile crash," she confided. "It all happened so quickly that I moved here and opened so many doors, that now, I live in a perpetual draft."

Another example occurred on our first dinner out together. Typically, Bob and I joined her for drinks in her apartment before Bob drove us to a restaurant of Louise's choosing, which she preferred to be far from her walkable Upper East Side neighborhood. We were in the car heading downtown on the FDR Drive to the old Fulton Fish Market, when Louise announced: "We'll go Dutch. If I treat, you will never feel comfortable asking me to go for dinner; this way, you can call whenever you wish." It seemed strange, at a time when I didn't even know the expression "wealth gap," but her advice proved to be a practical practice with many relationships.

In 1990, The Museum of Modern Art announced "the gift of an outstanding Matisse painting from 1905, *Landscape at Collioure,* from a generous trustee and noted collector, Mrs. Bertram Smith." In 1995, the museum published a book about her collection, *Masterworks from the Louise Reinhardt Smith Collection.* After her death in July 1995, the obituary in the *New York Times* included this quote from Agnes Gund, then-president of MoMA.

LOUISE REINHARDT SMITH, 91, PATRON OF THE MODERN,
IS DEAD

Louise Smith brought to art a real, true love. She cared nothing for the social status or the public attention that it could bring. The only people she wanted around her were those who felt for art the way she did.

I get carried away remembering Louise, whom I adored. She was a role model for me, and she influenced my appreciation of art and inspired me to visit Monet's home.

Giverny

When I traveled to France in July 1989, my little room at Le Meridien L'Étoile, near the Champs-Élysées—between the Arc de Triomphe and Porte Maillot—was outfitted as meticulously as a yacht. One morning, I chose not to sightsee because of the heat. Instead, I treated myself to a massage at Le Royal Monceau, which entitled me to day-long use of the spa facilities, including an indoor swimming pool surrounded by chaise lounges that opened out to a garden and a spa café, where I lunched. That trip was also my first opportunity to see the Musée d'Orsay, which had opened in 1986 within a former railway station and showcased the most beautiful Van Gogh room, 111 Degas sculptures and paintings, and a plethora of artwork.

As usual, I went to the Musée de l'Orangerie to see the Monet collection of *Les Nymphéas* hanging on the walls around that museum's grand, oval-shaped room. (I hadn't yet discovered the Musée Marmatton Monet, which also has a vast Monet collection, including its own set of *Water Lilies*. In 2024, I revisited both.) Because of work at the Place de la Concorde on the stands constructed for the Jeux Olympiques, the Paris 2024 Olympics, there was a detour to reach l'Orangerie, and I had to walk around the stands, into the gardens, and behind the museum; as a result, I walked ten thousand steps that day, which is all too rare now.

My priority that trip was to visit Giverny, where the artist painted on multiple grand canvases to capture the sunlight at different times of the day. I decided to go on the morning of the 14 juillet, to escape the Fête Nationale crowds, but even before 9:00 a.m. I could feel the building excitement in the métro as folks headed toward the Champs-Elysées to find a good viewing spot for the parade. I was traveling in the opposite direction, to Gare Saint-Lazare, where few people boarded the train west for the fifty-mile, one-and-a-half-hour train ride.

At the Vernon-Giverny station there wasn't even one taxi; obviously, drivers took the day off, a situation I didn't consider. And if a shuttle bus existed in those days, it wasn't working on that holiday morning, either. I asked someone in the station parking lot for directions to Giverny, and when he offered to drive me the four-mile distance, I chose to trust the nice stranger to take me there.

When Monet purchased his 2.5-acre parcel in 1893, it was already surrounded by high walls and planted with an orchard; the property sloped from the house to the road. The artist planted a garden, "full of color and symmetry," as he said, and ten years later dug the first pond, which was later enlarged. The Japanese prints he avidly collected inspired the wisteria-covered Japanese bridge, weeping willows, bamboo, and water lilies. World War II damaged the house and property; by 1980, less than a decade before my visit, the Fondation Claude Monet had restored and reopened the house and was still refurbishing the gardens with its distinctive bridge.

Inside the vine-covered cottage, the large dining room—with its checkered floor, fireplace, framed artwork on yellow walls, and French doors—was centered with a table for ten, big enough for the Monets' eight children. The blue-and-yellow country kitchen housed a massive stove, a fireplace, and a display of copper pots. That Giverny color palette made such an impression on me that, thirty-five years later, I still live amid blues and yellows. My front door, the wicker chair next to it, and all my ceramic pots on the porch are blue; inside, the color scheme continues in the living room, bedroom, and even with the kitchen accessories.

One room of Monet's home was turned into the gift shop, and it was where I first saw the silk "Giverny" scarf with water lilies, displayed with, if I recall correctly, a costly $180 price tag, at a time when my media rate for the Continental flight was $250. Usually, when I see expensive things that I'd like to buy but can't, I immediately forget about them. Not this scarf. For years and years, I was on a mission to find this Giverny scarf and asked for it wherever Hermès scarves were sold. I didn't know at the time that, like haute couture, scarf designs change seasonally. I endured the haughty, only-in-fancy-boutiques attitude of the sales help telling me that it wasn't available until one woman deigned to share the reason. (I will never understand why some of the people working for—and with—the very rich behave far snootier than the very rich themselves. Isabelle Huppert, in the film *Mrs. Harris Goes to Paris*, perfectly portrays their "how can you be so stupid" arrogance.)

In February 2021, while researching details about the silk industry for a chapter about Lyon, I read some Hermès history and said to myself, OK, it's time. I closed the Lyon file and started an online search for the "Giverny" vintage scarf. After ignoring two $1,200 listings, I found "Original Rare 1989 Hermès Silk Scarf 'Giverny'" posted by The RealReal online marketplace, for $262 minus a $25 "first purchase" discount. The text read:

> This tribute to Claude Monet was designed by Laurence Bour-
> thoumieux. Romantic, Luxurious, Authentic unworn original
> Vintage Hermès Silk Scarf and offered in its best palette Rose/
> Blue Border, unused in Box! Already a collector's scarf, don't
> miss it, in this superb fairy palette! Authenticity Guaranteed.
> This stunning scarf features hand-sewn, hand-rolled edges, and
> will be supplied in original Hermès Box. A stunning scarf for
> the discerning Hermès collector who loves that fabulous, classic
> Hermès style and outstanding artistry, a very special scarf for a
> very special lady. The scarf is 35" x 35" (90 cm x 90 cm) F162.

I didn't hesitate. I had wanted that scarf since first seeing it at Monet's home and typed in the credit card details, hoping that it would arrive in "very good" condition. It did!

chez moi: COMPÔTE DE PÊCHES

According to the cookbook *The Impressionist's Table,* by Alexandra Leaf, Monet grew his own produce at Giverny and loved fruit compotes, including peach. The "waste not, want not" credo advises cooking fruit before it gets over-ripe. Here's what I do before a trip: I simmer fruit in water with added wine, rum, or a liqueur, a vanilla bean, and a dollop of preserves and cook until soft but intact. It freezes well and I like to serve it warm.

Trains and Troubles

After a thirty-three-year career, I retired from teaching on February 1, 1994, to work full-time as a freelance food and travel writer. I traveled extensively during that following spring semester and spent almost as many days on the road as I would usually have been in the classroom. It was fun to take advantage of off-season, shoulder-season, promotional rates, and media travel opportunities.

Restaurant clips from a *New York Nightlife* and other magazines qualified me for membership in the International Association of Culinary Professionals. In 1996, I attended my first IACP convention in Philadelphia, where I was introduced to Julia Child, the major attraction at age eighty-four, and also met Graham Kerr. His daily *Galloping Gourmet* show kept Jeni and I company for lunch, when I raced home the year I was on split-session to meet her nursery school bus. Chef Kerr occasionally inspired me about new ways to cook the meat I was defrosting for the family dinner; once, Jeni helped me crack the peppercorns—which scattered everywhere—to replicate his *steak aux poivres.* During those shows, I would pour myself a glass of wine to toast with him!

The best part of the convention was when I met cookbook author Kate Hill, who signed my copy of her book *Culinary Journey in Gascony* and told me about the weeklong "foodie" retreat she was planning for that spring in Agen, in southwest France. I immediately decided to participate.

Just a couple of months later, when I arrived in Paris after the usual all-night flight, I headed toward Le Clos Médicis, a tiny three-star hotel on the Left Bank, where I had reserved a room for the one night before and one night after the week's session. The hotel directions said to take the RER train from Charles de Gaulle Airport to Luxembourg métro station and walk to 56 rue Monsieur le Prince.

As soon as I exited the subway, I realized that I had arrived on the corner of Boulevard Saint-Michel and rue Gay-Lussac, just footsteps from my former rooming house, and facing the building (Le Cercle Luxembourg now) where I used to eat upstairs in the cafeteria. The hotel was easy to find on a side street parallel to Boulevard Saint-Michel; I checked in and set out to explore the once-familiar quartier.

The following morning, I breakfasted early to get to the Marché rue de Buci, a famous outdoor food market, before heading to the *gare* for the high-speed TGV train to Bordeaux. I was delighted by the beautiful displays of produce, meat, regional products, and prepared items, especially the paella displayed in an oversize shallow black paella pan filled with colorful ingredients: dark sausage, saffron-shaded rice, golden chicken, green peas and red peppers, pink shrimp, and black mussels.

It surprised me that paella was so popular in centre-ville Paris, because the dish reminded me of my first authentic one on Mallorca, in 1973, where I spent a week during a six-month sabbatical and first tasted it with a family whom I met on the train and who invited me to join them for lunch. It was also the first time I saw how the Spanish serve snails, which arrived in a full basket accompanied by toothpicks—so different from in France, where they are served six to a platter, each in its own hollowed depression, alongside fancy silver tongs and a fork with long, skinny tines.

After the market, which was farther than expected and took longer than I planned, I rushed back to the hotel worrying that I'd be late for my train to Agen. I immediately collected my bag and went outside to find a taxi, though none passed the quiet little street. That's when I learned that in Paris, taxis go to special taxi stands and only a few major venues, so I asked the desk clerk to call one.

The driver who arrived proceeded down Boulevard Saint-Michel toward the station until he stopped at a red light just beyond the Luxembourg Gardens. He pulled to the right, turned off the engine, and announced in French: "*Je ne bouge plus.*" (I will no longer move.) "Give me _ _ francs." His body language was crystal clear: he wanted more money . . . lots more. This was ransom. I was dumbstruck. I opened my purse, paid the exorbitant sum, perhaps $50, and he slowly counted it. Eventually he continued en route, but I was quietly enraged and worried about missing my train and giving away a good portion of my week's worth of cash. (I probably brought $100.)

Inside Gare Montparnasse, I checked the information display, found the platform number, and raced to board. As I dragged my wheelie bag up the few steps to the passenger car, the doors silently closed behind me and disconnected the L-shaped strap holding my computer bag. I didn't hear the thud of my brand-new laptop falling onto the platform with the envelope containing all the trip informa-tion, plus my passport and ticket home. Fortunately, I had put the train ticket in my purse the evening before to have it handy.

By the time the conductor stopped by my seat, my angst was pal-pable. Pulling myself together, I stuttered in French and hoped he'd understand, "*Bonjour, Monsieur. J'ai un p'tit problème. Pouvez-vous m'aider?*" The conductor heard my request for help and seemed blasé about it; lost items were part of his daily routine. Before he vanished, he muttered: "*Madame, il ne faut qu'une.*" Essentially, "It only takes one." I realized he was right: one person can find and return it; or one thief can steal it. The phrase helped me regain my composure because it seemed profound; I've repeated this to myself countless times, because it's true: one person makes all the difference.

I took deep breaths—meditative ones that I had learned at spa sessions—and watched the rural countryside fly by to Bordeaux, where I paid careful attention to finding the correct platform for the regional train to Agen. Once on board, I worried about someone meeting me, because I no longer knew whom I was meeting, what numbers to call, or the address of the place I was going.

Happily, a driver was waiting: "Bonjour, Madame. Did you have a good treep?" I explained my predicament in Franglais, and he listened patiently; then, he disappeared to explain it to the station master. He even filled out the required documentation, which took some time, and was very generous about dealing with it all. Later that afternoon, he told me: "*Bonnes Nouvelles!*" (Good news!) The station master called me to say: "*Venez demain.*" (Come tomorrow.)

They had found the attaché in Paris, stored it safely, and would transfer it to Agen on the same train the following day. The following day, the driver took me back to the station and dealt with the station master himself, without requesting my participation, until he handed me the bag. Both were justifiably proud of their successful tactics, and I was much relieved and grateful.

IT ONLY TAKES ONE

The conductor who mumbled "*Il ne faut qu'une*" (it only takes one) announced a significant and correct theory, but he may have underestimated the number. In truth, it took an entire team to retrieve my bag—a village, as they say. A cadre of salaried civil service workers went beyond the scope of their job descriptions, without drama and with no expectation of a reward. They just made sure that a passenger's bag reached the rightful owner.

In Paris, someone found the bag and brought it to an office.

On the train, the conductor notified the Paris station master.

In Paris, the station master arranged to have it put on the same TGV the following day.

In Bordeaux, an employee transferred it from the TGV to the local train to Agen.

In Agen, the station master called Paris about the loss, contacted the driver, and retrieved my bag from the train. (I sure hope that I tipped that driver well for his part in the effort.)

Since then, whenever I hear insulting generalizations about the French, I tell them about the strangers who went out of their way to help me.

A caveat: There are exceptions! Exactly one week after the shakedown in Paris, I arrived back at Gare Montparnasse and went to the taxi queue. A cab pulled up and I stepped into the back seat and said: "Bonjour, Monsieur. Hotel Le Clos Medici, s'il vous plait, 56 rue Monsieur le Prince." Then, I settled back comfortably, glanced at the license, and stopped—startled—and stared at the driver's picture. It confirmed the coincidence.

He was the very same crook from the week before!

chez moi: PAELLA

In Spain, paella is typically prepared over an open fire; at home, it's a one-pot rice dish, though there are lots of ingredients that require careful timing. For years I considered it much too daunting for me to serve; in fact, my first attempt was more time-consuming than necessary because I shopped at the fishmonger, at the butcher, at the produce market, and at the supermarket. Once I started storing most of the staples in my pantry and freezer, I shopped only for produce and seafood, and it became a practical dish to serve company. To start, I sauté sliced chorizo sausage in olive oil, add boneless chicken thighs (skin side down), onion, garlic, scallions, and red peppers. Then, I toast one part

33

basmati rice in that same pan and add two parts hot chicken broth with saffron (it blooms in the heat) and wine. I cover the rice with a lid and wrap a clean kitchen towel around it, and cook until the liquid is absorbed, about 20 minutes. Off heat, I add clams (which open) and shrimp (which turn pink) and top it all with parsley. It's an impressive meal for a crowd of six to ten.

Alone, Twice, in Paris

In 2018, I traveled twice to France on separate three-week trips—spring on the Riviera and fall in Paris—sandwiching long weekends in the city after a pastoral stay in Burgundy and between two forays to Champagne. My first few days in the capital that September coincided with *La Rentrée,* the busy time after Parisians return from August holidays to a batch of business events and conventions, including Paris Design Week, when hotel reservations are notoriously difficult to obtain and costly.

HÔTEL ELYSA LUXEMBOURG

An online search showed one vacant room available at Hôtel Elysa Luxembourg, a three-star Best Western hotel located at 6 rue Gay-Lussac in the building where I had formerly lived. I immediately reserved a room with a cancellation option; I also tried to book the room directly with the hotel. I called and sent emails asking for a corner room on the *quatrième étage,* like the one I had stayed in, but to no avail. I kept the third-party-site reservation.

From the gare, the taxi crossed the Seine to the Left Bank, and I relived the day when a naïve, lovesick teen arrived. I was commit-

34

ted to four months abroad away from my boyfriend, and though I missed him every day, I had no intention of giving up my dream of learning to speak French in Paris.

The driver stopped, I entered the front door, and the receptionist gave me the key to a room on the *première étage*. When I asked him for help with the luggage, he refused: "*Madame, je ne peux pas quitter la reception.*" (I can't leave the desk.) Typically, three-star hotel service does not include help with luggage.

A flood of memories surfaced when I spotted the circular staircase and elevator; it was like a personal Proustian moment, except what replaced the author's indelible taste sensation was the pit-in-the-stomach anxiety of claustrophobia. This elevator, though newer, appeared as small as the old one that I recalled. So, I placed my luggage inside, pushed the button, and walked up the spiral stairs to fetch it.

The room was minuscule, noisy, and just above the street, yet it hardly mattered. There was a TV, air-conditioning, and a private bathroom almost the size of the sleeping quarters. I had made no dinner reservations and set out on foot to find the restaurant that was recommended online and was nearby. I saw empty seats on the terrace and at the bar, so I entered and greeted the barman and requested a table. He didn't even raise his head when he asked if I had a reservation, and when he heard my negative reply, dismissed me with a not-so-subtle wave, as if I were a fly on a glass. (The rejection reminded me, once again, to make—and confirm—every reservation.)

At a very hospitable café nearby, the host welcomed me so warmly that I imagine he probably owned the place. After a week's worth of big, bold Burgundian dinners, I was happy to order simple French favorites: *vin blanc, soupe à l'oignon, salade,* and *mousse au chocolat.* I ate well.

The next morning, at the hotel breakfast room on the lower level, an attentive waitstaff served an excellent full breakfast, and I chatted with a friendly mother-daughter duo at the next table. Afterward, I crossed Boulevard Saint-Michel and walked the short distance to the black wrought-iron entry gates into the manicured gardens that surround the Palais du Luxembourg.

It was a warm mid-September morning when I returned and walked a familiar path, next to elderly men in dark cardigans and berets and moms pushing strollers with one hand and holding a toddler's hand with the other. Cyclists in bright and oh-so-tight jerseys rode past holding baguettes under their arms. Two older women in housedresses and slippers caught my eye. They were chatting amicably and carrying white plastic grocery bags, and appeared so in tune with each other that I doubt they ever looked up from their animated conversation to notice the fashionistas parading by in their high heels and short leather jackets.

That morning in 2018 reminded me of the many after-class walks I took in 1958, when I strolled down the park's central *allée* to the fountain, or when I chose to sit and read by the *basin*. An employee was always available to open and wipe the folding chairs in those days; I remember giving each of them a few francs as a tip, but I don't think there was a cost. I'd read there, looking up from my book to watch kids steering their toy sailboats with long poles, and I absolutely adored feeling like I was part of a community experiencing daily life.

The intimacy of those everyday Parisian scenes always delights me. *Quelle joie!*

un peu plus: THE LUXEMBOURG GARDENS

That 2018 visit to the sixty-acre Jardin du Luxembourg, originally built for Queen Marie de Medici in the seventeenth century, sparked a memory from July 1990, when I was photographed there, near the Marie de Medici Fountain, for a feature in *Madame Figaro.* The "shoot" took place after the publisher of *Le Manuel de Survie de la Mere qui Travaille* (the French version of *You Can't Do It All: Ideas That Work for Mothers Who Work*) arranged a superb luncheon with the magazine's editor at Les Ambassadeurs, in the *haut de gamme* Hôtel de Crillon. They whisked me by limo to the gardens, where the photographer posed me as if I were a *vedette* (star). That day I wished there was someone I could tell about the memorable experience; if it had happened today, it would surely have been a "selfie" moment.

SHANGRI-LA HOTEL PARIS

By noon I had walked back to the hotel to pick up my luggage and taxi over to the Right Bank, where I planned an overnight at Shangri-La Hotel Paris. This *monument historique*, with its cast-iron gates, imposing porte-cochere, domed foyer, and grand stairway, is a true palace hotel, one of only twelve in Paris awarded that distinction. The restored one-hundred-room hotel was originally built in the nineteenth century for Prince Roland Bonaparte, the grand-nephew of Napoleon I, and showcases its original hand-carved mahogany, stained-glass windows, and authentic floorboards. He hosted opulent banquets in the Louis XIV–inspired, gold-leaf-gilded Grand Salon, where guests could view the Seine and see La Tour Eiffel at a very close range.

A Parisian spa acquaintance joined me for dinner that night at the hotel's La Bauhinia restaurant, where the tower soars over the adjacent garden. I slept in a room with a picture book tower view, and the following morning, indulged with a swim in the indoor heated spa pool followed by a facial. As I was walking through the elegant structure toward the reception desk to check out, I heard a loud, angry male voice yelling like a deranged, sleep-deprived toddler having a temper tantrum.

As I got closer, I saw the man facing the desk clerk and the woman standing near him next to a baggage cart on which designer shopping bags bearing names including Chanel, Dior, Hermès, and Louis Vuitton were hanging from the cross pole above the luggage. Sometimes, I envy those people who can shop so cavalierly in those stores, but on this occasion, I was hurting for that woman. She stepped back discreetly in small steps, as far from the man (whom I assumed was her husband) as appropriate and held tightly to her child's hand. She waited silently, but her expression had that stoic stillness recognizable to anyone who has seen a press conference with a wife standing beside her disgraced politician husband. I assumed that this wasn't the first time she had witnessed a comparable scene, and I wondered how she dealt with it. Who behaves like this in public and in such an exquisite place? I felt so uncomfortable with his yelling that rather than waiting to check out, as one normally would, I kept walking outside, as far from the noise as possible, and texted Uber. Happily, in May 2024, when I returned for a late afternoon spa service and dinner with Val at La Bauhinia, everyone behaved *comme il faut* (perfectly). In May, the landscaped garden was in full bloom and the tower soared above it like an enormous tree.

HÔTEL DU COLLECTIONNEUR

The Uber transported me from the swank boutique hotel across the Champs-Elysées to the smart Hôtel du Collectionneur, which is located between the Étoile (Arc de Triomphe) and the chic Park Monceau. I was en route to join a few British journalists there, and we were all going to attend that evening's launch of the hotel's newly refurbished restaurant. I met up with them near the monumental staircase in the art deco lobby before we had lunch in the stunning new restaurant, and again late that afternoon, for a champagne cruise along the Seine on a small private charter boat.

At the opening reception that night, I was introduced to our stunning host, Andréa Cohen, the CEO of the Gate Collection, who had personally overseen the new restaurant design.

The following day, the journalists were all invited to assemble outside at noon, where a series of shiny vintage Rolls-Royces were lined up in a row. We were instructed to choose one and climb in for an hour-long city tour by the driver/owner members of a Parisian auto club. After our tour, the journalists left for their flight to London, but I spent a second night there.

MUSÉE NISSIM DE CAMONDO

The next morning, I walked to the nearby house museum, Musée Nissim de Camondo, to be there when it opened. The former family home, which overlooks the greenery of le Parc Monceau, was built by Camondo, an Ottoman Jew born in 1860, who settled in France and loved the country. His family's story played out tragically, though. Camondo's son was a pilot in the French army and was killed in 1917, during World War I; his daughter, Béatrice, and her two children, Fanny and Bertrand, were deported and killed in

Auschwitz in 1943, during World War II. Camondo later donated his home—which resembles a miniature Petit Trianon and is filled with elegant treasures—to the French state.

That afternoon, on board the TGV to Reims in Champagne, I was still thinking about the father who had lost two children and two grandchildren in consecutive wars, totally unaware of the history that I'd soon be learning in Reims. I was en route to visit a city that was in the midst of commemorating the one-hundredth anniversary of the end of World War I.

HÔTEL BEL AMI

Just five days later, after a whirlwind winery tour of Champagne, I was back in Paris, unexpectedly having received a last-minute invitation to participate in a second Champagne experience by Louis Vuitton Moët Hennessy (LVMH). I had been able to change my flight but had no idea what I would do from Friday until Monday night, when the event began. Much to my relief, my host arranged for me to spend the weekend at a hotel in Paris and even had a car waiting for me at the station.

Usually when I'm in Paris, my meal-to-meal, museum-to-museum, spa-to-spa plans are set and often require moving from one quartier to another. For the first time, this particular weekend I had no plans, no assignments to research, no set itinerary, no appointments, no timed museum tickets, and no restaurant reservations. It was as exciting as if it were my first visit to the city, and I vowed to go everywhere on foot.

When I arrived at the Hôtel Bel Ami, I didn't yet know that the Left Bank hotel is just a short block from Boulevard Saint-Germain and its best-known cafes—Les Deux Magots, Café de Flore, and Brasserie Lipp—which were made famous by literati, including Ernest

Hemingway, Jean-Paul Sartre, and Simone de Beauvoir, whose notable *Memoirs of a Dutiful Daughter* was published in 1958. (It boggles my mind that the couple might have been seated there, arguing about freedom, the very summer that this naïve child-of-the-1950s was blissfully discovering the nearby neighborhood.) In 2018, my thoughts were equally frivolous. The hotel is so convenient to the cafés, restaurants, and boutiques in the quartier, that I stayed in the area to get my hair done and buy a sweater for the gala dinners in Champagne; after almost three weeks in France, the weather had started to chill from the warmer days of mid-September.

I lunched leisurely, in various nearby cafés, and stopped into others for coffee and to watch the world pass my table. For the first night's dinner, I crossed the street to hear music at Chez Papa Jazz Club, where I sipped wine and ordered the smoked salmon plate. One afternoon, I walked to Musée d'Orsay—which was farther than I expected—and had a cheese plate for dinner at its rooftop restaurant; because of the distance, I took a cab back to the hotel.

It was a sublime treat to be on my own. In fact, the only people I spoke to the entire weekend were the helpful concierge and the lovely hotel manager, Laurence Guinebretière.

The City of Light with Bob

———◆•◆———

PARIS HAS ALWAYS TOPPED MY WHERE-TO-GO WISH list, but in the early years of marriage, with babies, a new house, and a tight budget, Bob and I were lucky to take a road trip. In 1976, a dean at Dowling College, who knew I was teaching English as a Second Language, asked me to write a grant proposal for the college's first ESL program. I was as excited about the challenge as I was about the $500 fee, which almost covered the cost of two package tours advertised in a brochure that appeared in my school mailbox: "PARIS: $299.00 per person: 5 Nights, Airfare and Hotel."

I asked Bob: "Would you like to go to Paris? My treat." He beamed.

Just weeks before the vacation, he was headed on a sailing trip to reposition the thirty-nine-foot racing sailboat that he captained—and maintained—for the owner, and I joined him. Each morning, we attempted to leave Newport Harbor, in Rhode Island, but the fog was too dense to sail to Marblehead, Massachusetts. Bob was disappointed, and he puttered on board; I was beyond relieved to be safe at the dock and spent long, happy afternoons curled up in the forward "V" researching the *Michelin Guide to Paris*, for a special occasion restaurant, and *Fodor's*, for budget dining options.

Once in Paris, our low-cost package tour included a rather ordinary commercial high-rise hotel on the Boulevard Périphérique, the road that circles Paris, from which we had to take the métro everywhere. The first morning, we rode it to the Alma-Marceau station, where we boarded with all the other tourists and cruised the Seine on a *bateau mouche*.

My husband was an art lover, who admired Monet's *Nymphéas* (*Water Lilies*) at the Musée de l'Orangerie and *Two Young Girls at the Piano*, the Renoir painting that inspired my fairy-tale dreams of motherhood. One day, we walked from Nôtre-Dame and down Boul'Mich to 6 rue Gay-Lussac, where I showed him the place I had spent the summer eighteen years earlier.

Throughout the week, my partner smiled at everyone and eloquently used his five-phrase French vocabulary: *bonjour, bonsoir, au revoir, s'il vous plaît, merci bien*. When people talked to him, he nodded knowingly, as if he understood what they were saying, and responded with an authentic sounding *oui, oui, oui*. Whether they were aware of his inability to speak French or not, everyone treated him warmly. And he was happily enthusiastic about whatever I had planned. Back home, he adapted JFK's famous quote, substituting me for Jacqueline and announcing to anyone who would listen: "I am the man who accompanied Irvina to Paris, and I have enjoyed it."

I had prepaid for the trip and brought a little spending money, but I didn't have a clue how much cash my spouse would bring. Turned out, he had enough to treat me to a splendid late-night dinner at Maxim's, which was on my wish list for its décor and glamour more than the cuisine. It must have been a most successful evening, because one of the dated menus in my collection (February 1988) proves that I returned.

Off and on from the time of our first trip in 1976 and for almost thirty years after, Bob and I visited Paris together. We always spent a few days there before and after riverboat and barge cruises and road trips, too. Taking a morning cruise on the Seine after dropping off our luggage at the hotel became our little tradition. One hotel stands out as the most memorable: Hôtel de Crillon.

HÔTEL DE CRILLON

Hôtel de Crillon (in the 8th) has had a complete and gorgeous makeover in recent years, but the over-the-top former palace was utterly and completely impressive years earlier, when we checked in. Unfortunately, our unforgettable experience there is marred by a painful reminder of Bob's first serious health episode. He felt so sick when we arrived that he went to bed. When I felt his head, it was so hot that I called the concierge, who contacted an English-speaking doctor. The doctor arrived within minutes and recommended that Bob immediately be admitted to the American Hospital in Paris and made all the necessary arrangements.

I am still beyond grateful to have been at a hotel with a top concierge, a member of the prestigious Les Clefs d'Or (the association of best concierges in the world), who took care of the emergency. Anyone who gets sick, or travels with someone who gets sick, away from home is terrified and challenged when it comes to making medical arrangements. The way the concierge took care of Bob was exemplary.

Once, and I can't recall when or for what assignment, I was shown the room where Leonard Bernstein always stayed, where I stepped out on the terrace, feeling as if the Luxor Obelisk in the Place de la Concorde was within touching distance.

I clearly recall the piece I wrote about the hotel's magnificent renovation for the *Forbes Travel Guide* in 2018, for which I was not permitted any hosted experiences. In 2021, I returned to feature the Michelin-starred L'Écrin and the extravagant spa. In May 2024, Val and I stopped in for a drink at its iconic Bar les Ambassadeurs, within the space that once housed the formal dining room, where I had my book launch lunch in 1990. I sipped, smiled, and enjoyed the décor, but in my mind's eye, I saw Bob burning with fever.

Back to that emergency. When the taxi arrived at the hospital, someone took Bob straight to a room, while I was ushered into a small, swank salon and offered a high-backed upholstered chair facing a very polished woman seated at an antique wooden desk. (I remember curved legs; maybe it was Louis XV style.) She handed me paperwork to complete and asked for a deposit: "*Un p'tit dépôt, s'il vous plaît?*" I handed her my very new American Express card, and she promptly charged $1,000. OMG!

From the get-go, the patient was in good hands, well-cared-for, and unbelievably well-fed. He was released two mornings later, in time to taxi to the gare for the train to Dijon and the barge. During the entire week on board the barge, he avoided most physical activities and wasn't his usual energetic self. Still, he kept assuring me: "It was just a bump in the road." And I chose to believe that he had recovered. On land and on board, we managed to eat magnificently.

Gastronomic Multicourse Meals

During the last fifteen years of Bob's life, we worked together as a writer/photographer team. My restaurant articles featured his images of meals that we shared, many in Relais Gourmand restaurants within hotels affiliated with Relais & Châteaux. I remember almost all, except the name of a special Left Bank restaurant where I can still clearly envision the impressive antique duck press on display; it was a brass contraption with a wheel that turns, cranks, presses, and pulverizes the bones, innards, and carcass of a duck to make a *jus* for a sauce.

He may not have been healthy, but he surely ate as if nothing bothered him.

LE CINQ

The day Bob and I shared an outstanding Sunday lunch at Le Cinq in the Four Seasons Hotel George V, everything was perfection. To start, we were seated at a table covered in rose petals. My assignment for *Santé*, a wine magazine, was to feature Eric Beaumard, the sommelier credited with creating the hotel's prestigious fifty-thousand-bottle cellar, and whose accolades included Best Sommelier in France, 1992; Best Sommelier in Europe, 1994; and Best Vice Sommelier in the World, 1998. After a divine lunch, another sommelier escorted us to a small elevator, which went down to the historic cellars forty-six feet below ground. We toured the historic *cave*, which had been built when the hotel was constructed in 1928, within a quarry where stones were mined for the Arc de Triomphe between 1806 and 1836. The George V wine cellar was walled off to keep the Nazis from finding and taking the valuable collection during World War II. Our guide also pointed out the rare bottles lined up on a small table for a VIP guest.

ARPÈGE

One of the best of our fine-dining meals took place in 2002, at Chef Alain Passard's Restaurant L'Arpège, where I devoured the *tarte à l'oignon* at the three-Michelin-star vegetarian-focused, haute cuisine establishment. I had the sweetest, most delicious thinly sliced, golden caramelized onions served on a delicate crispy crust. I dream of it still and asked for it when I finally returned in November 2024, more than twenty years later. I was with my grandniece Lyndsey, and we both chose Le dejeuner des jardiniers, an exquisite, seasonal, twelve-course luncheon menu prepared with produce from the chef's farm and which, to my delight, included *Gratin d'oignons doux dorés au parmesan*. Lyndsey was enchanted with the carpaccio (thin slivers) of beets!

The chef-owner spent his childhood at his grandparents' farm, where he discovered farm-fresh ingredients and witnessed hearthside cooking. The chef is famous for his dedication to perfect produce, which he grows (Les Paniers d'Alain Passard). At the start of his career, Passard worked for the acclaimed Alain Senderens at L'Archestrate, at 84 rue de Varenne, a building he was able to purchase in 1986. A decade later, as an established culinary icon with three Michelin stars, he wowed the foodie world by sewing a half-duck and a half-chicken together to create a chicken-duck duo.

Then, he decided to elevate vegetables to be the focus of every dish, using produce that he was already growing outside Paris, well before vegetarian dishes appeared on the food scene. By 2001, when he stopped serving red meat entirely, the food world was in an absolute dither, because restaurant-goers still expected to find red meat on fine-dining menus. That might have been a career-killing risk for any ordinary chef. (It was still a gamble twenty years later in Manhattan, when Daniel Humm moved to an all-vegan menu at Eleven Madison Park.) Chef has retained his three stars ever since and added some fish and poultry to a menu in which produce still stars.

While searching online for the recipe for *tarte a l'oignon,* I came across a YouTube documentary referring to Passard as the "maestro of vegetable cuisine" and showing the chef-farmer in his garden speaking passionately about his produce. I read that he bastes fruits and vegetables with their own sugars, as you would meat, and have seen pictures of his bouquet of roses pie, for which he transforms long apple ribbons into intricate roses, sets them on a crust, and tops them with a *caramielle* (caramel made with milk and honey). Whatever his techniques and *trucs* (tricks), he transforms rudimentary, farm-grown vegetables into something ethereal.

I've also watched and rewatched *Chef's Table France* on Netflix, which featured Chef Passard in 2016, and shows him at his restaurant collecting the day's produce from the van. In his kitchen there are glorious images of his dishes. It also mentions that chef never writes down his recipes because he is always creating. I didn't know that information when I mailed him a handwritten, personal letter the old-fashioned way. *Et voilà!* In October 2022, I received a reply:

Chère Madame,

Je reviens vers vous suite à la réception de votre courrier. Voici la recette du gratin d'oignon jaune sturons, ainsi que sa photo.

A feu doux, faites fondre au beurre salé un oignon jaune sturons finement ciselé . . . Laissez l'oignon se faner quelques minutes dans le beurre chaud et le répartir finement dans un plat à gratin . . .

Parsemez d'un voile de parmesan et gratinez à la salamandre.

Servir avec un mesclun de pousses de moutarde!

Bonne table!

Here's my translation: Wilt chopped onions in salted butter for a few minutes. Spread them in a thin layer in a gratin dish and sprinkle with grated Parmesan cheese. Broil just until crisp. Serve with a mesclun of the smallest baby mustard greens available. Happy eating!

chez moi: TARTE Á L'OIGNON

And here's how I make it: Sauté Vidalia onion slices in butter until golden, not crisp, and spread them edge to edge on a prebaked puff pastry square (I'm told Dufour is best, but I usually can find Pepperidge Farm.) Then, I sprinkle the top with grated Parmesan and broil in a toaster oven. It's good—certainly not Passard good—but it makes me happy. Since tasting the gratin without the crust, my New Year's resolution will be to perfect the less calorie-laden version.

Paris Plus Friends
and Family

———◆•◆———

E VERY DAY WHEN I'M VISITING PARIS, I PLAN WHERE
to go before and after lunch, whether that be a museum, a
gallery, shops, or a spa. And I'm always doing research for
current assignments and to query future articles. Still, what I remember most are the meals like these that I've shared with good
friends and close relatives.

Chocolates with Val

By the mid-nineties, I regularly pitched story ideas about Paris,
which was a particularly hard sell because editors wanted to visit
Paris themselves and not give such a choice assignment to a freelancer. One bridal editor said as much when she rejected my "Honeymoon in Paris" query: "If someone is writing about Paris, it will
be me. Why don't you do a story about the Poconos?" It's certainly
reasonable that hardworking editors hoard the perks, so I decided
to propose less obvious ideas and rejoiced when this query earned a
positive response at *Chocolatier* magazine. It started like this: "Since
the time when the ancient Indians considered chocolate as a gift of
the gods and intrinsic to pagan rituals, the French have augmented

chocolate desserts to an art form." *Quelle chance!* (What luck!) It was my dream assignment to research and write: "The Best Chocolate Desserts in Paris." I invited Val to meet me in Paris and set about arranging reservations, managing to include some spectacular chocolate creations made by pastry chefs at the most fabulous restaurants that I'd heard about up to that point. At one restaurant, the superb Plaza Athénée, a breeze drifted across our table in the courtyard and the maître d' brought us each a lush cashmere shawl.

At a similar gastronomic venue, the waiter wheeled a trolley-size *chariot* with an assortment of decadent chocolate delights. It was an image to remember. Val looked up at the grand finale, smiled politely, and announced: "I don't eat chocolate. Do you have a baba au rhum?" I wanted to fall through the floor, I was so embarrassed, and I had no idea how to make the situation better. Val and I usually go Dutch when we're dining out, but on those occasions when I'm hosted at a "working" dinner, I remind my best friend to accept what is offered or explain "dietary limitations" in advance. (The waitstaff often asks guests about preferences or allergies.)

I sampled an abundance of creative and complex chocolate desserts. Restaurant Guy Savoy presented Chocolate Wafer Mocha Cream Bitter Chocolate Sorbet and Flower of Thyme Ice Cream Truffle with Chocolate Ganache Sauce; Les Ambassadeurs at Hôtel de Crillon included Crystallized Violets.

RESTAURANT MICHEL ROSTANG

The most unforgettable chocolate dessert was the Molten Chocolate Cake served within the art-filled Restaurant Michel Rostang, a former home in a swank residential quartier near the Arc de Triomphe, in which one room was dedicated to glass art by René Lalique. Michel Rostang, the fifth-generation culinarian, is the son of a star chef; he earned his first Michelin star in 1979 and a second by 1980. The family enterprise was a smoothly operating classic by the time I arrived in 1995, when Madame Rostang, Marie-Claude, greeted me at the entry and seated me adjacent to an open interior window where I could watch the kitchen *brigade* (team) in action. It turned out that they could also see me.

Someone must have noticed my it's-out-of-this-world expression when I tasted that dessert, with its warm, gooey chocolate center, served atop a pistachio sauce and accompanied by an oval-shaped scoop of pistachio ice cream. The dish has become ubiquitous on menus since then, but I had never eaten anything that sensual. "Aphrodisiac" became a word in my culinary vocabulary after that. When the chef came to the table, he invited me to return to the restaurant at 10:00 a.m. the following morning, saying, "The chef patissier will show you how easy it is to make."

This first foray into a Michelin-starred kitchen was exhilarating. Someone handed me a chef's jacket and a tall white toque and introduced me to the pastry chef, who claimed it was the simplest dessert to make. He melted bits of chocolate in a tiny copper pot over an ordinary pot of boiling water (no need for a double boiler). The whole process was done within fifteen minutes, and I decided to try it at home.

My delight in eating chocolate in Paris may have begun in the 1990s, but it is an ongoing joy. Michel Rostang's daughters, Caroline and Sophie, are now in charge of Rostang Père & Filles, and in May 2024, I savored a fabulous chocolate soufflé at Dessirier, their seafood restaurant. I also ate Fauchon *chocolats* and drank *chocolat chaud* (hot chocolate served with a bowl full of swirled Chantilly whipped cream) at Carette, facing Place des Vosges, in the Marais. Val ordered a non-chocolate-filled crèpe.

Ducasse with Near and Dear

In 1999, Alison happened to be traveling with her longtime friend Ellen while I was also in France. I was delighted that these two sophisticated women were willing to spend some time with me in Paris and at Versailles. We all stayed at a jewel of a hotel, which has since been transformed into the newly opened and ultra-tony Hotel 1, Place Vendôme, on the corner where rue Saint-Honoré meets Place Vendôme.

ALAIN DUCASSE AT PLAZA ATHENÉE

The high point of our togetherness took place at dinner at Alain Ducasse at Plaza Athenée. (Ellen still says it was her best meal ever and it surely ranks as one of mine.) We were greeted by the entire team when we entered, and after the superb meal, the staff presented us with a personalized printed menu, dated le 12 mai 1999 and listing each gastronomic dish, from Foie Gras de Canard (duck) to Homard (lobster) Breton, fromage (cheese), dessert, confisseries, and more. The record confirms indulgent wines, too: Champagne Paul Drouet and Chambolle Musigny 1er Cru 1992.

RESTAURANT LE MEURICE ALAIN DUCASSE

Bob and I dined at Le Meurice once in the early 2000s, when it had one Michelin star and before the venue became Restaurant Le Meurice Alain Ducasse, which currently holds two Michelin stars. Hotel Meurice sits in its grandeur facing the Tuileries Garden, and on the evening we were there, we learned some intriguing information about its World War II history, when the Nazis appropriated the desirable hotel as their headquarters during the German occupation of "*Gross* Paris" (greater Paris). According to the book *Is Paris Burning?*, Hitler wanted to destroy Paris before leaving and had ordered explosives to be placed under its most famous monuments, including the

Senate, the Assembly, the Eiffel Tower, the Louvre, and the bridges over the Seine. The book claims that a Swedish diplomat convinced General Dietrich von Choltitz to abandon the repulsive plan, and he surrendered Paris without obliterating the magnificent city.

If you walk along rue de Rivoli and happen to see long lines in front of the hotel, they are undoubtedly for Angelina, the grand patisserie-café next door, where hot chocolate is served with a full bowl of swirled whipped cream.

DUCASSE SUR SEINE

In the world of haute cuisine, Alain Ducasse has the lofty title as the current living chef with the most Michelin stars in the world—twenty-one now—and the only chef to have three-Michelin-star restaurants in three cities. At current count, he is involved with about thirty world-wide restaurants. This high achiever has been Chef Numero Uno in my book for decades, and I was lucky to have interviewed him in French in the early 2000s, after he made his New York début, and to have experienced his affiliated restaurants from Hong Kong to Saint Petersburg and in France, Monaco, and the United States.

In Paris, in 2021, Val and I were so lucky to have dined on the swank Ducasse sur Seine dinner cruise. It was a late-evening, five-course Nuit Étoilée (Starry Night) menu served with sommelier-selected wines and accompanied by the twinkling lights of the Eiffel Tower.

AUX LYONNAIS

Val and I also lunched at Aux Lyonnais, which replicates a bouchon in Lyon, including the workers'-priced *formule* lunch menu (about 32€ in 2024) that is handwritten on the blackboard. Marie-victorine Manoa heads the team, which prepared snails in puff pastry and *la volaille de Bresse au vinaigre,* the famous red-combed, blue-footed chickens raised in Bresse, outside Lyon, which have their own AOC (*l'Appellation d'origine controlee*; AOC legally requires that the bird be born, raised, and slaughtered in Bresse).

LE JULES VERNE

In 2013, my friend Susann and I celebrated our trip with lunch on the second level of the Eiffel Tower, at Le Jules Verne, which was then operated by Alain Ducasse. Yes, the food was gastronomic and lovely. Yes, the view of Paris on that clear day was outstanding. And, fortuitously, diners with reservations accessed a private elevator to the restaurant, a fabulous avoid-the-crowd convenience for those who can afford the prix-fixe meal.

A caveat: Do note that since 2019, Chef Frédéric Anton has led the team at Le Jules Verne, which a professional foodie guest on David Lebovitz's podcast highly recommended in late 2024. She claimed that the two-Michelin-star restaurant is far more worthwhile than simply as a venue with a view. For those who can handle the price tag or are looking for a special occasion restaurant, I consider the experience well worth it. But in November 2024, when I considered the cost for lunch-with-a-view for four after having already booked two other gastronomic lunches, I chose a less expensive option.

LES OMBRES QUAI BRANLY

For that November 2024 trip, my friend Françoise Rougé recommended the Ducasse restaurant Les Ombres Quai Branly, on the top level of the Musée Quai Branly - Jacques Chirac, for its perfect Eiffel Tower view and its proximity to our barge cruise on Bateaux Parisiens. We each ordered the least complicated lunch—there are others with five or six courses—and delighted in our meals. My cousins savored smoked octopus, Lyndsey was pleased with puff pastry with cauliflower, and I enjoyed agnolotti with spiced Bolognese. From amuses to mignardises, everything was exquisite—including the staff's willingness to substitute chicken for the pigeon on the menu.

April in Paris with Susann

I met my friend Susann, former managing editor at *Physicians' Travel & Meeting Guide,* in Italy in 1995 and we established an enduring friendship. As members of the same professional organization, The Society of American Travel Writers, we've traveled together to conventions in Dubai and Thailand and, on our own, to Saint Petersburg, Moscow, Las Vegas, and Miami. We share an enthusiasm for art museums and had talked about taking a road trip to the museums on the Riviera long before it happened.

An invitation from European Waterways for a barge cruise in April 2013 seemed like a perfect opportunity, and I asked her to join me for those few days. We planned an itinerary that started in Paris, with a continuation to the south afterward. Our visit to Paris was wonderful: we stayed at Hôtel Barrière Le Fouquet, on Avenue George V, and dined well at one of its restaurants, Le Diane.

As avid museumgoers *d'un certain age* (of a certain age), even ten years ago we taxied to all the museums and saved our footsteps for the grand, art-filled rooms. And we visited a smaller house museum, Musée Jacquemart-André (on Blvd Haussmann), with its collection of fifteenth- and sixteenth-century sculpture, eighteenth-century decorative arts, and paintings by famous artists, including Bernini, Botticelli, David, and Fragonard.

One afternoon, I had time to frolic in the indoor pool at Spa Diane Barrière, at Fouquet's, before my treatment, and later included the experience in one of my all-time favorite assignments, "Superb Subterranean Spas," which featured some of the underground spas with indoor heated swimming pools that I'd most enjoyed: George V, Shangri-La, Royal Monceau. For our last night, we moved to a hotel on Avenue de l'Opéra, where we met the other eight European Waterways passengers and where the van picked us up for the drive to Burgundy the following morning.

SPRING

During our stay in Paris, we were lucky to get a reservation at Spring, a tiny restaurant where American-born chef Daniel Rose had a market-driven menu before anyone else and his amazing talents attracted a Parisian following. We arrived early and nibbled on appetizers at the bar in the ancient *cave* downstairs. Once at the table, we didn't see a written menu. The waitstaff brought out one bright dish after another during the multicourse meal. Rose made such a splash that the American was credited with "One of the 10 Best Restaurants in Paris." Spring has closed, but Chef Rose reigns at La Bourse et La Vie in Paris and Le Coucou in New York.

A Culinary Triomphe with Emma

Can I tell you about *ma petite fille* (first granddaughter), Emma Lov Block? She was a musician in the crib, listened to classic music and rock 'n' roll in her car seat, and dressed up as a member of Kiss—with makeup and guitar—for her second Halloween. Emma entered first grade at an elementary school in Battery Park City just days before 9/11, and was so haunted by the "gray snow" falling from the World Trade Center towers that she wrote a song called *That Day* by the age of twelve. She started performing at The Bitter End (where Joni

Mitchell and James Taylor sang) in her early teens. Emma studied music at Manhattan's Professional Performing Arts Middle School, LaGuardia High School of Music & Art and Performing Arts, and Purchase College, where she formed a band LOOTE (LOv+ foOTE) that was signed by Universal and Island Records. When she decided to take a semester "off" to commit to her songwriting career, I saw the chance to spend time with her.

"Em, how would you like to take a two-week French 101 course in Paris and the Riviera?" She grinned agreement: "*D'accord!*" I felt beyond lucky to be able to introduce her to Paris. Each of my daughters had traveled there, alone or with a friend, and I never had the chance to witness their reactions.

Emma and I took the hour-long RoissyBus shuttle from Charles de Gaulle (CDG) airport, because it stops directly at the Palais Garnier, which faces The InterContinental Paris Le Grand where we were staying. We arrived with plenty of time to check in and freshen up before our 1:00 p.m. reservation at the hotel's Café de la Paix. The café terrace has a reputation as the place where "if you wait long enough, you'll meet someone you know," and, frankly, I didn't expect such an excellent lunch. It reminds me not to prejudge popular tourist destinations; in Paris, they are sometimes the best.

I had arranged to eat in two historic gems (Le Procope and Brasserie Fouquet's Paris), two tiny, newly opened restaurants (La Bourse et La Vie and Table Bruno Verjus), and a legendary favorite (Le Grand Véfour). And from that first meal to the last, our week was a culinary triumph, even though Emma eats a gluten-free diet, which I worried might be an issue. I told her to order anything she wanted. She did, and it worked out marvelously. We dined at the restaurants in the following order:

LE PROCOPE

Le Procope dates to 1686 and is situated in the 6th arrondissement, just off Boulevard Saint-Germain near the Comédie-Française theater. We loved the décor, the red walls, historic memorabilia, and portraits of literary and political greats, from Napoleon to Voltaire. A colleague, a travel consultant who happened to be in Paris and who had helped me secure our second hotel, Villa Maillot, joined us. We two well-traveled sophisticates committed the cardinal sin of ignoring the house specialties: onion soup, and classic seafood and beef dishes. We both craved coq au vin, requested it, and tasted it. After one bite, we looked up at each other and chuckled knowingly: "This old hen is older than we are, maybe as ancient as the restaurant!" Emma was delighted with her onion soup, without bread, and grilled fish.

LA BOURSE ET LA VIE

Daniel Rose had just launched his La Bourse et La Vie, a cozy twenty-nine-seat bistro in the 1st, where we started with huge gougères that Rose's wife, Marie-Aude, made. She is an accomplished chef who now owns La Mercerie restaurant in Manhattan. After a delectable foie gras served with onion jam, I tried my first traditional pot au feu, because I had heard so much about the slowly simmered meat and vegetable stew. Though I'm told Rose's version is lighter than the classic ones, I'm confident I would have been happier eating what Emma ordered: steak frites!

TABLE BRUNO VERJUS

At the second tiny bistro, Table Bruno Verjus, we sat at the counter and the owner served her a raw scallop fresh from the sea, which Emma loved. It was simple fresh-from-the-sea fare with a marvelous host who now holds two Michelin stars and was just ranked #3 in The World's 50 Best Restaurants 2024.

BRASSERIE FOUQUET'S PARIS

We also ate at an iconic restaurant: the widely popular, century-old gathering spot Brasserie Fouquet's Paris on the Champs-Elysées, which reopened after a sad two-year closure after a tragic bombing in 2019. The terrace is famous for people watching; the interior for its cuisine crafted by Michelin-starred chef Pierre Gagnaire. It was a thrill. This first meal by Pierre Gagnaire convinced me to dine at his namesake restaurant in 2024, which turned out to have been a marvelous choice.

LE GRAND VÉFOUR

During the pandemic, I rediscovered this signed menu from Michelin-starred chef Guy Martin of Le Grand Véfour.

Pour Madame Irvina Lew,
La cuisine du Coeur et de l'amitié
Merci de votre visite
05
10
15

The inscription translates to: "For Madame Irvina Lew, Cooking of the heart and friendship, Thanks for your visit 05 10 15" (October 5, 2015). It reminded me of the unique thrill of introducing Emma to Paris and of the epicurean lunch we had there.

Our meal at Le Grand Véfour is something we will both remember, so much so that I went back to dine there in 2024 (see the update that follows) and Emma took her boyfriend there when they were recently in Paris, just to take a picture and tell him about our meal.

Le Grand Véfour made its debut in 1784, when it was one of Paris's first society cafés, and soon became famous when Camille Desmoulins, a passionate revolutionary, issued his call "Aux armes citoyennes," there; his words, which begin the French national anthem, *La Marseillaise*, supposedly launched the storming of the Bastille (14 juillet 1789) and the French Revolution.

Its meticulously restored eighteenth-century interior showcases Louis XVI carved-wood paneling, an ornate Italianate ceiling, neoclassical frescoes, serene paintings, delicate mirrors, magical chandeliers and sconces, and imposing windows overlooking the arched arcade and Palais Royale gardens. Lush red banquettes identify the "who's who" list of guest gastronomes: Napoleon and Josephine, Victor Hugo, Cocteau, Jean-Paul Sartre, Simone de Beauvoir, George Sand, and Maria Callas. One regular, Colette, lived in an adjacent apartment; another, Julia Child, claimed the restaurant was her favorite.

Our multicourse gastronomic meal followed this typical fine-dining pattern:

amuse bouche (an hors d'oeuvre of one to three bites)
entrée (starter or appetizer)
plat principal (main course)
salade (usually served after the main course, if at all)
fromage (cheese)
pre-dessert
dessert
mignardises (petit fours or bite-size sweets)

Emma and I started the meal with *une coupe de* champagne and *foie gras canard en terrine*, a rich duck liver prepared in a loaf with a carrot preserve and a bright yellow carrot coulis. I continued with a perfectly pink fillet of roast lamb, while Emma chose blue lobster, which arrived with bright red edible flower leaves, sprigs of green, and tiny dices of mango, and a fillet of St. Pierre, a white fish topped with delicate purple leaves.

The sommelier selected the buttery Burgundy, a Meursault 2012, Clos du Domaine Henri Darnat, and a server brought us each a fresh baguette before the cheese course, with a dozen choices atop a silver platter. Pre-desserts arrived: four macarons on a narrow, elongated dish; six pieces of bicolored jellied candy—deep red-wine and blood-orange—decorating a rectangular plate; and three small glasses topped with whipped cream.

Dessert—a tall chocolate cube adorned with a purple-hued bonbon, decorative pistachio droplets, and a few burgundy-colored teardrops—was presented on a two-color plate, half white and half the color of red wine. Emma's *Physalis dans un biscuit* was a square phyllo dough sandwich filled with vanilla-touched crème Anglaise and served with ice cream, lime sorbet, and a lime gelée presented on a large, black-rimmed plate. The penultimate dessert, *gateau savoie*, a light, airy sponge cake from Chef Martin's native region, was served before *les mignardises*, the après-dessert sweets, petits fours, and a tray of thin, dry, and not-too-sweet chocolates plus one huge cacao bean in a silver bowl. Perfection!

I returned with Val in April 2024 and was aware that during the pandemic, when nobody could sit indoors, Chef Martin launched an outdoor, more casual terrasse menu and revised his gastronomic menu to include a two-course 58€, prix-fixe *formule*. The result is a livelier and less formal restaurant, still within an amazingly beautiful setting and with similarly exquisite cuisine and service. We chose from the à la carte menu and started with artisanal bread and the chef's special *amuse*: ravioli stuffed with seared foie gras topped with crème fraiche and truffles. I ordered a crab starter, which arrived in a cylinder wrapped with long paper-thin strips of cucumber, and a cheese plate; Val ate silky smoked salmon. We both ended with beautiful pastries.

———◆◆———

As for "kulcha," Emma and I visited two small museums that week. We strolled through the Picasso Museum inside the seventeenth-century Hotel Salé, where we viewed some of his five thousand works: paintings, sculptures, sketches, studies, drafts, notebooks, etchings, photographs, illustrated books, and films. It's in Le Marais, which became the Jewish quarter in the thirteenth century and is now quite trendy, with posh vintage stores, boutiques, cafés, and kosher restaurants on rue des Rosiers. We also went to the Frank Gehry–designed Fondation Louis Vuitton in the Bois de Boulogne, the city's largest park. To get there, we took a shuttle bus from the L'Étoile directly to its front door. The museum looks like a giant whale and features outdoor terraces with extraordinary views of the park and the Eiffel Tower.

Emma and I will always remember our time together in Paris.

Versailles

‹•••›

I IMAGINE THAT MOST OF THE TEN MILLION ANNUAL VISI-
tors to Versailles overlook eighteenth-century political drama,
excesses, and inequities and focus, as I do, on the palatial beauty,
with its hand-crafted furnishings, gorgeous gilt-framed mirrors, and
fabulous paintings, as well as its geometric-styled gardens, smaller
mansions, and expansive parklands.

At age nineteen, I thought nothing of taking the train to Versailles, waiting on a long entry line on a hot morning, spending the
entire summer's day touring the palace and park, staying on after
dark for the *Son et Lumiere* spectacle, and returning late to Paris.
The Sound & Light show that delighted me then still enchants tourists: lights illuminate different parts of the palace as French actors
narrate history. Baroque music plays in the background, water jets
shoot from fountains, and *feu d'artifices* explode in the sky just as
in the time of Louis XIV, when the king provided lavish entertainment—including fireworks—to keep his courtiers too amused to
plot against him!

The motivation for my next visit to this charming suburban
commune was to dine and write about Gérard Vié's restaurant, Les
Trois Marches, which was housed at the Trianon Palace between
1970 and 2007.

WALDORF ASTORIA VERSAILLES-TRIANON PALACE

When I first arrived, in 1995, it was called Trianon Palace. I was beguiled by the beautiful belle époque villa, with its high ceilings and black-and-white checkerboard-patterned entry gallery. Its twentieth-century history impressed me, too: George Clemenceau had stayed there in 1919, when he signed the Treaty of Versailles, and General Eisenhower used it as his post–World War II headquarters.

My stay was dreamlike, with a visit to the palace, a swim in the indoor heated pool that opens out to a garden, a spa treatment, and glorious meals. Even my last morning walk was memorable: I entered the gates to the palace estate, within footsteps of the hotel, but somehow missed a turn toward the palace, where I was headed. The path I took circumnavigated the cross-shaped path around the Grand Canal, and I ended up walking the 5,479-foot-long path there and back, plus the distance around each of the 3,000-foot crossbars, for a total of about four miles. As fit as I like to think I was thirty years ago, that was more than my usual morning trek.

I was truly thrilled with my room, where I felt as if I had stepped back in time because it overlooked sheep grazing in the fields at Le Hameau, the miniature farm that Marie-Antoinette created in 1783 as a bucolic escape from the daily protocol of court life.

un peu plus: MARIE-ANTOINETTE

I had always believed that Marie-Antoinette dressed like a farm maiden to play shepherdess on her little farm, until I read information online that claimed it was a myth. Historians don't dispute that she frivolously said: "*Qu'ils mangent de la brioche*" (Let them eat cake.) They agree that she disdained the plight of starving peasants who couldn't afford flour to make bread and certainly couldn't buy eggs and butter needed for the cakelike brioche. Some say that enemies of the monarchy took out their anger on the imperious queen and beheaded her in 1793, during the French Revolution, and some months after her husband, Louis XVI, met his fate at the guillotine.

In April 1999, Alison and her friend Ellen joined me at Trianon Palace, and again, our rooms had that idyllic view. Two nights earlier, we had shared a gastronomic dinner at Alain Ducasse at Plaza Athenée and, although I was hopeful that they'd be willing to accompany me to dinner at Les Trois Marches, they nixed that second extravagance. Not I! I had loved my first Gérard Vié meal and wasn't about to miss this one.

LES TROIS MARCHES

In June 1976, I saw Chef Vié pictured in *Paris Match* among eight celebrated French chefs whose reputations were already familiar to me: Paul Bocuse, Alain Chapel, Michel Guérard, Alain Senderens, and Jean Troisgros. By then I had generated a long bucket list of top French chefs to experience, and he was added. By 1980, Gérard Vié had seven starred restaurants, 140 employees, and success as an author, consultant, founding member of the Chambre Syndicale de la Haute Cuisine Française, and, in 1985, he was named Best Chef of the Year 2002 by Johnson & Wales University.

It took almost twenty years before my first dinner at his Les Trois Marches, but it was his remarkable *haute cuisine minceur* (elevated spa cuisine) lunch menu that impressed me most. In the mid-1990s, I specialized in writing about healthy eating, particularly spa food, and at that time the typical US spa-goer was served broiled fish or chicken breast, steamed broccoli, iceberg lettuce, and a lemon wedge!

So it was an awakening when I was introduced to Chef Vié's beautifully presented cuisine, which he developed for sophisticated, health-conscious patrons who frequented the Trianon Palace spa. He incorporated locally sourced seasonal ingredients with very little butter, cream, or sugar in inventive, gastronomic spa fare; others are famous for similarly special dishes now, but it was new to me in 1995.

I remembered owning his cuisine minceur cookbook but couldn't find it. During an online search to reorder *Manger équilibré: 100 recettes pour garder la forme (Eat Well-Balanced Foods: 100 Recipes to Take Care of Your Body),* I found a *New York Times* review of Le Trois Marches from January 24, 1999, written just a few months before my second meal there in April.

That night, I sat at a well-spaced table set with fine linen, crystal, and china, under crystal chandeliers hanging from high ceilings, and spent far more time sipping a "coupe de champagne" and studying the menu than I ever would have if I had been engaged in conversation with someone else.

I recall rejecting one appetizer because the word *lapin* (rabbit) was listed as an ingredient, and I don't eat bunnies. The dish was called *gateaux de poireaux,* which I translated wrongly as pear cake (*gateau*=cake, *poire*=pear), not knowing that *poireaux* are leeks! Instead, I requested familiar specialties: *le foie gras de canard poelé au pamplemousse rose* (a seared slice of foie gras with pink grapefruit) and *la canette fermier de Challans,* a young farm-raised female duck from Challans, in La Vendée.

Dinner was exceptional, and I saved the dated menu, with its *Haute Cuisine Française* logo, and the twelve-by-seventeen-inch, poster-size beverage *Carte des Cafés et des Thés,* with its illustrations of Ethiopia, Kenya, and Ceylon, where tea and coffee are grown. The French text notes that Soliman Aga, the Turkish ambassador to France, introduced Louis XIV to his first taste of coffee in 1669, and it was an immediate hit: *le success fut immediate.*

The review I mentioned was by Jacqueline Friedrich and called "Choice Tables; Hard by the Château, Royal Eating"; coincidentally, she referenced a dish that I rejected because rabbit was mentioned as an ingredient. She obviously had no problem eating it:

". . . His *gateaux de poireaux*, a compact mound of leeks, bacon, foie gras, and mushrooms, is equally delectable and comes with rabbit, pounded and wrapped around cabbage, flavored with thyme and bacon, as well as a wealth of rabbit liver and kidneys."

By 2021, when Val and I arrived to overnight at Trianon Palace, via an Uber from Paris, it was called Waldorf Astoria Versailles–Trianon Palace, and we were both looking forward to our stay and our reservation for dinner at Gordon Ramsay au Trianon. We were also looking forward to touring the palace again, and had purchased timed-entry tickets to the château.

After we checked in, I hurried to see the room, which happily overlooked Le Hameau, although we didn't see any sheep grazing there. We lunched in the lovely glass-roofed Winter Garden adjacent to Le Hameau fields, and afterward walked out through the hotel's wrought-iron gates and turned right toward a *parc* entry, just a few steps away.

We didn't want to risk getting lost on the two-thousand-acre palace grounds and being late for this visit, so I carefully followed the concierge's instructions to the palace.

We arrived without difficulty, waited only a few minutes on a short line and, once inside the palace, wandered around the royal apartments and admired the glamorous Hall of Mirrors and the *Coronation of Napoleon* painting, which conveys more about Napoleon's psyche than most other historical data.

un peu plus: CORONATION OF NAPOLEON

The *Coronation of Napoleon* is by the emperor's favorite painter, Jacques-Louis David. Napoleon himself commissioned the famous painter to produce a large-scale work depicting a key moment in the ceremony. The classic scene on view shows Napoleon wearing a laurel wreath and standing, his back to the pope, holding Josephine's crown as she kneels before him. During the coronation ceremony, at Nôtre-Dame in Paris on December 2, 1804, Napoleon took the first crown from the pope and placed it on his own head, then crowned Josephine with a smaller one. It was quite the controversial power gesture, as if to show his superiority over His Holiness. We'd previously seen the first rendition, which was moved from Versailles to the Louvre in 1889. The second version was painted later and is considered the better of the two.

At the end of that visit to and through the palace, my feet hurt so much that the taxi stand was too far away for me to walk, although it was located just beyond the cobblestone courtyard on the far side of the street. I hobbled toward the nearer side street to the closest restaurant, Café Bleu Roi, where we rested, glass of white wine in hand. We were tired, and if not hungry, ready enough to eat something; besides, it seemed only proper to order food before asking the *patron* to call a cab for us. Val chose her usual mozzarella and tomato salad; I craved onion soup, and we relaxed, then asked him to call the taxi.

I faded as soon as I was back in the room, and even an hour later, couldn't get out of bed to dress for the dinner we had reserved weeks earlier from the States. As eager as I was to dine at the Gordon Ramsay restaurant, I had to call and cancel.

I dread canceling a reservation and restaurants certainly resent it, particularly at the last minute, which is why so many take credit card authorizations and charge for no-shows. I can count the times I've missed an appointment or canceled a meal, but it has happened. Once, I suffered so from a migraine in Paris that Bob had to cancel a hard-to-get reservation at Tour d'Argent; and on that same 2021 trip with Val, I was so tired before a much-awaited 10:30 p.m. reservation at Joël Robuchon that I couldn't get up to eat, even though it's located next door to Hotel Montalembert, where we were staying.

It happens rarely, but when my body says *no mas*, I listen. In Versailles, I suspect that late-afternoon glass of wine messed with my head and my digestion.

AIRELLES CHÂTEAU DE VERSAILLES, LE GRAND CONTRÔLE

I was fine the following morning, and we got up early to taxi the short distance to Airelles Château de Versailles, Le Grand Contrôle. To research this "new-new" Parisian hotel for *Hospitality Design* magazine, I had arranged a *visite* of the hotel. Then, Julien Révah, the general manager, generously invited us to breakfast there and join hotel guests on an exclusive docent-led tour of Le Grand Trianon an hour before it opened to the public.

We taxied from Trianon Palace, at one far edge of the palace grounds, past the distinctive gold-and-black wrought-iron gates in front of the château, to the opposite side of the palace. There, a costumed valet, wearing a waistcoat and breeches, greeted us at the gated entry court (it reminded me of the eighteenth-century-style dress in Williamsburg, Virginia). All the men were similarly garbed, including house painters on ladders, by Marie-France Croyeau of Terre et Ciel, who authentically outfitted each of the one hundred employees.

Le Grand Contrôle is the first hotel built on palace grounds and is housed within a building originally designed in 1681 by Louis XIV's favorite architect, Jules Hardouin-Mansart, who, according to Wikipedia, named his famous mansard roof design for his great-uncle François Mansart. One of Louis XIV's officials, Paul de Beau-villiers, was the first to live there, and future finance ministers for kings Louis XIV, XV, and XVI, enjoyed the same prestige housing. Unlike most courtiers, who lived in palace apartments, they were allotted a private—albeit attached—home, making it easy to scurry indoors when the king summoned.

The hotel conversion, which took four years and entailed precise artisanal work, created the fourteen rooms and three suites, and added the necessary high-tech, twenty-first-century infrastructure within three connected seventeenth-century mansions. Architect-interior designer Christophe Tollemer transformed the interior, reinstating the authentic décor so that every element—the gilded walls, wallpaper, mirrors, sconces and chandeliers, marble and parquet floors, fabrics, and rare antique furnishings—reflected what existed in 1788, the last date for which inventory records exist.

DUCASSE AU CHÂTEAU DE VERSAILLES AIRELLES

Alain Ducasse was charged with creating a culinary program that nods to the period. In August 2022, I watched a documentary, *The Quest of Alain Ducasse*, streaming on Amazon Prime and YouTube, that shows him impeccably researching the minutiae to incorporate into a royal dinner at Versailles. That dinner took place years before the hotel opened, but it foreshadowed his intimate involvement with the hotel project. In the documentary, a waiter sounds the bell at 8:30 p.m. to summon guests lucky enough to dine at the five-course, carefully curated Royal Feast, accompanied by the music of Bach and Vivaldi. Costumes and candlelight add to the theatrical event.

When we arrived for breakfast, we were escorted to the exquisitely appointed dining room, where our upholstered chairs flanked a breakfast table facing Le Nôtre's famed L'Orangérie in the royal gardens. I peeked at the underside of the beautiful Limoges china to see the back stamp: Ancienne Manufacture ROYALE fabricated at Sèvres, which refers to the famous, and still operating, eighteenth-century porcelain factory that I had toured as a student. I took pictures to record the information: one plate was made for Louis XV; another was dated 1833, when Louis Philippe was king.

Artfully prepared pastries, including croissants, pain au chocolat, and sliced breads, along with a variety of butters, sliced fruit, and a platter of meats appeared at the table. The waiter served freshly squeezed orange juice and made-to-order omelettes. The presentation hinted at what the hotel's Sunday Royal Brunch buffet might be like. The original royal ritual was called Le Grand Couvert, and the king and queen dined in front of the public. They began their meals, as King Louis XVI did, with a glass of warm vegetable broth, known as the king's soup, and continued with classic dishes.

LE GRAND TRIANON

Toward the end of the meal, we were invited to follow a costumed valet out of the back of the hotel, near the imposing one-hundred-step staircase that connects the manicured, geometrically precise gardens with the château. Next to a string of golf carts that guests can use to explore the two-thousand-acre park were two vans waiting to drive us to Le Grand Trianon, the one-story, pink-marble hideaway that Louis XIV commissioned in 1670, and which Jules Hardouin-Mansart erected in 1687.

Our guide told us about the château's history, including the fact that when General de Gaulle restored Le Grand Trianon in 1963, he lived in the north wing, and hosted foreign dignitaries there. Having once walked around the entire Grand Canal, I wasn't a bit surprised when she told us that the Sun King cruised there in a gondola, when he fled courtly life in the formal palace to rendezvous with Madame de Montespan in their love nest.

We felt lucky to have seen the hotel, breakfasted there, and toured with hotel guests, who can also "sip" at the Marie-Antoinette afternoon tea; "sup" by candlelight on a meal presented on gold, silver, or vermeil dome-covered dishes; "stay" in a Maison Pierre Frey–decorated room named for a period icon; and "spa" at the Valmont.

My Instagram tag #sipsupstayspa reflects those preferred travel activities, but I don't always get to experience every single one.

chez moi: CLASSIC FRENCH OMELETTE

As an unabashed fan of Jacques Pépin, I am familiar with how he swirls and rolls an omelette and have practiced his technique. (You can watch on YouTube.) Here's how: I add a drop of water, milk, or cream to three beaten eggs (or two yolks and three whites) and pour it into a nonstick pan with lightly melted butter. I swirl to the desired doneness, fold, and slide onto a plate.

THE RIVIERA

———◆◆———

Looking out from the kitchen terrace of our rental apartment in Cannes, in May 2024, I watched a cruise ship moor just beyond where our street—Rue Macé—meets the Mediterranean. What struck me speechless that day was the intense color of the sky above the neighboring six-story buildings. The magical blue imitated the vibrant luminescence that first lured plein air artists to the French Riviera. The beau monde followed them and so, eventually, did I.

The French Riviera, aka the Côte d'Azur, is considered the most beautiful part of France and, after Paris, its second-most-visited tourist destination. My first trip there was my chance to pay homage to my favorite artists: Bonnard, Chagall, Derain, Matisse, Léger, Picasso, Renoir, and Signac, who each relished the regional light. Yet what overwhelmed me as the plane descended in 1990—my first opportunity to see where they lived, dined, and created—was an immediate, palpable reaction to the region's topographical beauty. The morning sunlight reflected off mega yachts in the sparkling Mediterranean; it glistened in the swimming pools behind villas strewn like jewels along the mainland to the tip of Cap-Ferrat, and glimmered off the commanding, snow-capped Alpes Maritimes. I was so smitten I had goosebumps, which the French call *chair de poule* (chicken flesh). From that day on, I've returned often and traveled alone, rented cars, cruised with Bob, taken a road trip with car afficionados from Grenoble, and toured the coast with Susann, Emma Lov, and Val. I attended the annual *Jazz à Juan*, and have visited Saint-Tropez, Èze, Terre Blanche, and beyond.

I started renting apartments for three-week periods in 2018, with each of my daughters and, subsequently, with Val. No matter where I stay, I always find my smile on this oh-so-lovely coastal corner of France.

First Timer on
the Riviera

———◆◆◆———

MY FIRST TRIP TO THE RIVIERA, IN 1990, WAS FUNDED by an unexpected book advance from FIRST, inc., the French publishing company that bought the rights to my book *You Can't Do It All: Ideas That Work for Mothers Who Work* (Macmillan, 1986; Berkley, 1987). At a time when my school salary was allocated to family expenses, I assigned the extra funds ($1,500) to my long-awaited trip to the south of France. The check arrived in June, not long before the last days of the school year, when I was busy with the flurry of exams, and grading tests, averaging marks, and completing attendance reports (none of my favorite tasks). I didn't have the bandwidth to organize every minute detail, but I did create a Riviera road trip itinerary based upon visiting art museums in and around Nice.

My travel "advisors" for the adventure weren't trusted travel agents or savvy colleagues, but a bevy of oh-so-stunning strangers— single fashionistas who worked near the Gottex wholesale outlet in Manhattan, where Val, who worked in the garment center, took me to shop for resort wear. In that open-to-all changing room, women were chatting knowledgeably about their annual vacations in Saint-

Tropez. One woman advised me to take the helicopter from Nice to Monaco, where I planned to start my trip.

Landing in Nice was—and always is—a rarified experience. (Beyond the topography, the airport is welcoming and surrounded by flowers.) I took the helicopter from the airport to Monaco, where I spent an idyllic few days, which I describe in a future chapter, before boarding the train at Gare de Monaco Monte Carlo, carrying three cumbersome, soft-sided Lands' End bags that I had purchased for my book tour in 1986 (and which they monogrammed gratis).

Thirty-two minutes later, in Nice, I encountered *problème numéro un*, the challenge of maneuvering my luggage from the train to the upper-level exit. At that time, there was no escalator or elevator at the station, no Red Cap valet to help, nor a *chariot* (baggage cart) in sight. I was standing on the platform staring at the steep stairs and contemplating how to carry one bag at a time up the long flight, when one person after another (they all walked by me and up the steps) warned me about pickpockets—*"Attention aux voleurs!"*—but not a soul offered to help (this may be why I still always offer to help overloaded travelers, young and strong ones as well, if only to watch their bags).

I waited for the crowd to disperse and dragged the bags up, one by one. By the time I crossed the parking lot to the car rental agency, I mocked myself for having over-bought and over-packed as I tried to stuff all three bags into the ridiculously teeny, stick-shift Renault. I understood then that I'd never be able to manage that luggage on trains between Nice and Lyon and Lyon to Paris, and decided to send home as much as possible, including all that resort wear. I got in the car and set out to find a big box.

At a nearby *supermarché*, I picked up the first large, sturdy carton that I thought would be suitable for my extra clothes, deposited it into the back seat, and drove along the seaside Promenade des An-glais and admired the belle époque seafront villas built for the British and Russian aristocracy who originally wintered there.

I knew that the Musée Matisse was closed for a major renova-tion, so I drove to the Musée Chagall, where I stopped at Buvette, the little outdoor café in the museum's gardens, which was designed by Chagall himself, and ordered a hearty croque monsieur, the French version of a grilled ham-and-cheese sandwich. In France, it's topped with a bubbly, cheesy béchamel sauce. I don't know how long I spent viewing some of Chagall's four hundred paintings, but I can assure you that seeing the plethora of his artwork is life-enhancing. I was still lingering in front of a romantic image of a fanciful Chagall fe-male embarking on a phantasmagorical flight, when I realized that it was past 5:00 p.m. and time to set out for my hotel.

As I crawled along in big-city rush hour traffic, I was still under the impression that Le Relais Impérial, in Saint-Vallier-de-Thiey, a charming and economically priced two-star hotel, was only eight miles from Nice—so I thought it would be a short, easy drive. Oops! I was doubly mistaken: it is located eight miles from Grasse, on hilly Alpine roads north—and thirty-five miles away—from Nice! It's usually an hour's drive, but not during rush hour and certainly not in the deluge that began shortly after I got on the narrow, curvy hillside roads. Between gear-shifting—and stalling—I was trying to feel around for the windshield wiper switch, which I finally found, and the defogger, which I never found. Of course, there was no air-conditioning, so I had to open the window just to see between the raindrops. The final trek in that dark rainstorm was scary.

When I finally arrived, the innkeeper greeted me: "*Desolé, Ma-dame*. You didn't call to confirm. I just gave your room to someone else. " He was polite and welcoming, but firm. He led me to the only vacant room, which was so small that the bidet almost touched the bed. (In 2024, Val and I lunched at Relais Impérial, which the innkeeper's granddaughters now run, and I saw that tiny room again.)

The innkeeper cordially agreed to dial my husband in the United States from the front desk. Moments later, when the phone rang, I was sprawled across the bed and sobbing. "I don't think I can do this by myself," I whined. Bob was supportive, as usual, and said all the right things: "You're a great driver." He tried to boost my spirits: "You know how to handle cars better than most people, even around the mountainside and alone." He continued, "Once you get more familiar with the car, your 'ordeal' will be over." He was sensitive, but neither of us acknowledged what it took me some years to accept: when I'm challenged, my psyche plays tricks on me and sometimes I create my own stress.

The following morning, when I opened the car door to bring the empty box up to the room, the intense odor hit me. After an overnight in the hot, closed vehicle, the smell that I hadn't noticed at the grocery store or while driving clearly announced itself: I had unwittingly grabbed a box previously used to transport whole hams to the market. With hopes that the breeze would fumigate the box in the four days before its slow transatlantic voyage to the States, I placed it on the sill of an open window facing nonstop tourist and trucker traffic on the famous Route Napoléon. Unfortunately, a few days of fresh air did not diminish the stench; when the carton finally arrived on Long Island six weeks later, I had to hand-wash every item again and again and line dry it all, in the sun, as my mom had taught me, before my odorific fashion finery became wearable!

Cap d'Antibes

The morning after arriving at the Relais Impérial, the weather was sublime, so I decided to follow Gottex-gal-pal advice: "Spend the morning poolside at the famed Hôtel du Cap-Eden-Roc." I started early from Saint-Vallier-de-Thiey and drove south on the Route Napoléon twenty-five miles to the coast. In those pre-GPS days (and still) I studied maps before getting into the car; in 1990, I followed the clearly marked road signs and cruised downhill along the picturesque roads beyond Grasse (the perfume city), and Mougins (where I would one day dine solo at Moulin de Mougins, just so I could sample master-chef Roger Vergé's signature zucchini blossoms stuffed with black truffles).

I continued through Vallauris, where Picasso created ceramics and lived in a house called La Galloise (c. 1948) with Françoise Gilot and their two children: Claude and Paloma. Once on the coast at Golfe-Juan, I followed the seacoast through Juan-les-Pins to Cap d'Antibes and drove along the waterside on the verdant, villa-studded peninsula until I spotted Boulevard J. F. Kennedy and the drive to the fabled hotel. I knew that the hotel had been a favored paradise among the world's most privileged for more than 150 years, especially for Americans, including Hollywood legends who flock there during the Cannes Film Festival. Val saw Roger Moore, Eva Gabor, and Merv Griffin there; we both spotted Michael Douglas in 2019.

HÔTEL DU CAP-EDEN-ROC

I pulled into the entry at Hôtel du Cap—a twenty-two-acre botanical garden by the seafront—and stopped at the valet stand in front of the 118-room Napoleon III–style palace building, c. 1870. The valet directed me toward *La Grande Allée*, and I strolled beneath massive

Aleppo pine trees next to manicured lawns and formal gardens on the idyllic walking path that connects the majestic main structure and the waterfront pavilion.

I recall paying an exorbitant sum to enter the pool, equivalent to a night's room rate at my little two-star hotel, but I didn't even wince; such is the price tag for the experience. As the pool boy directed me to a chaise lounge, we passed strikingly good-looking couples, among which several women were sunning topless. Clearly, I was the only singleton at this amazingly romantic retreat! Once settled, I averted my eyes from the "beautiful people" and focused on the scenery. The extraordinary infinity seawater pool had been hollowed out of the surrounding basalt rocks from which a series of circuslike trapezes were hanging high above the sea. It was my first time swimming in an infinity pool, and I leaned against the far edge to admire the extraordinary expanse of sea and the dock, where the dockmaster and his crew were helping guests onto a small boat that sped out to their mega yacht moored offshore. Other guests in swimsuits boarded dinghies that took them out for water sports, and the ones in chic sportswear boarded wooden-hulled speedboats. I imagined they were being shuttled to Cannes, where they would shop in haute couture boutiques on La Croisette, that city's famous seafront boulevard, and lunch, perhaps seaside, at one of the belle époque hotels.

That poolside pleasure was surely worth the cost; in fact, I later learned that I was lucky to have been admitted to the pool at all, as it's usually reserved exclusively for in-house guests. Still, my Sancho Panza self—the practical, down-to-earth, budget-minded me—cringed at staying for a high-priced lunch. I dressed and left the lap of luxury on a quest to find something to eat before visiting the Musée Picasso in Vieux Antibes. Almost immediately, I spotted a side-of-the-road beach shack, where I stopped and ordered the most typical sandwich in all of France: *le jambon fromage,* ham and cheese on a lavishly buttered baguette.

un peu plus: F. SCOTT FITZGERALD

A decade or so later, when I was sipping wine at the stunning Fitzgerald Bar at Hôtel Belles Rives, in Juan-les-Pins, I inquired about its name. The barman explained that it honored F. Scott Fitzgerald, who had lived at the villa with his wife, Zelda, in 1927, before it had been transformed into a five-star hotel. Later, I learned that Fitzgerald was one of the many famous residents on Cap d'Antibes and that the villa at Hôtel du Cap inspired the setting for *Tender Is the Night,* F. Scott Fitzgerald's fourth and final novel.

Daughter Jen was with me in 2018, when I next returned, on assignment to feature the Spa Eden-Roc. Touring the gardens, we saw the two outdoor *cabines* reserved for spa services and the collection of quaint, sand-fronted cabanas available to guests, where Marc Chagall used to sketch. We walked under a floral, vine-covered, trellis-topped path through a garden near the tennis courts to the small stand-alone spa. It was all too lovely to leave, and I suggested lunching on the terrace of Eden-Roc Grill, the more casual of the two seafront restaurants.

We each started with a glass of wine, fabulous bread served with beautiful *Bordier* butter from Brittany, and a regional gazpacho, the cold tomato soup, here made with *brunoise* (tiny diced) vegetables. I might have skipped directly to dessert had we not noticed the waiter carrying a tray of burgers to the three teens at the next table. During the time it took to order, wait for, and eat our burgers, I became engrossed in the family drama at the adjoining table and, without knowing the truth of their situation, imagined this scenario.

A middle-aged (fifty-five- to sixty-five-year-old) man sat at the table head next to a young woman, who looked to be the same age as the eldest of three girls also seated at the table—that I assumed were his daughters. It seemed as if the man and his female guest didn't know much about each other. He asked: "Do you eat this? Do you like that? Will you have wine?" When he spoke, she responded with yeses and nos and not much more. She appeared to be the outsider and certainly made no eye contact or conversation with the girls. As for the teens to twenty-somethings, they kept their eyes on their phones and, when served, ate in silence. The "dad's" attempts to speak to them resulted in the kind of eye-roll disdain that anyone familiar with teenagers recognizes. They were more detached than overtly rude and ate quickly, rushing to make their escape. I imagined—with no proof—that the outsider was the new girlfriend that the father had brought along on a vacation with his daughters.

Far more pleasant interactions were taking place at the table on our other side, where we noticed luncheon guests stopping to greet a young man and ask for his autograph, which he affably signed. I assumed he was a professional tennis player after one man told him that he had brought his tennis-playing daughter to attend the Monte Carlo Masters tennis tournament.

I imagine the terrace was full of accomplished people.

CHEF OLIVIER GAÏATTO

The following summer, in 2019, I was writing a feature about Chef Olivier Gaïatto, who had recently been elevated from cook to *chef du restaurant* at the gastronomic restaurant Eden-Roc, the formal restaurant on the building's upper level. He had just won a Michelin Plate for "Exceptional Standard." Chef Gaïatto isn't comfortable speaking in English, so I had prepared questions in French for our before-lunch interview. We met in the formal salon outside the restaurant, where the chef spoke about his childhood on the Riviera and mentioned growing up eating his grandmother's *soupe de pistou*, a typical Niçoise dish. (*Pistou* is like a Provençal cousin to Italian pesto).

Gaïatto credited his mentor, the hotel's longtime executive chef Arnaud Poëtte, with being the one who influenced his cooking techniques, and providing his access to a great kitchen staff and to the best culinary sources. And he acknowledged that his most impressive learning experience was when he worked four *stages* for multiple-Michelin-star chef Alain Ducasse; he said those four two-week sessions in the famous chef's kitchen taught him about discipline, purity of flavor, dedication to perfect ingredients, and attention to detail.

I asked him three specific questions designed to help home cooks like *moi!*

Q: What garden-fresh herbs do you choose for fish?
A: Freshly picked rosemary, lemon thyme, and *sariette* (savory).
Q: What temperature do you consider perfect for grilled or poached fish?
A: 55 degrees Centigrade [131°F].
Q: What do you use to stuff the *fleurs de courgettes* (zucchini flowers)?
A: Caponata or ratatouille Niçoise, "the way we like it in Nice," with cooking juice, Taggiasche olives, and grilled cébette onions (they are something like scallions).

In the kitchen, he introduced his *équipe* (team): "*Nous sommes famille.*" (We're family.) He showed me how he uses layers of individual flavors in his dishes to enhance taste; for example, carrots simmer in carrot water and whiskey. Then, he explained the ratatouille preparation. He dices each onion, pepper, tomato, zucchini, and eggplant into equal-size small pieces and cooks them individually in olive oil, because each vegetable takes a different amount of time to become tender yet stay intact.

I always love the energy, concentration, and focus that takes place in a kitchen, where the *brigade,* an entire team, works individually yet together, like an orchestra. Here I had the pleasure of seeing and smelling huge pots of simmering stocks that cook for hours, and watching a *commis* (a junior cook) strain the *jus* from an enormous pot of beef bones to use as a base for sauces. I learned a technique for my own kitchen by watching another *commis* prepare the chef's version of a bouquet garni: instead of tying the herbs with kitchen twine (as I do) or using flavorless cheesecloth, he tied the herbs—thyme, bay leaf, peppercorns—inside a long leek leaf. Chef declared proudly, "Everything in this kitchen is made in-house, many dishes from the kitchen's on-site and sustainable *potager* [herb and vegetable garden]," and continued, *"Je n'achète rien de l'extérieur"* (I buy nothing from the outside)—except for langoustine, lobster, butter from Brittany, and wild salmon from Scotland. Likewise, Chef Patissier Lilian Bonnefoi prepared all the breads, croissants, pastries, chocolates, cakes, and tarts in-house.

Once seated, he sent a sample portion of *soupe de pistou,* which he prepared especially for me. It was a delicate and delicious garlic-enhanced, minestrone-like broth filled with chickpeas, beans, teeny cubes of carrots and celery, baby basil leaves, and vermicelli. And it was served in style: The bowl arrived under a glass *cloche* (dome).

In 2019, the subsequent extravagant, wedding-worthy buffet that Val and I had at Eden-Roc was irresistible. I managed to taste only a fraction of what was at the ready and was too full to try the pasta, which was being prepared to order! After tasting the *soupe de pistou* and stuffed zucchini flowers (chef stuffed them with ratatouille), I sampled some salads and shared a platter of langoustines. Val was delighted with *Gillardeau* oysters, the homemade pâté en croute, and fresh burrata with red, purple, and yellow tomato segments and basil. Add the house-made smoked salmon, Culatta ham, and a whole fish, and there was simply too much for one meal. Our waiter offered to save dessert until after my spa service and guarded my raspberry tart. My takeaway lesson from that all-inclusive buffet was that, albeit expensive, it was cost-effective for anyone planning to order a multicourse meal.

In 2023, when we returned to Cannes, Val and I couldn't wait to go back to Hotel du Cap, and I arranged for another spa assignment to feature the Dior Spa Eden-Roc, which launched three weeks earlier as a merger of two iconic brands: the fabled Hôtel du Cap-Eden-Roc and Maison Dior, the luxury fashion and perfume house that Christian Dior created, which is now part of LVMH.

To reach the newly reconstructed, stand-alone Dior Spa facility, guests follow a red-tiled path under a vine-covered trellis. The transformed spa features marble, light woods, luxe furnishings, fabulous floral displays, and Dior's signature *toile du Jouy*–patterned fabric in black and white. The updated outdoor patio features the same toile fabric—albeit in blue and white—on the umbrellas above the two chaise lounges, which face a tiled wall in the same pattern. A curvilinear staircase connects the refurbished lower level, which houses locker rooms, a sauna and hammam, an ice fountain to stimulate circulation, and an onyx affusion hydrotherapy room with an onyx table used for the tailor-made Roc Affusion Ritual, with its sequence of water jets.

Outside, the private Dior Gazebo centers a verdant lawn adjacent to the spa, but my favorite choice for outdoor treatments is in one of the two cabanas that are hidden within the park, near a pathway located closer to the Mediterranean Sea. Along that seafront path, there are cabanas with sandy frontage for guests, and a restaurant, Giovanni's, a new-in-2023 casual, outdoor café, specializing in pizza, pasta, and Italian fare. Walking along these shaded paths and catching views of the sea between the greenery feels like a meditative, magical experience.

We reserved a table for a second epicurean buffet in May 2023. While it was nice, it was glaringly obvious that Olivier Gaïatto was no longer in charge of the kitchen. I asked about him and was told that he had opened his own restaurant, Le Safranier, nearby in Antibes. It was too late to get there that trip, but I arranged a lunch for 2024, which turned out to be the best meal of our stay.

LE SAFRANIER

In 2024, I reserved a midday table at Olivier Gaïatto's restaurant, so Val and I could visit the Picasso Museum and the market before lunch. We arrived early enough to also explore the adjacent Cathédrale Nôtre-Dame de la Platea d'Antibes. We walked along the main street to the tiny square, also called Le Safranier, where we spotted the charming stand-alone cottage that houses the restaurant. Passing tables on the terrace, we climbed the porch steps where there were more tables. Blackboards posted the menu items in handwritten—half-print, half-script—lettering:

ENTRÉES: Aspèrges de Provence, Oeuf mimosa, Œuf parfait, Courgettes . . .
PLATS: Poulpe grille, Pomme de terre a la Gallega, Chou fleurs, Pintade roti, Joue de bœuf comme sauce Daube, Gnocchis
DESSERTS: Pavlova aux Fraise, Moëlleux au chocolat, Brioche Perdue

It was wonderful, and when Olivier came to the table to greet us, I noticed a grinning, seemingly younger, more relaxed version of his former, more formal self. The chef whom I met in 2019 was no longer heading a huge team in a high-pressure, five-star palace-hotel kitchen; at Le Safranier, Chef Olivier appeared to thrive.

chez moi: PISTOU

I use homemade chicken broth as the base (or a boxed low-sodium organic broth) and instead of painstakingly dicing the carrot, celery, garlic, and onions in a brunoise, I pulse them a few times in a food processor. Then, I add a can of rinsed chickpeas. About ten minutes before serving, I add the vermicelli. Once it's in the bowl, I top it with torn basil.

Vieux Antibes

———◆◆◆———

PICASSO WAS MY RAISON D'ÊTRE TO VISIT ANTIBES IN 1990; since then I've learned that, in addition to F. Scott Fitzgerald, the city has hosted many famous residents, including novelists Jules Verne and Graham Greene, and artist Paul Signac, who later settled in Saint-Tropez.

Driving dilemmas continued during that first Riviera road trip in 1990. Since Covid, it feels inappropriate to label them car "catastrophes" or "calamities," which exaggerate my minor inconveniences. As a fan of alliteration, I've decided to call them: "car quandaries." Hopefully, reading about them will inform, intrigue, and, perhaps, amuse you.

In France, museum visits and markets are always determined by an inflexible *horaire* (schedule), so I timed that first visit to the Picasso Museum for after its two-hour midday closure, when it reopened at 2:00 p.m. I followed the signs announcing the Musée Picasso toward the ancient neighborhood built upon the foundations and ramparts of the even more ancient Greek town Antipolis, and when I noticed them posted more frequently, I decided—albeit with no real data—that I must be very close. I stopped, parked on a narrow street in Vieux Antibes (Old Town), and started walking, assuming I was nearby.

MUSÉE PICASSO

Eventually, I found the honey-hued building, which was erected in the fourteenth century atop a Roman fort and the former home, Château Grimaldi, of the reigning family in the Principality of Monaco. In 1925, the City of Antibes bought the château and created the Grimaldi Museum; in 1946, city officials offered Picasso a six-month stay in the château in return for some of his artwork. That was a brilliant move because the prolific artist, who was living with Françoise Gilot at the time, was unusually productive. Between mid-September to mid-November 1946, the artist created twenty-three paintings and forty-four drawings, all of which he donated to the museum, which became Musée Picasso in 1966.

The current treasure trove also showcases the cache of Picasso ceramics that he created from 1948 until his death in 1973, including works from Vallauris, where he met his future second wife, Jacqueline Roque Picasso, who generously added them to the museum's permanent collection. Among regular temporary exhibits, my visit once coincided with a display of photographs of Picasso by David Douglas Duncan, who had captured the daily life chez Picasso and Jacqueline in the 1950s, when they were living at Villa La Californie in Cannes.

My late husband collected photography books, and the oversize volume of Duncan's photographs of Picasso was a favorite on our own bookshelves and where I first saw pictures of Picasso gingerly removing an entire fish skeleton from the fillet and pressing it into a ceramic platter. I used to carry that heavy volume to school for an annual Picasso-themed show-and-tell.

At the end of my first visit to the art mecca, I left through the museum store—the film *Exit Through the Gift Shop* comes to mind—but once outside, I forgot where I had parked the car and even what color or make it was. The joy I felt facing Picasso's works vanished and I was stymied. But the keys on the Budget/Avis key chain in my hand included the license number, so I hiked up one side of each historic street and down the other, trying to retrace my footsteps while looking for matching letters—if not numbers—on each license plate. I stopped, squinting in the sunlight, trying to read the plates any time I saw a little "ordinary" car that might have been mine. I wandered—forever, it seemed—but finally found the match. I just stood there staring at the nondescript vehicle, attempting to memorize its shape and color. After this experience, I began taking a photo with some sort of place detail in case I forgot where I parked.

LE MARCHÉ PROVENÇAL

I had so little time for research before my end-of-school-year trip to the Riviera in 1990 that I was unaware that Le Marché Provençal, in Old Antibes, was one of the region's most noteworthy markets or that it is located just footsteps from the Antibes Cathedral and Musée Picasso. Had I known, I would have sped past the beach shack to the market before its 1:00 p.m. summer closure, where I could have tasted my way through the aisles, munching on a baguette and some charcuterie, nibbling on teeny black Niçoise olives and a box of raspberries. Then I could have lingered at a nearby café waiting for the 2:00 p.m. museum opening.

In 2018, when Alison, a foodie and award-winning cookbook designer, joined me for the last week of my rental, we arrived at the Picasso Museum early enough to have time for gift shopping at Le Marché Provençal: Provençal linens, herbes de Provence, herbal soaps, and cans of foie gras were some purchases. We also strolled the narrow cobblestone streets of Old Antibes, with its cafés, boutiques, mom-and-pop stores, and English-language bookstore.

Nice and Cannes have outstanding daily markets too, and every village has its market day(s) for food. Some use the marketplace for flowers or flea markets (*bricantes*), which sell *bric-à-brac,* furnishings, accessories, and clothes. The *horaires,* or schedules, are listed online, in newspapers, and are available in tourist offices.

chez moi: PERSILLADE

Parsley is an ordinary fresh ingredient that I always purchase at produce markets and grow seasonally. I make and serve *persillade* the way I've ordered it at restaurants: *pommes persillade* (potatoes), *poulet persillade* (chicken), *langoustines persillade,* although I use large frozen shrimp instead of langoustines (small lobster-like Mediterranean shellfish). It's so easy to make the pesto topping in a blender: add garlic, olive oil, a pinch of salt, and some lemon juice to the flat-leaf parsley, and use it to accompany meat, fish, or vegetables. I also mash it into softened butter, which I roll, slice, and freeze in zip-top bags and pull out as needed to throw into a skillet or flavor a sauce.

Hillside Art

———•••———

THE COOL AND INVITING HILLSIDES BEHIND NICE AND above the coast are dotted with medieval communes and walled villages that attracted artists to live and work. Three art-filled venues—in Vence, the Matisse Chapel; and in Saint-Paul-de-Vence, the Fondation Maeght and Colombe d'Or—have repeatedly enriched my life since I discovered them on my first visit to the region.

Vence

Vence, a historic village, has its own laid-back, small-town allure, and the gated old city is ringed with medieval structures. There's a wonderful market at Place du Grand Jardin and the lovely Place Clemenceau, where there's a view of the church. Dufy, Soutine, Matisse, Chagall, and Dubuffet chose to live amidst its ancient architecture and enjoy its grand views. In 1990, I arranged my weeklong itinerary according to the few days and hours when the nuns who staff *La Chapelle du Rosaire*, known as the the Matisse Chapel, accepted visitors. (The current "horaire" is more generous: Tuesday to Saturday, 10:00 to 11:30 a.m. and 2:00 to 5:30 p.m. And during services.)

MATISSE CHAPEL

The Musée Matisse in Nice—known for having the world's largest Matisse collection—was closed for renovations in 1990, and I was concerned that the chapel might be my only chance to see the artist's use of color, patterns, and *decoupage*—the cutouts that he created while disabled—near to where he lived and created them.

On the scheduled date in 1990, I set out, downhill, on the Route Napoléon. This time, when I reached Grasse, eight miles away, I turned left and followed the road signs across the backcountry for about a dozen miles to Saint-Paul-de-Vence and five miles farther to Vence.

The small white church sits on a steep hillside not far from the villa where Matisse lived. Inside, steps lead to the minimalist chapel on the lower level. Simple wooden doors open to a small chapel with a few dozen straight-backed wooden chairs, where visitors and worshippers sit facing an altar and a superb stained-glass window, an abstract representation of the Tree of Life. The intimate space is flooded with light from three more boldly tinted stained-glass windows at right angles to the altar. Intense yellow, free-form leaf shapes signify the sun; verdant green represents lush vegetation; and brilliant blue curved pieces mimic the sea and sky.

The artist created three religious murals for the Chapel of the Rosary, including *Saint Dominic, The Virgin Mother and Child,* and *The Stations of the Cross.* The figures, rendered in outline form, are drawn with thick black lines on stark white tiles. (I read that Matisse sat in a chair and drew the shapes with a piece of charcoal at the end of a long stick and that his friend Picasso introduced him to a ceramicist who helped execute his drawings onto tiles.)

un peu plus: LA CHAPELLE DU ROSAIRE

I think it's a heartwarming to know how this tiny, yet strikingly stunning La Chapelle du Rosaire came to life. Henri Matisse was seventy-two in 1941 when he was diagnosed with abdominal cancer and had surgery that required a long, sedentary recovery. To avoid the wartime aerial bombardments between 1944 and 1948, the artist moved from the swank Cimiez neighborhood of Nice to Villa Le Rêve in Vence. He hired a young nurse, Monique Bourgeois, to care for him, and they remained in contact after the artist had regained his health and she became a nun in the local Dominican order. Now known as Sister Jacques-Marie, she persuaded Matisse to help her local order decorate a little chapel they wanted to build nearby.

He accepted the project as an expression of the gratitude he felt for Monique, who had no idea, in late 1946 when Matisse started the venture, that he would become deeply involved in the undertaking, overseeing every single bit of the creation, from its construction to the interior furnishings and décor, even to the design of the gloriously colorful chasubles, or vestments— decorated with leaf patterns, crosses, and other shapes—that the officiating priests wear. (For readers interested in the chasubles, duplicates are displayed at the Vatican Museum in Rome, and *maquettes*—original paper patterns—are on view at the Musée Matisse in Nice and the Centre Pompidou in Paris.) The artist later claimed the chapel was his greatest masterpiece.

A few years after my first visit, I spent the morning in Vence before a planned midafternoon meetup with Val in Cannes. When I realized that I'd be late and had no way of contacting her, I parked in the first empty spot I saw in front of STE Malnati Peinture—a wallpaper and decorator shop—greeted the shopkeeper, and asked to use her phone.

Ms. Malnati was lovely and let me leave a message at Val's hotel. After thanking her, I mentioned that I was looking for a house rental for my daughter and son-in-law, who were planning a trip to the area. A mature gentleman who was standing nearby unexpectedly responded: "I have a little cottage that I rent. Would you like to look at it? You can follow me there, *c'est pas loin*." (It's not far.) I smiled, thanked him, and said: "*Desolé, monsieur, merci*. I can't go to look at an empty house with a stranger." Ms. Malnati giggled and assured me, saying "*Pas de problème, c'est mon père*." (No problem, he's my dad.)

I followed Monsieur to his hillside cottage, which Alison and Kenny ended up renting for two months. Alison still has an enduring passion for Vence.

In 2018, when Alison and I last visited the Matisse chapel, she bought me an image of a lovely face, drawn in characteristic Matisse style in one continuous black outline. I love it, and it's the closest I'll ever get to owning a "real" Matisse. Chatting with the nun who handled the transaction, I learned that she had been very young when she joined the order and that she remembered Sister Jacques-Marie. I felt as if history was alive all around me.

CHÂTEAU SAINT-MARTIN & SPA

After our chapel visit, Alison and I headed to lunch at Château Saint-Martin & Spa, a boutique hotel that's so dreamy it was awarded the "Palace" de France distinction. Its long history dates to its original Roman fortification: it was home to the Bishop of Tours, the Count of Provence in the year 350, and he bequeathed it to crusaders returning from Jerusalem who constructed the château on foundations built by the Knights of the Templar, a Catholic military order, in 1150. It was purchased from monks who made wine there in 1740 and became home to eleven generations of titled families.

Today's sprawling, white stone structure has red tile roofs and a panoramic view from the Alpes-Maritimes to Vence. It's a super-luxe mountain retreat—with pool, tennis courts, and private villas—on a 35-acre landscaped park perched high on a rocky hillside.

We enjoyed an elegant lunch-with-a-view on the terrace, prepared under the direction of Michelin-star triathlete chef Jean-Luc Lefrançois, who served an exceptional amuse, a special swirl of smoked salmon, which I was determined to try to make at home. I also ordered a carpaccio, a platter of thinly sliced raw beef with shaved Parmesan on top, which was perfect.

Leaving the restaurant terrace, I noticed six gilt-framed and matted Matisse prints displayed on the wall of an adjacent lounge, which I recognized from his famous book *Jazz*, a limited edition of prints created from Matisse's cut-paper collages—plus the artist's handwritten text—published in 1947 by art publisher Tériade éditeur. I once owned (and lost) a small—about nine-by-five-inch—horizontal book called *Jazz* that illustrated the prints and sayings. A year after seeing them on the wall at Château Saint-Martin, I found an oversize boxed set of the prints from *Jazz* in the Livraria Lello bookstore in Porto, Portugal (famous for its red staircase), which I bought. (I still plan to give framed pages to each of my daughters and granddaughters.)

After lunch, I walked down an arched stone-walled passage en route to the ground-level spa, where I was having a treatment to feature in my article. I lingered with delight during a facial, while Alison waited impatiently, because she eagerly wanted to return to the medieval quartier of Vence, where eventually we spent a couple of lovely late-afternoon hours.

chez moi: SMOKED SALMON ROULADE

Instead of a presentation of the usual thin slices, Le Saint-Martin served the smoked salmon rolled around a soft, cheesy center—a cream cheese or burrata-type cheese—like a rose petal and topped with microgreens. At home, it tastes great but it's never as appealing as at Château Saint-Martin, even when I add caviar or capers. When smoked salmon is on a hotel buffet, I eat it; when it's on the menu, I usually order it because fine-dining kitchens source better quality salmon than I can access (unless I order it online from Russ & Daughters in Manhattan). And it's usually a better choice than poorly cooked eggs, high-calorie breakfasts, and many other menu items.

Saint-Paul-de-Vence

Saint-Paul-de-Vence is a picturesque walled village perched on the hillside about two miles from Vence and fifteen miles behind Nice, with views that extend down to the Mediterranean. The medieval village is the region's oldest and attracts two million tourists a year to its narrow, steep streets lined with tiny boutiques filled with treasures. The recently reopened Place du Général de Gaulle is also called Place du Jeu de Boules. It's the sandy square in front of a café near the entry to the village and where locals (including the late singer, Yves Montand) play *pétanque*, the traditional French game of *boules*. (Two players on each of two teams compete by throwing three metal balls as close as they can to the target.)

On Wednesday and Friday mornings, it's where the minuscule market takes place. Women staff a few tables topped with vegetables and homemade confiture (preserves) and tapenade, and, when I was last there in May 2023, one lady squeezing oranges by hand prepared a delicious fresh juice for me. On the far side of the market, I noticed a young man next to the open back of a parked van equipped with a pizza-style round oven. He was making the traditional Niçoise chickpea pies called *socca*, which he broke into pieces and sold in little bags.

Next to him, a farmer who grew her own zucchini was staffing her stall next to a stack of large rectangular bins filled with bright yellow zucchini blossoms (*fleurs de courgette*). On the counter, she had a large plastic container filled with pancake batter and, as we chatted, she dipped each blossom in and deep-fried five at a time in an adjacent electric fryer filled with vegetable oil. She called the crisply fried blossoms "beignets" and served them in a paper cone, selling five for five euros. They were fabulous!

As appealing as the village is, my reason for making it a repeat destination is as an art "fix," because so many of the artists whom I admire lived here or nearby and their and other artists' output is readily available to witness firsthand; for example, Marc Chagall set up a home and is buried here, Henri Matisse lived nearby in Vence, and Pablo Picasso frequented the village.

FONDATION MAEGHT

Fondation Maeght, considered the world's greatest twentieth-century sculpture collection, is a major reason to visit the village. Art dealers and collectors Aimé and Marguerite Maeght established it in 1964 after visiting some inspiring American foundations, such as the Barnes, Guggenheim, and Phillips collections. The couple were friends with the artists whom they represented, including Georges Braque, Alexander Calder, Marc Chagall, Joan Miró, and Fernand Léger.

The most exciting objects for me to see are the skeletal sculptures by Alberto Giacometti, which resemble—and remind me of—the *Walking Man* piece that my friend, Louise Smith, placed at the foot of her bed. The sculptures are on view in massive, high-ceilinged indoor spaces and outdoors—in gardens, patios, terraces, and along paths and next to fountains—on the vast wooded, parklike grounds. Of all my visits there, including in May 2024, when Val and I were lucky to have revisited, the best fun was with my granddaughter Emma Lov in October 2015, who amused herself by posing me next to works by Calder and Miró.

COLOMBE D'OR

The traditional, family-owned Colombe d'Or, located just inside the entry gates to *le village perché* (the perched village), houses a museum-worthy art collection. I considered it an essential part of my inaugural art-focused road trip in 1990, and I have favored it enough to have returned alone and one-on-one with Bob, Alison, Emma, Susann, and Val.

Artist Paul Roux and his wife Babtistine ("Titine") added food and three upstairs bedrooms to the inn they opened in 1931, in what had formerly housed a *ginguette* (tavern). They called the auberge Colombe d'Or. Paul decorated the walls with his own artwork and became friendly with, and exchanged hospitality for art with, a cadre of creative locals, notably Pablo Picasso, with whom he was particularly friendly and who often ate *poulet* there and once traded a painting for a green earthenware dish he admired. The inn lured a galaxy of greats, among them Marc Chagall, Henri Matisse, Pablo Picasso, Georges Braque, Jean Cocteau, Sonia Delaunay, Raoul Dufy, Alberto Giacometti, Fernand Léger, and Joan Miró. Alexander Calder left an *oeuvre* after every stay. In the 1940s, when the South of France was a free zone, Churchill frequented the venue; Jean-Paul Sartre and poet Jacques Prevert were often patrons, and the guest book is also filled with clever designs by Charlie Chaplin, who drew a comic self-portrait. Yves Montand met Simone Signoret there in 1949 and married the famous actress at the restaurant two years later.

During my first solo lunch there in 1990, I so enjoyed the art and the house-made, locally sourced, farm-fresh regional dishes that Colombe d'Or has remained my go-to Riviera restaurant. Before email reservations, I used to call from the States to book a table just after I confirmed my flights. As I reflect on those meals, I recall that several of them involved some rental car drama.

In April 2013, with Susann, I reserved a slightly larger midsize, more practical car from the Budget/Avis rental agency at the Nice train station. Instead, they handed me the keys to the only automatic shift car available, a much-too-large, difficult-to-maneuver SUV.

We arranged to stay near Saint-Paul-de-Vence at Le Mas de Pierre, a lovely Relais & Châteaux affiliate, and I booked a table at Colombe d'Or for our first full day there. I remembered to ask the concierge to confirm our reservation at the most prominent restaurant in the area and we left early enough—or so we thought—for our 1:00 p.m. table. Within a few minutes, I dropped Susann at the entry and headed to the adjacent underground public parking garage, where I drove down the spiral, wincingly narrow one-way lane into the bowels of the building, looking for a space. When I finally found one on a lower level and tried to drive in, I got stuck; I couldn't go forward, I couldn't back up. Then, when I finally achieved the impossible and got out of that space, I had to search for another. That took forever, as did the walk to find the elevator to street level.

The valet, who had opened the door for Susann, saw me coming across the street from the garage and said: "Madame, when you have a reservation, you don't need the garage. I'll park the car." It was an informative detail that the innkeeper at the nearby five-star boutique hotel didn't bother to tell me and which would have avoided the entire unpleasant ordeal.

When I finally arrived à table, Susann was already eating, because the waiter advised her that the kitchen was about to close and that she should order. I had been dreaming about the whole grilled fish, but that was out of the question. I was so late that the waiter didn't even bring the colorful handwritten menu that Paul Roux had designed, since it would have been a waste of time.

Fortunately, the soft bread had a crisp crust, the sweet local butter was fabulous, and so were the perfect black Niçoise olives. I sipped the dry white wine he'd poured and looked forward to whatever the *chef garde manger* had prepared: a *panier de crudités*, a basket filled with tiny mushrooms, baby cucumbers, cherry tomatoes, baby radishes, celery stalks, and an endive, served with a garlicky aioli, house-made paté de foie gras, dessert, and coffee. It was all very satisfying.

By the time we finished, other diners were gone, and we were able to walk around alone, staring, as if in an empty art museum. I admired the paintings hanging between arched windows with wooden shutters and the artwork studding the white-stucco-walled room with its sunken banquette framing a fireplace. I ducked outside to the pool deck to greet the Calder stabile with its bright red flags, which always reminds me of the *Le Guichet* stabile at Lincoln Center in Manhattan, where my young daughters and I used to play follow the leader singing "Tiptoe through the Calder" together.

The aesthetic satisfaction of being in the same room with those marvelous paintings didn't last long. A few minutes later, at the garage exit, I couldn't find the ticket needed to raise the gate. Impatient drivers honked their horns, passengers yelled, and someone got out of his car and started waving a fist; I didn't dare make eye contact. I got out of the car to find help; Susann waited in the car in silence.

Recently, I asked Susann if she remembered the ten-year-old incident. She did, vividly. She assured me that the wait, perhaps ten to fifteen minutes, "felt like a week" and told me her story for the first time. "After you got out of the car to search for help, I was repeatedly harassed by aggravated drivers who had no way of getting past our car on the one narrow exit lane." She claimed she sat, face forward, without daring to face her nasty-tempered accusers. "One driver yelled, another walked to the car and screamed at me through the window, another raised an insulting finger. I was scared silly and seated with clenched jaw and tight fists. And you were already too upset for me to tell you about it."

While Susann was waiting in the car, I had my own adventure searching for an agent to explain my problem. After I found someone, I had to hike back up the ramp and around to the entry gate. Eventually, a uniformed employee appeared and raised the gate. We sped away.

My worst-ever car quandary happened with Emma two years later and the day before we planned to lunch at Colombe d'Or. We had checked out of the lovely Royal-Riviera Hotel and were headed toward the Matisse Museum for a visit, before continuing up the hillside to a hotel in Saint-Paul-de-Vence where we had reservations for dinner and an overnight. The rental car sparked flames, sputtered, and stopped just before a busy bus stop on boulevard Cimiez in Nice, adjacent to the park and museum.

Avis answered my first call and said they'd send someone to help us, but no one showed up and Avis never answered my repeated phone calls. There we sat. I was hoping to have spent that hour inside the ten-room, seventeenth-century Genovese-style villa looking at fabulous Matisse works; instead, we were watching buses go by and staring at the gorgeous, ornate former Regina Hotel, which was built as a residence in 1897 for Queen Victoria's winter sojourns and now houses exclusive, privately owned apartments.

By midafternoon, I canceled our dinner and hotel reservations, assuming that the situation would never be resolved in time to get to the backcountry before dark. I also called the Royal-Riviera, explained my predicament, and requested another night's stay. To our delight, reception called the general manager, Bruno Mercadel, who serendipitously happened to be nearby and who came to our rescue. Our hero verified that there had been a fire and called Avis and a taxi, which took us to the airport where I rented another vehicle. I'm familiar with concierges who go to great lengths to help guests, but M. Mercadel's generosity was beyond what any guest could expect! Avis, on the other hand, disappointed, from that first call until many hours later—and didn't even reimburse the charge for the day we couldn't use the car or for the expensive taxi ride to the airport.

On a recent phone chat, Emma reminded me of our *panne* (breakdown) and how fearfully I was still driving days later. "Grandma, do you remember driving up to Terre Blanche on those narrow, curvy roads, and all the cars behind you honked because you were driving too slowly? You were still driving nervously when we went to Saint-Paul-de-Vence." Guilty as charged. That's me, the slow driver who pulls to the side and lets cars pass, especially on mountainsides.

When Emma and I arrived at Colombe d'Or the day after the fire, I dropped the car off with the valet and we were well-seated in the center of the outdoor terrace. Her chair faced the vibrant, ceramic-mosaic Léger mural that covered the interior side of the wall separating the restaurant from the street. I chose a *salade de homard* (lobster salad). Emma had grilled local sweet peppers bathed in olive oil and *saumon fumé avec ses toasts* (smoked salmon with toasts).

After lunch, when she walked inside to the lavatory with me, my Manhattan-public-school-educated nineteen-year-old granddaughter recognized many of the artists' works, just as she had at Fondation Maeght, because of annual school outings to The Metropolitan Museum of Art and the Museum of Modern Art.

I returned to Colombe d'Or in May 2018, with my daughter Alison, after a visit to the sculpture garden; nothing diminished the pleasure. It was her first meal at the restaurant, and our side-by-side seats at a table against an outer wall faced amazing paintings on the three interior walls. We also had a clear view of what was on the platters that the waiters carried, including an alluring dish of fat white asparagus spears topped with a maize-colored Mornay drizzle, which we decided to share.

We also shared the whole grilled fish. Dominic, an attentive server whom I remembered, deboned it at the table. Using two forks, he precisely carved the herb-topped, olive oil–scented fish, moving the herbs away from the body. He removed the head and tail, trimmed the sides, divided it for two, and served it on a plate garnished with a simple parsley-flecked boiled potato and half a lemon. Like the professional he is, and with credit to his charm, he acted as if he remembered me. (A skill that's more difficult to perfect than deboning fish!)

For dessert we shared the house specialité, the *Tarte de la Mère Roux*, the traditional apple tart with a delicate crust that honors the original baker: Babtistine Roux.

In 2023, as usual, I had made my Colombe d'Or reservation months in advance. I entered before Val arrived, and the maître d' led me through the lovely terrace where I'd eaten with Emma to a table hidden behind a huge potted plant, in the rear corner. Although I prefer a table facing artwork, I said nothing knowing that Val would leave the restaurant and stand at a counter eating a crêpe before she'd sit at this table. When she showed up, she took one look at me, and another at the tree, and turned around to find the host.

The maître d' wasn't very enthusiastic about it, but he did find a table in the middle of the room facing the famous mural.

It was a repeat of restaurant experiences that plague *dames d'un certain age* and with which I've become familiar, unless I enter as a "food writer," in which case I am greeted like a VIP. It sure puts the hierarchy of hospitality in perspective. If Dominic had been our waiter, it would have been a warmer experience; still, the ageist snob hasn't been born who could spoil my delight in being in the same room with that artwork.

As always, the food was as I like it and, when I dilly-dallied en route to the *toilette* and later stood captivated in front of remarkable paintings, I was thrilled. I even stepped outside to the pool deck to say hello to the Calder, although I obeyed the Private-to-Hotel-Guests sign and returned inside.

I've certainly had my share of stressful rental car situations in Saint-Paul-de-Vence, but not on my first journey to the region in 1990. I drove downhill from Saint-Vallier-de-Thiey, turned left at Grasse, and arrived quickly and with nary a problem. I found parking easily, and even the little rental car functioned *comme il faut* (as it should).

On another solo trip, in the pre-cell-phone era and while I was still teaching, I spent my last night on the Riviera at Hôtel Le Saint-Paul, a superb boutique hotel in a restored sixteenth-century building, on the narrow, thousand-year-old main street of the pedestrian village, where vehicles are not allowed. When I drove into the village, I followed cars to the outer road and searched for a parking space next to the thick medieval ramparts. I squeezed my miniature car into a skinny space and set out on foot to find the hotel.

That stay, I enjoyed a sweet lunch at Colombe d'Or and window-shopping in the teeny, open-door galleries and boutiques bordering the jam-packed cobblestone streets. I ate dinner and an early breakfast at my hotel, both served to me at the same tiny rectangular table on the hotel's narrow terrace overlooking verdant hillsides.

As I readied to check out to drive the thirty-some minutes to Nice Côte d'Azur Airport, the desk clerk formally proclaimed, "Madame, the gendarme called to tell you that someone found your keys. You must go to the gendarmerie to retrieve them." What? I had no idea that I had lost my keys and still have no clue about how the gendarmerie knew the name of that hotel. (The car rental agency didn't know the names of all the places that I was staying during that trip.) I raced to the gendarmerie worrying about being late for my flight, recovered the keys, and rushed to the car, which was blocked in by larger automobiles. I tried to back out and tried again. Passersby used hand signals to direct me, shouting "*tout droit*" (straight ahead). The trouble was, if I went forward I would have driven off the edge of the cliff.

I started sweating, was scared about having an accident, afraid of missing my flight, and fighting tears. Eventually, I managed to extricate the vehicle, with nary a scratch, and departed the scenic little village, though I was still shaking at the airport as I searched for the return car lot. I had calmed down considerably by the time I boarded the plane. (Missing a flight is less stressful now that I don't have a set work schedule or have to watch every penny.)

chez moi: BEIGNETS DE FLEURS DE COURGETTE

I never see zucchini blossoms at my produce market, but because they are easy to grow I have enough from my garden to pick for this seasonal treat. I mix 2 eggs with 1 cup skim milk and 2 cups Bisquick, then add baking powder and seltzer to lighten the batter, which I like to season with slivers of chives or scallions or some red pepper flakes. I stuff them with duxelles: chopped mushrooms, onions, and herbs. Coat them in the batter and fry until golden in a high-sided large skillet with ½-inch hot oil. Next summer I plan to use jarred chopped truffles as an homage to Chef Roger Vergé, even though I'm confident he would avoid using "jarred" anything.

The Back Country: Fayence, Terre Blanche in Tourrettes, Seillans

I first visited the quiet, inland corner of Provence, known as the L'Arrière-Pays, when Bob and I visited Terre Blanche in 2004; on a subsequent trip, I returned on a day trip from Nice. My friend Françoise Rougé, who has a travel design company, is extremely well-connected, and she put me in contact with a colleague who had just launched a one-woman travel service. I called her number from my hotel and the lovely woman, whose name I've forgotten, spoke in English: "I'd love to show you the Var, the backcountry. It's a less touristy part of the Riviera, and I can introduce you to Fayence, where we can stop for lunch." I readily accepted because it was a rare opportunity for me to spend time with a local and discover an authentic French village.

FAYENCE

One of those sweet medieval perched towns, Fayence is also the name-sake for the famous majolica-like, tin-glazed earthenware known as faience, which is said to date to the pre-ninth-century Middle East or, some claim, to Egypt some fifty centuries earlier. The area is studded with olive groves and sprawling vineyards on limestone hills, and the quaint village is special for its ancient churches, little plazas, a communal oven that dates to the sixteenth century, and simple stone houses with blue shutters and flower-filled window boxes. Of course, there's a village market. Like other little Provençal villages, it's a place to just be and cherish, though there's plenty to do if you like nature, golfing, wine tasting, or markets.

The destination has become increasingly popular since I was first there and is an expat haven where foreigners buy and renovate little—or very grand—villas.

TERRE BLANCHE IN TOURRETTES

The late Sean Connery, a passionate golfer, purchased the storybook setting in 1979, near where his wife, Micheline Roquebrune, was raised and her family has lived since it was an undeveloped rural region. The vast Monaco-size, 740,000-acre "Domaine" property in Tourrettes boasts sloping hillsides covered in grand oak, cypress, and Mediterranean pines. It's a huge forest studded with lakes and rivers that link the mountains to the sea. The celebrated Scottish-born star's dream was to build Europe's finest golf club there, along with one thousand homes, but that never happened. The actor sold the estate to a business tycoon who went bankrupt, and in 1999, German billionaire-entrepreneur Dietmar Hopp acquired it. The tycoon developed it into the luxurious, ultra-hospitable Four Seasons Resort Provence at Terre Blanche, where he displays some of his eye-popping private art collection, including world-class sculptures by Niki de Saint Phalle, Joan Miró, and Anthony Gormley.

The luxe resort, just an hour's drive from Nice Côte d'Azur Airport, launched in 2004, and because it was brand-new, I was able to get assignments featuring it. Bob and I arrived there by car for the last night of our Paris to Nice car trip. The following day, we planned to return the rental car at the airport in Nice, take a taxi to the cruise port, and board the Wind Surf for a week's voyage to Barcelona.

I've stayed at Terre Blanche five times but only drove there myself twice, and I wish I could say never. The curvy, narrow Route de Bagnols-en-Forêt frightens me, but not locals who speed along as if they're on a straightaway. I always feel I must pull to the side whenever a speeding vehicle approaches—trouble is, there's not always room at the side of the road. I refuse to go fast on those curves and, in 2015, with granddaughter Emma, I was still traumatized from our breakdown in Nice. When I returned with Alison in 2018, the drive was less stressful, but be assured, I was very relieved when I arrived at the gates of the Domaine.

Every arrival at this *porte cochère*-fronted contemporary main building is special because the entry leads to art-filled public spaces. After lunch on the terrace, I always relish strolling on the meandering paths, where scents of lavender, mimosa, and thyme magically mingle, and where the vines that I saw planted in their first season now produce grapes. The pathways lead to about fifty stone-walled, terracotta-tiled, ochre-colored villas, where each light-filled suite has a bedroom and living room opening out to a terrace with a view, and boasts a textural décor with woods, stone, rattan, and woven fabrics.

When the resort added a magnificent art-filled, stand-alone, 35,000-square-foot spa facility in 2007, set among terraces and gardens overlooking the golf course, I returned to write about it. My jaw dropped inside the entry of the two-story lobby, viewing the seventy-nine-foot indoor lap pool bordered by columns to its vaulted ceiling. When I'm under that soaring ceiling—and swimming through the curtains to the sunlit outdoor extension—I feel like the luckiest person in the world. When Emma and I were at the swimming pool in 2015, I chatted with a retired British woman who told me that she was a spa member who lived just ten minutes away in Fayence and came every day to swim.

The building houses a state-of-the-art gym, a Zen studio where fitness classes and private sessions are held, ice fountains, an indoor dry-heat room known as a laconium, and a hammam (steam room), plus a jet-strewn vitality pool. The upper level houses his/hers locker rooms and fourteen treatment rooms—all equipped with showers, hydraulic beds, and heated blankets. The VIP suites offer double whirlpool baths, steam showers, and private terraces.

Because beauty is paramount in France, and skin care is a cherished tradition, there's an extravagant spa treatment menu, including some that incorporate natural ingredients, such as sugar and white heather, honey, lavender, and aloe vera. It ranks high as one of my favorite spas in the world.

And I love the fresh, local, natural, sustainable, and environmentally friendly foods, with a bevy of Provençal bounty, including truffles, tapenade, and Mediterranean seafood. I recall meeting Chef Philippe Jourdin, a protégé of Roger Vergé at Moulin des Mougins, at a marvelous luncheon buffet. In 2018, when Alison and I stayed there, we lunched at the Golf Club, where she ordered a carpaccio of thinly sliced seasonal red, yellow, and green tomatoes topped with small burrata rounds and a few croutons the size of baguette slices.

The dish I most enjoyed was one of only two perfect Niçoise salads during my entire three-week-plus trip.

In 2021, Christophe Schmitt, an award-winning chef, took over as chef de cuisines at what is now called Terre Blanche Hotel Spa Golf Resort.

SEILLANS

On our way home from Terre Blanche in 2018, Alison suggested we stop at the scenic village of Seillans, which she and her late husband, Kenny, had visited, before heading downhill to Juan-les-Pins. Kenny, who was also an artist, was a great fan of the German surrealist painter/sculptor Max Ernst, who had lived in the tiny commune with his fourth wife, artist Dorothea Tanning, from 1964 until his death in 1976. Ernst had fled to New York in 1941 to escape the German occupation of France during World War II and married Dorothea in California in 1946, in a double ceremony with Man Ray.

The couple bequeathed their artwork collection to the city, and it is on view at Maison Waldberg, aka Musée Ernst. Unfortunately, the museum was closed during our spontaneous visit, so while Ali explored the cobblestone hillsides on foot, I browsed the boutiques. In one wonderful little shop, we both bought sun hats that are almost transparent and fold beautifully for packing (I lost mine and miss it). Ali, who doesn't share my affection for luxury spa resorts, admired the appealing traditional hotel, Hôtel des Deux Rocs, in an authentic limestone building with blue shutters; she'd be very happy to take her watercolor paints and spend time there.

Afterward, we drove to a second little hillside village where we bought cheese, charcuterie, and wine for dinner. I followed the signs to exit the village, which directed me down a steep, super-narrow street to a dead end, where stanchions stuck up out of the ground and stopped me. What to do? The buildings were only inches from the sides of the car and there wasn't even enough space for Ali—who was concerned—to get out and direct me. I told her that I could handle it and started in reverse, backing up the semi-vertical street slowly and cautiously. Just as I approached the top, a man stepped out of his doorway and pointed out a hidden drive where I could safely make a right turn to the main departmental road home. Whew!

It was a traumatic experience, but Alison reminded me—just as her father once had—"Mom, for a fearful driver you have very good skills." That kudo from Alison confirming my driving proficiency felt great, and she swears that she is going to share the story about my uphill reverse-driving abilities at my funeral.

I hope she does, and I hope everyone laughs!

chez moi: SALADE NIÇOISE

My best salade Niçoise is served when French breakfast radishes, tomatoes, and cucumbers appear in my garden and includes torn shreds of Romaine lettuce, blanched young green beans, boiled new potatoes, red onions or scallions, tinned anchovies, tiny cured Niçoise olives, and canned or jarred spears of tuna in olive oil. Because some of my guests don't eat hard-boiled eggs on salad, or anchovies, I often serve the dish "deconstructed," with the greens in a big bowl, all the ingredients in small individual ones (I salt and drain the tomatoes and cucumbers separately, and soak red onions to tame the flavor), and a pitcher of vinaigrette (three to one olive oil to wine vinegar, some Pommery whole grain mustard, and garlic). Traditionally, according to Rosa Jackson, author of *Niçoise: Market-Inspired Cooking from France's Sunniest City* and owner of Les Petits Farcis cooking school in Nice, the dish contains mostly tomatoes, tuna and/or anchovies, plus crunchy raw vegetables and Niçoise olives. Escoffier, she claims, added the greens. I don't know who added potatoes, but I think they are essential.

Mediterranean
Cruises

———◆◆———

OR YEARS, I DREAMT OF TRAVELING ON THE CÔTE
d'Azur with Bob, but until 2002, the closest we got to sharing its pleasures was once on the phone, when I called him via
BlackBerry from Juan-les-Pins to listen to Norah Jones with me during Jazz à Juan. Some time later, my spa colleague and good friend,
Bernard Burt, described his marvelous Mediterranean voyage on a
sailing ship, and it occurred to me that cruising would be the ideal
way to introduce Bob, an avid sailor, to the region. I started sending
queries to editors pitching a "Spa at Sea" story.

Bob was not an ordinary "I like sailing" mariner (and surely not
a fair-weather one like me!). He was a yachtsman, a racing sailor who
lived to compete locally, in Newport, and in the Bahamas. He studied celestial navigation at the American Museum of Natural History
and earned a 50-ton captain's license. Writing about cruising the
Med was so obvious, I wondered why I hadn't thought of it earlier.

Bob was also an ardent photographer who illustrated all my
boating articles in *Yachting* and *Southern Boating* magazines, and
whose food photos had accompanied my restaurant pieces since the
eighties. Ultimately, cruises that featured the MSY *Wind Surf* became some of our happiest times together.

MSY *WIND SURF*

The *Wind Surf* is the largest of the three five-masted staysail schooners in the Windstar Cruise Line, and one of the world's largest sailing cruise ships. Still, there are only 150 staterooms and a capacity of 342 passengers, so it's ranked as a small ship. (On our voyages, the staff of 210 tended about 185 to 200 guests.)

The ship was powered primarily by sail and that was the obvious first reason to choose it. Once on board, Bob appreciated that Mark Boylin, the captain, was a true sailor who only turned on the engines in an absolute necessity. Happily, he commanded all three weeks. I was grateful for wind power for a different reason entirely—motor vibrations give me *mal de mer* (seasickness).

We preferred its smallness because the ship can maneuver into little ports, such as Villefranche-sur-Mer, and tiny harbors on small islands, where we enjoyed exploring sleepy fishing ports, learning about their unique histories, and seeing varied landscapes that ranged from rocky to sandy and salt marshes. We delighted in touring Corsica and Sardinia, though we missed seeing Ibiza due to bad weather. And we treasured the walk on the isolated beaches in Porquerolles, one of the Îles d'Hyères off the coast of Port d'Hyères, where the pristine national park between Cannes and Marseille covers 80 percent of the three-thousand-acre island and there are very few year-round residents.

We liked that the ship was large enough to have multiple dining rooms with fresh, uncomplicated, healthful options and small enough not to require assigned tables. (We easily reserved a table for two, four, or six on the same day.) I liked that it was large enough to maintain a spa, with employees trained to do multiple services. And Bob, who commuted for twenty-plus years in a tie and jacket, was relieved that they were not required. Neither of us cared that there was limited nightlife, an amenity that larger vessels provide.

We cruised two concurrent weeks from Barcelona to Nice and then to Rome in 2002; and another from Nice westward to Barcelona in 2004. On board, we had a predictable routine: I exercised and, when possible, headed to shore. Bob preferred to stay on the ship, but I didn't realize it was health related. I never questioned his preference when he said, "I'd rather hang out on the bridge." I was fine exploring alone, then meeting Bob for a drink among locals at a café in the late afternoon after the tour buses had departed.

Saint-Tropez

———◆◆———

WHEN ANYONE ASKS ME TO NAME MY FAVORITE world destination, the answer is always Saint-Tropez. St.-Trop is a petit, pastel-colored, fairy-tale village, a dreamlike destination where cafés with outdoor terraces face the docked mega yachts in the old port. I love its narrow cobblestone streets that climb up the hillside, leading away from the semicircular harbor and lined with one-of-a-kind mom-and-pop shops and designer and pop-up boutiques. At night, as if by magic, teeny tables and chairs appear and alleyways are transformed into outdoor cafés frequented by a myriad of resort-clad visitors. It's the kind of place where it's as much fun to stand at a crêperie window (my favorite is on a narrow alleyway next to the Le Petit Pointu restaurant on rue des Remparts) as it is to "dine."

The prime yachting destination lures summertime tourists who refer to it as a "beach" resort, though there are only a few minuscule beaches on the north-facing harbor, which view mountains beyond the broad bay. Beach aficionados looking for long, languid afternoons on the sand must drive—or be driven—to the world-famous Pampelonne and Tahiti beaches in Ramatuelle, long east-facing stretches of sand on the Route des Plages (Beach Road). Cars, vans, limos, luxury yachts, and chartered speedboats transport the haut de gamme luncheon crowd for luxe lobster lunches under tented decks at snazzy beach clubs perched on the sand. For some, an afternoon lingers through drinks, dinner, and late-night dance clubs that stay open until early morning.

MUSÉE DE L'ANNONCIADE

I am not among those who dance the night away, but in daylight, the one thing I always do in Saint-Tropez is visit my favorite small portside museum, the diminutive Musée de l'Annonciade, a restored and refurbished former fishermen's chapel, where paintings by Dufy, Matisse, and Signac decorate white arched walls.

I like to roam alone and sit for a while in a big leather chair upstairs, near a favorite seascape by Signac that echoes the maritime vista outside the adjacent window. I just look, breathe, linger, and feel gratitude. In August 2019, I bade farewell to some of the artwork, thinking it might be my last visit. (It wasn't! I returned joyfully on a Sunday morning in 2023.)

* * *

Val and I first visited Saint-Tropez in summer 1993, because we hated our hotel in Cannes and, by the second night, mused about moving on to Saint-Tropez, where neither of us had ever been but where the fashionistas we had met at Gottex three years earlier always vacationed. We checked out of our hotel the following morning. Though we were in our fifties and considered ourselves savvy travelers, we never considered making reservations, even though it was high season.

I recall the scramble searching for correct change for the toll booth as I drove along La Provençale (Autoroute A8). About an hour and a half later, when we arrived inside the village, we followed hotel signs up the hill to Hôtel Byblos, on avenue Paul Signac—named for the artist who settled there—which directed me to turn right. At the valet stand, we descended the curved outdoor staircase with its impressive wall of verdant vines, entered the hotel, walked to the reception desk, and requested a room. Of course, the prestigious hotel was fully booked and, were it not, the price in high season would have been prohibitive.

We left, started walking, and, just a few doors away, saw a villa that had been transformed into the appealing Hôtel Ermitage. We entered through its shaded courtyard, passing guests lingering on the patio at breakfast, and walked to reception. To our delight, there was a charming small room available, and we stayed there for a few nights. (After a long closure, Hôtel Ermitage has been upgraded and transformed into a luxe little venue. On subsequent visits, Val and I stayed at other small but lovely and less expensive hotels near Byblos: B Lodge in 2019, and Hotel Le Y in 2023).

From the hotel, we walked downhill to the port village to a café where we, along with most of the other tourists, stared at the grand yachts, where the crews wearing T-shirts bearing the boats' names were the only people visible. Later, we spent hours strolling among the European tourists, jet-setters, wannabes, and shopaholics, going in and out of designer boutiques and pop-ups. (There's a lot of A-list fashion, from Chanel, Dior, Fendi, Gucci, Hermès, Loewe, and Louis Vuitton, among others.)

The next day we walked in the other direction along avenue Paul Signac, beyond Byblos, and stopped at a sign that read *Plage des Graniers* posted on the street at the head of a narrow, rocky path. It led us down to a teeny-tiny beachfront shack-restaurant, with tables set up on the sand just footsteps from the water. We were seated at a wooden table topped with ceramic plates, real silverware, and cloth napkins, and buried our toes in the sand. It was one of my first encounters with beach shack elegance à la française. Lovely. And lunch was truly good. (Almost thirty years later, I took a solo stroll down that same path to the restaurant and noticed that it boasted a Michelin Bib Gourmand recommendation.) We walked through the adjacent Cimetière marin de Saint-Tropez, the sprawling seaside cemetery, past the historic Citadelle, and to the port, where we stopped for coffee before my first visit to the Musée de l'Annonciade.

When Bob and I took our first cruise in 2002, I was thrilled to read that Saint-Tropez was listed as a port of call. I loved the port village and knew that he would enjoy seeing the mega yachts that dock there. Unfortunately, the weather was rough, and the ship had to moor somewhere safer along the coast. I suggested that we rent a car and drive there for the day, not knowing the distance or the amount of traffic. He drove for almost three hours in a Hamptons-like crawl along the coastal road, but we arrived in time for our lunch reservation at Résidence de la Pinède, a five-star beachfront hotel on a sliver of sandy beach at the edge of town, which joined the prestigious Cheval Blanc group in 2019.

After introducing Bob to l'Annonciade, there was still some time to stroll the shop-lined streets, where I noticed a woman wearing a colorful bright blue, white, and red blouse in multi-flag patterns, featuring the American Stars and Stripes, and the French, Belgian, British, and Italian flags, too, and said: *"C'est super!"* She stopped, thanked me, and pointed to the nearby shop where she had just bought it. We went in and found only one similar style on the rack. It was too large and long for me, but I've been wearing it as a bathing suit cover-up every July Fourth ever since.

On our return cruise to Saint-Tropez Bay in 2004, all three ships—the *Wind Surf* and its two smaller, five-masted sister ships— the *Wind Star* and the *Wind Spirit*—were scheduled to anchor there on the same date. Bob and I were amid throngs of onlookers on shore who delighted at the sight of the trio with a total of fifteen sails flying.

That day, we lunched on an elegant, Italian-influenced meal at Villa Belrose in Gassin, a boutique hotel within a converted manse just outside the village. During lunch on a terrace overlooking both the bay and a vine-studded hillside, someone confided that Brigitte Bardot had stayed at the villa. I wonder if it's true, because I've never been able to confirm it. Was she an owner? A houseguest? As reigning queen of Saint-Tropez, either could be true.

HÔTEL BYBLOS

After that first peak at the iconic Byblos in the 1990s, I return whenever I'm in Saint-Tropez, if only for lunch or drinks poolside, facing what resembles a perfectly planned, pastel-shaded, palm-tree-studded, mini-Mediterranean hillside neighborhood. To me, Byblos is unique as its own *petit* village-within-the-village called Saint-Tropez. It also has a captivating history.

un peu plus: JEAN-PROSPER GUY-PARA

A Lebanese billionaire businessman, Jean-Prosper Guy-Para, designed and constructed this extraordinarily romantic destination as a labor of love. Its intricate tilework, inner courtyards, and trickling fountains were inspired by the splendiferous nineteenth-century Beiteddine Palace in Beirut, and one room, Le Salon Libanais, was created by Guy-Para as a stone-by-stone replica of a parlor at the original palace, with a geometric-patterned ceramic-tile floor ringed with marble banquettes topped with deep upholstered cushions and decorated with fabulous inlaid tables, bronze lamps, and authentic accessories. This entire Arabian nights-like stage set was created as an ultra-extravagant attempt to woo, enchant, and entice Brigitte Bardot, the mid-century French film goddess, who lived nearby and who single-handedly made Saint-Tropez a glamorous world destination. Unfortunately, the 1967 Six-Day War thwarted the creator's dream of romance. He had to sell the property shortly after the hotel opened. He offered it to entrepreneur Sylvain Floirat, who bought the venue and whose family continues to operate it and maintain its impeccable hospitality. (Today, Antoine Chevanne is CEO of Groupe Floirat, and Christophe Chauvin is General Manager at Hôtel Byblos.) Even though Byblos never served as the setting for M. Guy-Para to seduce Ms. Bardot, romance has always been at the heart of the hotel and many people honeymoon there, including Mick and Bianca Jagger in 1971.

In April 2012, I had the opportunity to stay there. My room had a *petit balcon* overlooking the pool deck, and the next day we lunched on a tented deck at the chic Le Club 55, on the *plage mythique* Pampelonne Beach in Ramatuelle. Two food items impressed me most during that stay: Tarte Tropézienne, the iconic cream-filled cake that the pastry chef introduced, and Citron Pressé, which my friend Janet ordered at every opportunity.

Six years later, on assignment to write about the spa, daughter Sharon and I checked in on a late-April morning just after the hotel's annual winter closure, when there were hardly any guests. Perhaps that's why we were led to a suite with a living room, a small side room fitted with a desk, chair, and a console filled with amenities, and two balconies that overlooked the landscaped pool terrace. Details included wonderful wallpaper behind the bed, fabric-covered electric cords the same color as the wall, so guests wouldn't be disturbed by ugly black television wires, and a fabric newspaper holder attached to the entry door, so guests need not bend to get their daily news.

I've lunched poolside at Byblos, ordering Salade Byblos, their version of salade Niçoise, on enough occasions to vouch that it is wonderful. Sharon agreed that the resort's version—with fresh grilled tuna atop greens studded with a bevy of Niçoise olives, whole anchovies, tender haricots verts (green beans), and small potatoes and tomatoes—was better than any of the other salades Niçoises that we tried that week.

The hotel's fine-dining restaurant is down a series of long staircases from the pool on the hotel's lowest level, just footsteps from Place des Lices. For many years, the hotel has partnered with Alain Ducasse, the 21-Michelin-star chef, whose Ducasse-experienced chefs add their individual creativity to his distinctive Mediterranean influences, details, and high standards. The venue has changed names but what's constant is a *tropézienne* culinary universe that features the best local, market-fresh ingredients.

Vincent Maillard was executive chef on two different occasions when I was there: in 2012, when the restaurant was called Spoon, and in 2018, when it was Rivea. Sharon and I drank Bertaud Belieu Prestige, a lovely rosé, and our "amuse" included green olives, charcuterie, and socca, the regional specialty pie. We shared a boule of creamy burrata atop red and yellow tomato quarters, and vitello tonnato, an Italian-influenced tuna dish. I relished linguine with tiny clams; Sharon indulged in a half-salted cod à la Marseillaise. (Chef Maillard currently heads the kitchen at Lily of the Valley, a nearby wellness hotel.) Well after midnight, I entered Les Caves du Roy, the dark, music-filled, super-chic *boîte* (supper club), which was jam-packed even on the first weekend of the season.

In August 2019, during a rare visit in high season, the restaurant was called Cucina Byblos, and Val and I had a 10:30 p.m. dinner reservation, which is particularly early for Saint-Tropez (Monday nights are no exception). We were seated outside on the terrace, where twinkling lights were hanging from grand old trees surrounded by vine- and plant-covered walls. We could watch the "beautiful people" arrive until we left at 1:30 a.m., when two groups of four were just sitting down at two tables.

Executive chef Rocco Seminara welcomed us and gestured to the waiter to bring us glasses of Veuve Cliquot. He had come from the Hôtel de Paris Monte Carlo, where he had a long career working with Chef Ducasse. Chef suggested sharing his specialties, a black-truffle–topped pizza from his wood-burning pizza oven and a blue lobster salad on a pesto with orange segments, followed by a rare T-bone steak with seasonal vegetables.

Byblos has its own *potagerie* (kitchen gardens) near the pool deck, and chef had also established a vertical vegetable and herb garden on the terrace walls, which he invited me to tour before dessert. The produce is all *bio*, what the French call organic, and included tromboncino squash, red berries, wild thyme, dozens of species of aromatic herbs, and who knows how many cherry tomato plants that he had planted vertically and that, he assured me, he picked himself.

Our grand finale featured two specialties: the *sgroppino*, two slices of Neapolitan cake surrounded by a circle of cherry halves, and the pizza al cioccolato, made with white, light, and dark chocolate. The room was still full when we left to climb the outdoor staircase to Les Caves du Roy, which was at capacity and in full swing.

For my spa article in 2018, my treatment took place in the most exquisite exotic space: the Salon Libanais. The hotel placed two massage tables in the middle of the room and I don't think they altered any other detail. When I was there, the masseuse warmed the oils beforehand. She covered my eyes with a silky mask that I removed when I was face up, so I could stare at the dark painted-wood ceiling. A massage has a special pleasure in an ambiance like that one.

When I returned in May 2023, the Sisley spa had been expanded, with new waiting and changing areas, marble and wood accents, more treatment *cabines*, and the "Eaux Rêvées" water journey, with Turkish baths and waterfalls curated to prepare guests for their subsequent treatments. The interior courtyard in the spa, where a Jean Dorval–designed, ceramic-tiled patio floor surrounded a centuries-old olive tree, had been repurposed from lounge to workout space where three women were stretching. The new lounge area had moved to the outdoor terrace overlooking the pool deck.

Whatever the year or name of the Ducasse-affiliated restaurant, Byblos is a perpetual delight.

HÔTEL DE PARIS

In 2013, Susann and I overnighted in Saint-Tropez just shortly after Hôtel de Paris opened at the entry of the village, close to the Musée de l'Annonciade and the port. The lobby is exciting and designed so that guests can look up and see the rooftop pool!

My pictures remind me that our rooms were accented by purple, with a wide stripe around the bedroom wall, on pillows, and the hanging lamp—and the corridors were lined with images of the famous local sailing regatta *Les Voiles de Saint-Tropez*. Our dinner fare was influenced by the consulting chef, Michel Rostang, who had served me the memorable molten chocolate cake in Paris years earlier.

Val and I ferried from Cannes to St.-Trop in 2019, which is by far the nicest way to arrive there in season. We always try to be there for the amazing open-air market that takes place at the plane-tree-shaded plaza, Place des Lices, on Tuesday and Saturday mornings. This market is more exciting than most: it's not just foods, shoes, cashmere, and clothes. There are a plethora of treasures like vintage Louis Vuitton trunks. After spending the morning and too many euros at the market, we lunched at the hotel's rooftop terrace, called Les Toits (the roofs). Our table faced an open window wall abutting one short edge of the pool, and it felt as if we were sipping a bubbly *coupe* and eating hot-from-the-oven bread and langoustines almost inside the pool, yet in shaded, air-conditioned comfort.

The creative chef layered flavors in different dishes by repeating one ingredient with different preparations: both raw sliced artichokes and cooked artichoke quarters were incorporated in one appetizer; tomatoes in different sizes and colors—red, yellow, green, and purple—encircled burrata; a plate dotted with strawberry sauce was centered with a strawberry tart topped with baby strawberries; and a frosted Victoria pineapple was stuffed with pineapple sorbet and topped with sliced pineapple. It's an effective and appealing culinary *truc*.

After our poolside lunch, we picked up our overnight bags from the valet and pulled them the short distance to the new harbor and the midafternoon ferry back to Cannes. It was a perfect trip.

In 2023, Val and I traveled from Cannes to Saint-Tropez via car service. The ferry wasn't yet running for the season, and we opted not to deal with the complications of a train, taxi, ferry, and another taxi. We did what we love doing there: sitting in portside cafes, browsing the shops, exploring little streets, going to galleries (one artist had an exhibit in a beautiful church). We spent Saturday morning at the market and dined at a recommended seafood restaurant at the port that night. On Sunday morning we returned to the Musée de l'Annonciade.

After a quiet hour amid those breathtaking paintings, we still had a few minutes before calling an Uber to take us to a 1:00 p.m. brunch reservation, which I planned as our "final" special meal. We were walking the short distance toward the new port when we passed a stunning restaurant terrace where, from the sidewalk, we could see four shiny white steps framed in brass going up to a long white table. We walked up the path to L'Opéra Saint-Tropez and found the interior décor equally striking. Without skipping a beat, Val reserved a late-night table. I called the Uber.

AIRELLES SAINT-TROPEZ, CHÂTEAU DE LA MESSARDIÈRE

Our reservation for Sunday brunch took place at La Table de la Messardière, in the fabulous resort Airelles Saint-Tropez, Château de la Messardière, one of the thirty-one hotels in France awarded the "palace" distinction, because it is so exceptional that it is considered beyond a five-star venue. We brunched outdoors overlooking expansive parklike grounds with exquisite views of the sea and listening to live music: a singer accompanied by a four-piece band. It was perfection! The bountiful buffet was extraordinary, with a series of table displays that occupied two entire interior dining rooms: one room offered a vast selection of seafoods and salads, and the other was devoted to an inordinate number of gorgeous pastries.

L'OPÉRA

By 9:00 p.m., when we were dressing to go out, we were starting to feel hungry enough to eat, again; by 10:00 p.m., we entered L'Opéra. It was as empty as if we'd arrived in midafternoon, and we probably could have booked a table for midnight or later, when the cognoscenti arrive. Moments after we were seated, performers climbed wide white steps, like those we had seen outside, and performed on an adjacent tabletop, dancing and singing. Their costumes replicated the seductive ones in one of the room's enormous, albeit quirky, photographic murals. Later, we noticed that they changed costumes for each "show" and that they looked as if they had stepped out of whatever mural they were portraying.

Even the waitstaff was costumed, so to speak, wearing stylish black jackets emblazoned on the backs with large white painted letters: "I'm the best f---ing waiter (or waitress or sommelier)! Throughout the meal, the entertainers continued with solos, duets, and group dancing and singing on various tabletops around the room. The food was far better than one would have expected at a dinner theater with a sexy show. It was all a bit shocking and amusing and thrilling. As a restaurant L'Opéra is good. What's more, it's great fun and *un peu risqué!*

chez moi: CITRON PRESSÉ

With the abundance of lemon trees in the region, the popularity of citron pressé should be no surprise, and it appeared so often that I usually requested it. In France, it's not at all like the sugary-sweet Southern-style lemonade. Instead, this healthy thirst-quencher is designed for individual taste buds, with each ingredient served separately: freshly squeezed lemon juice, water—with ice in warm weather—and no sugar (if you must have sugar, use as much as you like). I make mine according to my friend's instructions. "Citron pressé uses very fresh lemons, squeezed in a nice squeezer to get the most juice in a glass, and filled with your favorite flat water. You can add sugar, but I don't!"

Marseille and Collioure

———◆◆◆———

I N 2004, AT A LUNCHEON WITH TRAVEL WRITERS, I GOT up to leave to catch a train home when the man sitting next to me said: "You mustn't leave now. They're about to announce the raffle winners." I listened to Michael—who has since become a close friend—and minutes later, they called my name: I won two tickets on British Airways from New York's JFK to London's Heathrow. That November, I used them for a three-week vacay with Bob: a stay in London, the Eurostar to Paris, a drive through Burgundy and Provence to Nice, and another cruise aboard the *Wind Surf* to Barcelona.

Marseille

Among our ports of call on that trip was Marseille. My major interest there, during the few hours of that first visit, was to eat the most authentic bouillabaisse I could find. The briny fish stew, which became the city's signature dish, was originally prepared by fisherman to make use of their unsold fish. With so many cafés lining the Vieux Port, it's plausible that one prepared a worthy rendition, but I didn't know which one and I wasn't about to risk my one chance to find the best.

LE PETIT NICE PASSEDAT

I knew from studying my Relais & Châteaux catalog that both chef-owners at Le Petit Nice Passedat, a family-owned property since 1917, had two Michelin stars: Jean-Paul Passedat earned his by 1981; his son Gérald Passedat was awarded his third in 2008, just four years after my first visit. I assumed that I'd find the best bouillabaisse there and asked a taxi driver at the port to take us to the restaurant. Because it was still morning, I asked him to show us a bit of the city before dropping us off.

He drove along the quai bordering the harbor and headed to the Abbaye Saint-Victor, a former Roman sanctuary that contains a crypt with the fourteenth-century relics of Saint-Victor. He continued up the highest hill in the city—450 feet above the harbor with an amazing view of the Old Port—to Notre-Dame de la Garde, a nineteenth-century basilica that started life as a chapel in 1214.

Our brief cultural excursion completed, the driver took the curved coastal road to Le Petit Nice Passedat, perched high on a wave-washed bluff above the Mediterranean.

It was still too early for lunch, so we sat at the bar chatting with the bartender. When I told him about my mission, he said *"Desolé!"* (the restaurant was closed for Sunday lunch). When chef-owner Père Jean-Paul Passedat arrived, the barman introduced us. During a conversation about our mutual contacts in the Relais & Châteaux family, I told him about my disappointment at not being able to dine there and my hope for a special bouillabaisse.

Without missing a beat, he instructed the barman to tell the concierge to make a reservation for us under his name at his favorite place for bouillabaisse, Restaurant Chez Michel, a multigenerational family restaurant that opened in 1946 (*his* multigenerational family business launched in 1954). It makes sense that the two local eateries send clients to each other, but what was so big-hearted is that I wasn't even a guest at the hotel!

CHEZ MICHEL

At Chez Michel, the owner greeted us at the front door standing next to a presentation of fresh fish in straw baskets atop a white halved fishing boat trimmed in blue and named "Michel." He wore the typical blue-and-white-striped fisherman's shirt, welcomed us warmly, and seated us personally. Soon, the formally attired maître d' brought the menu from which we each ordered the *specialité*. He soon returned carrying a tray of whole raw fish on ice to show us each specific specimen that would soon be poached in a saffron-rich broth. There may have been rockfish, daurade, sole, and mullets on the tray, but I can't be sure. I can only identify fish local to Long Island (flounder, striped bass, and tuna) and salmon. What I can assure is that there was nary a shellfish in sight.

The maître d' ultimately returned wheeling a *chariot* holding a covered soup tureen and a separate platter of cooked fish. First, he ladled the brick-colored broth into our dishes, then added individual pieces of fish. He placed the extra pieces on a separate platter next to the covered tureen. Immediately, a waiter arrived with a plate of round croutons, which looked like crostini slices, and two small dishes: one with *aioli*—a golden garlicky blend with emulsified egg yolks and olive oil—and the other with a rusty-hued *rouille*, another garlicky emulsion in which the olive oil was spiced with hot red peppers. The waiter returned regularly to refill Bob's bowl—he ate most of the fish. I set about spreading aioli—and, alternately, a bit of rouille—on each crouton, which I floated in the broth before scooping up and enjoying. Although I wasn't sure about the correct etiquette for eating bouillabaisse—and was too intimidated to ask—

it tasted perfect. A YouTube demonstration at Chez Michel instructs the diner to top each bite of fish with sauce, dunk it in the soup to hydrate, and devour, just as I did with the croutons.

I like to gaze around a dining room to get the feel of a place and move around the room. Like a smoker who gets up for a quick drag, I use the restroom as an excuse to look about. Women were dressed in silk dresses and low heels, men wore jackets and ties, and children were equally well-attired. In this place, I felt like a fly on the wall at the local country club during an after-church Sunday brunch, where everyone greets one another like old friends. We were probably the only out-of-towners, certainly the only Americans, which made that uber-satisfying culinary and cultural discovery even more gratifying.

Almost ten years later, in April 2013, my friend Susann and I returned to Chez Michel, and I found dinner as pleasingly perfect as my earlier lunch. Susann loved the saffron-rich flavor of the dish but missed calamari. Like many people who order an authentic bouillabaisse Marseillaise, she didn't realize that there's no shellfish in the traditional seafarers' supper.

That year, Marseille was one of three European Capitals of Culture, and the city had made many improvements, including some newly built and newly renovated museums, which was why we decided to spend three nights there before going to Nice for our art-focused Riviera road trip.

INTERCONTINENTAL MARSEILLE-HOTEL DIEU

One of the new editions to the port city was the soon-to-open five-star InterContinental Marseille–Hotel Dieu. I had secured two assignments to feature the hotel, which was built in a former eighteenth-century hospital facing the port, so they took me on a hard-hat tour of the property. The transformation added skylights and every modern convenience, but what impressed me was what the architect kept intact: the original staircases, stone tiles, vaulted passageways, and sections of limestone walls—one of which dated to the Renaissance.

RADISSON BLU

Susann and I stayed at a new, nice, well-priced Radisson Blu hotel, located port-front on the quai on the opposite side of the harbor from Hotel Dieu. A public bus stopped outside the hotel door, and we used it multiple times during our short stay to sightsee. That's how we traveled up and around the coastal road to Restaurant Chez Michel for bouillabaisse. We also bused to and from the railroad station, where we boarded a regional train for the hour-long trip to Aix-en-Provence to see Paul Cezanne's studio. We only had the chance to pass the stunning Fondation Vasarely, which has a façade that resembles one of his cubist paintings.

Our final evening in Marseille, we took the bus up to the bar at Le Petit Nice, where I asked if M. Jean-Paul Passedat was available, so I could say hello. The lifelong hotelier was gracious enough to come downstairs to greet us and even sounded pleased to hear about—and feign memory of—his kindness to Bob and me a decade earlier.

Although we both would have liked to have had a full Gérald Passedat culinary experience, after the day trip to Aix and back we were too tired for a formal multicourse prix fixe dinner. Instead, we drank wine and sampled some of his lovely appetizers—I recall mozzarella-stuffed zucchini blossoms and Susann's favorite, octopus—in a room overlooking waves breaking on the rocks. Then we taxied back to our hotel early to pack for the morning train to Nice and our Riviera road trip.

un peu plus: GÉRALD PASSEDAT

I recently bought Gérald Passedat's beautiful cookbook, *Flavors from the French Mediterranean*, hoping to find a bouillabaisse recipe. Instead, his "Bouille Abaisse" recipe is for a seafood terrine that's far more daunting than anything I'll ever attempt. It was interesting to read his explanation of the name, which comes from the verbs *bouillir* = to boil and *abaisser* =to lower, and means: "when it boils, lower the heat."

Collioure

Collioure was a true "discovery" on the last cruise Bob and I took. I was familiar with the name but couldn't place it and was completely unaware of how lovely a spot it is. The ship moored at Port Vendres, and we disembarked and taxied two miles along the Côte Vermeille to the small fishing village in Languedoc-Roussillon, France's largest wine-producing region, in the far western Basque country, where grapes thrive between the shore and the Pyrenees mountains. It is located only twelve miles from the Spanish border and is just two and a half hours by train from Barcelona.

The picturesque village, with its lemon-and-peach-colored, terracotta-roofed stone homes facing the harbor, has the imposing Pyrenees as a backdrop, in addition to a decorated carousel; a pebbled beach, Plage de Port d'Avail; a church, Nôtre-Dame des Anges, which had formerly been a lighthouse; and Château Royal, an eight-hundred-year-old medieval castle. Notably, its cobblestone streets bear historic place names: rue de la République, avenue du General de Gaulle, rue Pasteur, rue Colbert, rue Voltaire, rue Vauban, and the main street, rue de la Democratie.

While ambling along the shorefront walking path—the Chemin du Fauvisme (Path of Fauvism)—I was taken aback and surprised to see nine reproductions of flamboyant panoramas captured on canvas and posted for all to admire. Unexpectedly, I was face to face with copies of seascapes painted by my favorite Fauves, including André Derain and Henri Matisse. Even with their exaggerated palettes of raspberry, ochre, vivid red, and royal blue hues, it was easy to identify the precise scenes of the boldly brushstroked, brightly painted, primary-colored seascapes.

One picture showed the nearby lighthouse; another replicated the pastel stone houses facing the harbor. Images of the distinctive painted sailing/fishing boats copied what the boats moored nearby looked like, though it had been created a hundred years earlier. I was absolutely thrilled to view what my much-admired Fauve geniuses observed and interpreted.

It wasn't until I saw those images that I remembered that I first heard the word Collioure when Louise Smith showed me *Landscape at Collioure, summer 1905*, by Matisse, a striking abstract work with short blue and green, Van Gogh–like brushstrokes. The place name appeared again after her 1990 bequest to MoMA (Museum of Modern Art) in New York. Matisse, who had discovered Collioure in the early twentieth century, memorialized it on canvas. The Collection Musée d'Art Moderne de Collioure has a Matisse ink-on-paper drawing called *Bateaux et Poulets, Collioure, 1906* among its treasures.

Braque, Chagall, Derain, Dufy, Maillol, Marquet, and Picasso were also drawn to paint the village's bluer-than-blue skies and fleets of thirty-foot wooden fishing boats, called *catalanes*, for the neighboring Spanish region. The distinctive watercraft inspired the artists because they are brightly painted—in combinations of sun yellow or sea blue—and have unusual folding masts, triangular sails, winches, and nets.

un peu plus: FAUVES

At the 1905 Salon d'Automne, one critic's reaction to the shockingly bold and energetic primary-colored artworks—including some by Maurice de Vlaminck and Kees van Dongen—was to call the artists Fauves, or Wild Beasts, a name that stuck. It referred to André Derain, Raoul Dufy, Henri Matisse, and Georges Rouault, among others. (Kandinsky attended that exhibit, which influenced his work.)

Collioure so impressed me that I advocated an overnight there when my friend Cara Greenberg, an author and editor, told me about a solo train trip from Barcelona across the Mediterranean coast in 2015. I told her, "Who knows if I'll get to see Collioure again, but I hope you consider it a must-do." Here's Cara's blog entry, which she called the *Colors of Collioure*:

"MY FRIEND IRVINA WAS SO RIGHT. Irvina Lew, a career travel writer who's been a lot of places, told me the Mediterranean seaport town of Collioure, France, where Derain, Matisse, and others famously went to paint—and where the vivid colors they were inspired to use gave rise to the movement known as Fauvism—was a 'must' for my European itinerary, 'even if you only get there for a couple of hours.'

"I was a little surprised by her insistence. I'd never even heard of Collioure (though I love Fauvism, which comes from the word fauve, or wild). But it was a convenient place to stop for the night between Zaragoza and Arles—about four hours by train from each. So I made a one-night reservation at the Hotel les Templiers, which looked suitably artistic, and prepared to be wowed. Wowed I was. Collioure is vibrant and charming in the extreme, rather quiet in the off-season with just a few French vacationers. The weather for my one-day stay was perfection, the blue sky offsetting Fauvishly the oranges and yellows of the old stucco houses and the surreally pruned sycamore trees casting sharp shadows in the bright sunlight."

Route Napoléon

———— •••• ————

I N 2004, I RECEIVED AN INVITATION FROM THE FRENCH
Government Tourist Office to participate in a four-day road
trip, the *Rallye de l'Empéreur ROUTE NAPOLÉON*, in vintage
cars. I was thrilled that the journey started out near Nice and accepted the invitation before the second fortuitous event, when I won
the two round-trip tickets on British Air.

The souvenir poster still hanging on my office wall attests to
the dates: *du 1er au 4 septembre 2004*, and until I arrived, I wasn't
aware that the drive was organized by a group of dedicated classic car
owners, members of *L'Association Amie de l'Automobile Ancienne de
Grenoble* (Antique Automobile Club of Grenoble) or why they chose
to plan the rally for September 2004. I imagine they did it because
the weather was more suitable for the convertible vehicles than it
would have been on December 2, 2004, the actual bicentennial of
Napoleon's coronation, or near March 15, when the region honors
Napoleon's March 1 landing at the Vieux Port (old port) of Golfe-
Juan with a re-enactment of the event: *Vallauris Golfe–Juan fête le
débarquement de Napoléon du 1er mars 1815.*

Naturally, I was thrilled at the prospect of returning to the Riviera and learning about classic cars, meeting new people, and discovering historic venues along the Route Napoléon from Golfe-Juan to

Grenoble. History is as integral to the coastal region as is its beauty, and from a historical viewpoint, the major French figure, Napoleon Bonaparte, is the most important element. One interesting factoid is that his name might well have been *Napoleone di Buonaparte* had his birth taken place before 1769, while Corsica was still under Italian rule. Skipping through time from his birth to his coronation and eventual exile omits much of his lifetime; still, his escape and subsequent journey on what is now called *Route Napoléon* introduced me to a fascinating weeklong historical period known as *le Vol d'Aigle* (the Eagle's Flight).

un peu plus: THE EAGLE'S FLIGHT

On February 26, 1815, Napoleon had been in exile for less than a year when he escaped from the eighty-six-square-mile isle of Elba, located just thirty miles east of Corsica where he was born. The former French leader and twelve hundred faithful troops set sail on a seven-boat flotilla and headed to the small fishing harbor of Golfe-Juan, between Antibes and Cannes. His goal was as clear as the Mediterranean: Return to Paris, reclaim the throne (from King Louis XVIII), and regain control of the French Empire.

He addressed his men with these words: "The eagle with the national colors will fly from bell tower to bell tower as far as the towers of Nôtre-Dame." The entire incident has such historical significance that the French still commemorate *le Vol d'Aigle*. For the two-hundredth anniversary of Napoleon's death, it was even the theme of the summertime 2021 *Son et Lumière* (Sound and Light) show at Les Invalides in Paris.

When I arrived at Nice Côte d'Azur Airport, there was nobody there to greet me, which happens now and again. When it does, I always tell myself: Don't worry. Have no fear. It's daylight. It's not raining. You have a credit card. You have cash. It will be OK. In France, I also remind myself that I can make myself understood. Talking to myself sounds ridiculous, but it works for me. So I took a deep breath, convinced myself that I'd be fine, and promptly walked to the information desk and asked the clerk to call the hotel. She did willingly and assured me that someone would soon arrive.

Eventually, a dapper gentleman walked toward me, identified himself as a member of Quadruple A (i.e., AAAA), apologized for waiting at the wrong terminal, and said: "*Allons-y!*" (Let's go). He drove a short distance on the scenic coastal route along the wide, palm-lined Promenade des Anglais through Nice, past the elegant white belle époque villas facing the sea that I always admire, and beyond the distinctive Le Negresco Hotel to Vieux Nice, where he turned left through an ancient arch into the old city and parked outside the colorful flower market in Cours Saleya. We lunched at a picture-perfect café, which I have never been able to find again, although I remember that it was near the bold yellow Misèricorde Chapel. When a regional rosé appeared followed by fresh baguette, I was in heaven even before I ordered my first salade Niçoise in Nice.

My host explained some of the challenges that members of Les 4A faced in transporting their vehicles to the coast, where the *rallye* would begin. Their plan was—as he clarified—to form a parade of vehicles, one after another, and drive north from the coast in formation following France's most picturesque road, the two-hundred-mile mile-marker-studded Route Napoléon, which had been officially inaugurated in 1932. He told me that our journey was planned to begin the following morning in Golfe-Juan, the harbor where the former emperor had anchored and where a reenactment ceremony would take place. Afterward, the cars would follow the sea-to-mountain corridor, on the same path that Napoléon's troops marched up to Grenoble. Our "expedition" along RN85, I later learned, would pass through forty-two little communities, known as *communes*, and take four days, although motorists can make the coast-to-Grenoble trip in about four-plus hours if they drive speedily on the autoroute.

Grasse

After lunch, my host drove from Nice to Grasse, the perfume city, which I had visited alone on my first trip, and where Bob and I once toured a perfume factory. The industry dates to the sixteenth-century time of Catherine de Medici, who complained about the stench of her leather gloves, which were handmade at a Grasse tannery. Entrepreneurial artisans tried to please her by collecting roses and lavender from nearby fields and infusing the leather with a more pleasant floral aroma. Perfume as an industry was subsequently established in the mid-1700s by Galimard, then Fragonard and Molinard.

When the charming gent and I arrived at the aptly named Hôtel des Parfums, he sped off to work in the club's temporary headquarters, and he was so occupied with operational tasks during the entire trip that I rarely saw him.

An international assortment of people—driver-owners and other AAAA members, a half-dozen journalists, and local bigwigs— all assembled on the terrace that evening for a pre-sunset view of the Mediterranean, about a dozen miles south. The inaugural dinner party was hotel-elegant, but the ambiance had the camaraderie of a frat party, with men singing enthusiastically and loudly accompanied by an accordion played by Georges Dini (I later discovered he was the proud owner of a twin Ford Model A Roadster). Amid all the partying and noise, it was hard to meet anyone at the event, but with servers continually pouring wine it was easy to drink too much. I overslept the next morning and woke up to the sound of motors buzzing down the driveway. By the time I got down to the lobby, everyone was gone. I had to hire a taxi for the fifteen-mile drive to Golfe-Juan harbor.

Napoleon Festival at Golfe-Juan

Once at sea level, the coastal road passes modern five-story apartment houses with seafront terraces facing Golfe-Juan's cruiser-lined marina. September flowers were blooming and flanked the entry to the old harbor where the taxi dropped me off. I never got to watch the cars as they lined up in formation, and if the rest of the group arrived in time to see the traditional ship sail into the harbor that morning, I did not.

The bivouac was an "imperial" village with numerous tents, a parade of fifes and drums, dance demonstrations, and some extraordinary formal festivities, with speeches and toasts. Most boys and men wore imperial uniforms, and costumed soldiers marched in black or red jackets with white crisscrossed bands, shoulders adorned with gold epaulettes, feet in tall black boots, and heads with even taller hats. Women dressed according to nineteenth-century social status: some wore long, workaday muslin dresses, and others were in fine gowns paired with pearl tiaras. Mini market stalls displayed Napoleonic memorabilia overflowing with every appealing souvenir, but having already overspent on the costly cab ride, I didn't shop.

While I searched the crowd for a recognizable face, I spotted the Napoleon *imitateur* (look-alike), positioned exactly where he would have disembarked and posing for photographers in front of a monument inscribed with these words: "Here landed Napoleon on March 1, 1815." Finally, while listening to the speeches, a colleague noticed me. As soon as these concluded, she led me to our posse near the display of AAAA cars.

It was an unabashedly remarkable thrill to see that collection of beautiful cars lined up together. *Hélas* (alas), I was as ignorant about the twenty vintage automobiles as I was about the history of *le Vol d'Aigle*, and if not for their colors, I'm not sure I would have been able to distinguish one car from another or remember which driver drove what. I recall Christian Simonetti's royal blue 1935 Delahaye Course, Philippe Salamand's cream-colored 1950 Salmson Cabriolet E72, René Verbiest's 1928 Cadillac Cabriolet Fisher with a crest that had been trucked from Belgium, and Mustaffa Laiche's 1957 Porsche Cabriolet 356A, but there were lots more.

The AAAA Rallye

Our twenty-car convoy started its first journey amid much commotion and followed the route that Napoleon had traveled the day he arrived in Golfe-Juan. The little corporal was in a big rush to get on the move before being attacked, because as soon as he landed, he sent some troops on a scouting trip to Antibes and learned, within hours, that they had been captured by local royalists. He is quoted as having said: "I have to move faster than the news."

Napoleon rode while his soldiers marched the six miles to Cannes to a place where he stopped, prayed, and slept on land that first night. The location is close to the Palais des Festivals, City Hall, and Le Suquet, and is now home to the church built in 1865 called Nôtre-Dame de Bon Voyage (Our Lady of the Good Voyage), where

I noticed the bronze plaque referring to Napoleon on the outside wall of the church.

Our first procession passed places that I recognized from my previous visits: the fishing port at Vieux Cannes, the street where the drivers turned north toward Le Cannet—where I have since visited the wonderful Bonnard Museum—and Vallauris, a town famous for faience—glazed earthenware pottery—and for its Picasso Museum, housed in an old château. It continued toward Mougins, where I had once tasted Chef Roger Vergé's stuffed zucchini blossoms at Le Moulin de Mougins, and where Picasso spent the last twelve years before his death in 1973.

We continued upward, past lavender fields and through the rocky alpine foothills to Saint-Vallier-de-Thiey, passing Le Relais Impérial, where I had stayed on my first trip to the Riviera in 1990, without realizing that the "Impérial" in the hotel's name referenced Napoleon. At that time, I had been so focused on visiting art museums and lunching in high style that I failed to understand the significance of the Route Napoléon or its nineteenth-century military history. Had I taken time to explore the tiny medieval town outside my hotel door, I might have noticed the column topped by a bust of Napoleon and the little stone seat that commemorates where he rested in the shade, taking a moment to drink some water, before mounting his horse and heading onward. My loss. (During the car rallye, I decided to explore the little village someday, and I did, finally, in 2024, as my next pages remind me.)

Those first hours were in familiar territory and recalled great experiences. Our small group of international journalists was instructed to change cars at each stage (étape), when the cars stopped in communes that were at about twenty-mile intervals. These changes gave me the gift of meeting an array of fascinating drivers. I had about an hour of one-on-one conversation with each to ask some obligatory car questions and then about what really interested me: their lives. Some of the older drivers had been youths during—or just after—World War II and had endured wartime and postwar hardships. I'm convinced that their youthful dreams contributed to their passions for owning the vintage cars they collected, their lust for life, and *bonhomie* (friendliness).

Had iPhones been available, I could have made a video of what is etched in my mind's eye. Several times each day, the cavalcade pulled into a teeny commune and the same marvelous choreography occurred. The motorists followed a protocol that had probably taken decades to perfect, lining their automobiles up next to one another like a precision marching band, in the *place* (central town square) that fronted the *hôtel de ville* (town hall). As if by rote, each man took out a clean chamois cloth and shined his beloved vehicle in a circular motion, as if he were imitating Marcel Marceau, the great French mime.

un peu plus: MARCEL MARCEAU

I recently learned from the true-to-life film *Resistance* (2020) that Marcel Marceau was more than a mime and artist. During World War II, he was a valiant hero who helped at least seventy orphaned Jewish children cross the border into Spain and escape to freedom.

Within minutes of arriving in each little commune, the mayor, town dignitaries, and guests appeared behind a reception table decorated with the *Tricoleur, the drapeau français* (the French flag). We stood attentively, facing them, listening to their welcome speeches as they toasted the drivers with a regional sparkling wine and feted us all with local culinary specialties. These welcomes—with between-meal receptions—occurred multiple times a day as we journeyed north up RN85, along a road that was a treacherous path through the Alps in 1815 when Napoleon traversed it. He made the strategic decision to risk the round-about, steep route to Paris via Grenoble to avoid the even more dangerous royalists, near Marseille, who wanted to kill him.

At one dinner, at Le Coin Fleuri in Digne, we started with foie gras, had a wonderful rack of lamb, and drank an excellent local Domaine La Blaque 2003. It was quite a party. After dinner, Jean-Pierre Martinetti—a Corsican like Bonaparte—showed a short clip of Rod Steiger's film *Waterloo*. When the club members bellowed their usual song, the man sitting next to me was distinctly outraged and claimed that it offended Italians. I learned how and why some months later, from author George Semler's article in *Forbes*: the group didn't sing the original lyrics; they substituted salty—and politically incorrect—ones in the familiar folk song. Here's how George described the scene: "Christian Simonetti introduced us to the Quadruple A (Association Amie de l'Automobile Ancienne) theme song, a scatological tribute to the cultivation, consumption, and eventual, um, digestion of 'la bella polenta,' rendered in Italian."

George is the only person whom I met that week who is still a friend. He's an American guidebook author who has lived his adult life divided between winters in Barcelona and summers in his hometown in Maine. Here's what he wrote about another driver: "Jean Prestail sat calmly in his pristine 1935 Ford Roadster, an even dozen years older than his automobile and, like his machine, humming flawlessly on original parts. Jean couldn't stop smiling. Behind the wheel since 1939, when all the men were off in the war and the driving age was lowered to sixteen, he's clocked five million kilometers between rallies, road trips, and normal commerce. 'And never filled out an insurance claim,' he crowed, 'never had an accident.'"

On the last day, we gathered just sixteen miles outside Grenoble, at Laffrey, at the *Prairie de la Rencontre* (the field of the encounter), where, on March 7, 1815, Napoleon was blocked by royalist troops from Grenoble. Napoleon famously told his men to lower their weapons and walked out to face his adversaries, announcing these legendary words "Soldiers of the Fifth, you recognize me," said Napoleon, unbuttoning his tunic. "If there is a single man among you who would kill his Emperor, may he do it now. Here I am!" The troops shouted, *"Vive l'empereur!"* and embraced him.

Our get-together there was somewhat less dramatic but impressive, because the antique cars, which were assembled in precision formation as usual, looked even more striking adjacent to the grand statue of Napoleon astride his horse. For our final lunch before we arrived in Grenoble, a costumed Napoleonic band from Belgium serenaded us. Best of all, France's most famous chef, Paul Bocuse, had driven ninety minutes from Lyon to host us at a gala special occasion *pique-nique* buffet outside the historic Château de Vizille, with its expansive gardens and Grand Canal. I was thrilled.

A DAY TRIP ON THE ROUTE NAPOLÉON

Driving the Route Napoléon is considered the most scenic journey in France and is rich with natural and historic venues: thermal bath towns, parks, ancient churches, and mountain cliffs. If you are a confident and competent driver—or are traveling with one—I recommend replicating Napoleon's trek from the sea through those high cliffs up to the Alps in Grenoble. It will be memorable. If you are less ambitious, as I have become, do a day trip as we did in May 2024, partway through the Alpes-Maritimes along the route marked with commemorative plaques and monuments. Val and I were passengers, and I instructed the driver where to go. It was, as is said: *Une bonne idée* (a good idea).

We started at the Route Napoléon sign in Golfe-Juan, followed the road up to Vallauris, where we stopped and visited the National Picasso Museum, which has an extensive collection of the artist's ceramics. We also saw his famous mural *La Guerre et La Paix*, where Picasso's war and peace work is displayed on the curved ceiling of the ancient castle's chapel. (There's a virtual visit available online!) The important Madoura studio, where Picasso learned and practiced pottery and which has an amazing exhibit, was not open when we were there.

Next stop was in the perfume city of Grasse, where twenty-eight-hundred pink umbrellas were strung across the city's historic streets (and in the Villa Fragonard gardens) to celebrate the town's annual Fête des Roses. Then, as had happened so many years before, we drove in the rain for an additional nine miles to Saint-Vallier-de-Thiey, where we stopped at Le Relais Impérial, my first-ever hotel on the Riviera. After a hearty lunch, we walked toward the famous column with the bust of the emperor and saw the imposing elm tree with its circular stone seat, where Napoleon rested that winter day in 1815.

We followed the road back downhill and departed from the official route when we turned left at Grasse toward Saint-Paul-de-Vence, where we visited the Fondation Maeght, which had reopened since its closure the summer before.

Our final stop was close to the coast, at the Pierre Auguste Renoir Museum, in the artist's former hillside home on a farm with groves of olive and orange trees. In 1907, the artist bought the domaine, in Cagnes-sur-Mer, called Les Collettes, and built the villa there that viewed the sea, with fewer obstructions then. The first time I visited his studio, in 1990, it was set up as if he had just left the room, with his easel, with accessories that I recognized from his paintings, and the artist's wheelchair. I was moved to tears. Now it's updated and has original Renoir paintings on view, which I don't recall seeing years ago. After our visit, while on our way to the autoroute (A8) toward Cannes, we passed an open store-front window where crêpes were sold. We stopped for the welcome treat.

chez moi: CRÊPES

Crêpes originated in Brittany, in the north of France. Poor farmers were not taxed for buckwheat, which didn't make good bread, so they ate the nutritious and fast-growing grain in buckwheat pancakes, called *galettes*, made with buckwheat, water, and salt. They served them plain or topped with sucré (sugar), *salé* (salted) caramel ice cream, fruit, or as a savory dish stuffed with ham and cheese and/or an egg. My technique is to slowly incorporate the wet ingredients—skim milk, eggs, and seltzer—into a blend of one-quarter buckwheat and three-quarter all-purpose flour, whisk to eliminate lumps, and let the batter rest overnight in the refrigerator. I use a Cuisinart nonstick crêpe pan, which came with an authentic T-shaped stick to spread the batter and a long, skinny wooden spatula, but read that an old-fashioned cast-iron pan gets hotter and makes a better crust. You can watch crêpe-making tutorials on YouTube to see how to pour the thin batter on one side of the pan and move the pan around to cover the entire bottom. I make an extra dozen, stack them between wax paper, and freeze them.

Riviera Apartments

---◆---

FOR AS LONG AS I CAN RECALL, WHENEVER I STEPPED foot into a French market, I wanted to buy some of the dazzlingly displayed ingredients to take "home" to eat. While I felt grateful to experience fine dining and for the many restaurant experiences, there were times that I just wanted to have a refrigerator to open and easy access to food, instead of two-hour lunches and three-hour dinners.

Then, in the fall of 2017, my youngest daughter, Jen, had emergency gall bladder surgery. While her sisters, Alison and Sharon, and I were waiting nervously for the doctor's post-op report, Ali said: "Mom, you're not getting any younger, and you've always wanted to rent a house in France. You should get on it before it's too late."

I realized that she had deliberately changed the conversation away from the heaviness of the moment, but I also recognized her point. If not then, when? I had wanted to rent a house in France for years, but Bob never shared my enthusiasm. Now that he was gone, I no longer envisioned a house as home base and renting a car to drive from place to place. What I preferred was an apartment in a flat, walkable, seafront city on the Côte d'Azur, near a produce market, bakery, butcher shop—preferably one with freshly skewered chickens on a rotisserie—and cafés, restaurants, and boutiques.

Her suggestion encouraged thought about my savings for "old age," and I decided that some could be spared to make memories.

Within the week, I had transferred my American Express points to my Delta account, because Delta flies nonstop from JFK to Nice. Then, I searched VRBO for an apartment with two "master" bedrooms. My well-traveled middle-age daughters were not going to be happy with a second bedroom with a futon, twin, or bunk beds! I hoped to find two full-size bathrooms and a terrace big enough for two to sit with a cup of coffee or glass of wine, and found a great spot in Juan-les-Pins, a coastal party town in summer, but which is quieter and less costly off-season. I booked it mid-April to May.

That Hannukah, I gave each of my daughters sixty thousand Delta miles and invited them to spend a week with me separately on the French Riviera. Happily, they all accepted.

Juan-les-Pins

Jen and I landed in Nice for her first trip to the coast, and I drove along the Promenade des Anglais that separates the grand belle époque villas from the seafront, past the port where Bob and I had boarded the *Wind Surf,* and directly to the oh-so-plush Grand-Hôtel du Cap-Ferrat, a Four Seasons hotel, in Saint-Jean-Cap-Ferrat, where we spent two ultra-luxe nights before heading to Juan-les-Pins.

On the third afternoon, I drove to the apartment building on Avenue Amiral Courbet, where I had to park on the street and wait for the landlord, who promised to give me the fob to access entry into the garage. The patron of the little *marché* next door saw me struggling to put money in the parking meter and helped me. When the apartment manager arrived, he gave me the garage fob and instruction to head down the ramp to the narrow, underground parking space. I had some trouble maneuvering the oversize SUV into it, much to Jen's concern, but managed.

Minutes after he had finished showing us around and sharing the necessary instructions, Jen hurried out the door to the same adjacent market on a mission to buy the best ingredients that she could find. The owner helped her choose fat white *asperges,* a mango, and an avocado. (Days later, I was there when he helped her choose a second avocado and heard him ask: *"Pour ce soir ou demain?"* (For tonight or tomorrow?)

She returned with all the basics—extra virgin olive oil, wine vinegar, *herbes de provence,* bottles of wine, charcuterie, and cheese—plus so many flowers they filled three vases. She was so happy shopping in each little store that she set out again, this time to the local supermarket to buy paper goods and cleaning supplies. That evening we shared the exact stay-in supper that I had always fantasized about, complete with wine, fresh bread, charcuterie, cheese, crudités, and pastries.

The next morning, my youngest suggested that we take an Uber to Antibes, and I didn't object. We went directly to the Picasso Museum, where I bought two placemats for our terrace table that reproduced his famous bouquet of flowers. Then, after waiting years for the pleasure, I shopped for more produce at the famed Marché Provençal, buying beautiful ingredients for salade Niçoise: jarred capers, *les anchois* (anchovies), tuna spears packed in olive oil, baby-pink French radishes, little red new potatoes, tiny tomatoes on the vine, skinny *haricots verts,* and tiny black Niçoise olives.

Afterward, with market goodies positioned on an adjacent chair, I sipped espresso in a café and watched the world pass by while Jen explored the historic Vieux Antibes quartier. She stopped into the English-language bookstore, where an author happened to be giving a talk about her newest oeuvre, which Jen bought for me.

un peu plus: RIVIERA DREAMING: LOVE AND WAR ON THE CÔTE D'AZUR

This book, by Maureen Emerson, is an eye-opening account about two architects who designed some of the region's most spectacular seaside mansions during the high life after World War I. The era's excess and abundance changed into absolute tragedy—including death by starvation—during World War II and the Nazi occupation. The book captivated me when I read it on that stay, and I've gone back to it several times since.

When Jen and I weren't off sightseeing, she was happiest on a rental chaise at the beach, where the mid-April weather was perfect for sunbathing. She started each morning searching for the best croissants and sampled them at different boulangeries until she settled on her favorite, which happened to be close by. They were presented amidst a display of baguettes, brioches, sept grains, and the traditional *pain de compagne*, but they also sold tartines, napoleons, éclairs, and tartes tatin, plus sandwiches, pizza, and pissaladière (a Niçoise-style olive-topped pizza). The saleslady was so patient, especially with non-native French speakers, that when I asked for an éclair au chocolat, thinking that the chocolate was the topping not the filling, she noticed my disappointment, asked for it back, and offered me a *crème à la vanille* with a smile. *Merci, Madame.*

Jen also wanted to eat crêpes, so we searched for them. There were ample options had we been willing to stand at an open window, but we wanted to sit and linger. We found a café terrace with a chalkboard menu that listed crêpes with *jambon* and *fromage*, and which was located across from La Pinède, the famous seafront park, where we watched locals playing *pétanque* under pine trees. (The morning Sharon left Nice-Cote d'Azur airport on the same plane that brought Alison, we drove directly to the market in Vieux Nice, where we ate crêpes for breakfast; the saleslady topped mine with her own homemade raspberry preserves.)

My typical Riviera lunch is salade Niçoise. There was a place in Vieux Nice that was recommended, but when we arrived, the *patron* (owner) appeared at the front door and announced: "The food is finished. I'm closing." I had assumed that a Niçoise would be good everywhere, so I hadn't done my usual extensive research and was most disappointed with what was served, either with mushy tuna, old greens, or overcooked eggs. I preferred my own and prepared it for lunch, which we ate on the terrace. Sharon, who loves this salad too, and remembered eating wonderful ones on her business trips, was surprised that they were mediocre. I reminded her that those lunches took place in posh hotel restaurants. As it happened, hotels were the only places where we were served excellent salades Niçoises.

My favorite cooked French food is a rotisserie chicken, and I spent those three weeks dedicated to selecting, buying, serving, and eating them. I didn't have to look to find them because, with morning coffee in hand on the front terrace of the apartment, I could see the young assistant roll the portable rotisserie to the front of the *boucherie* (butcher) across the street; in the late afternoon, I watched him wheel it back inside. I eagerly bought my first poulet for our second night's supper, which cost 15€, if you please: three times more than at my usual supermarkets and one hundred times better. The next time I bought a hot-from-the-oven bird, my purchase included a few farm-fresh eggs, which were sold individually from a basket next to the register.

One day, when he had sold out of chickens, I had to change the menu and noticed a sale sign, 9.9€ a kilo for steak. The butcher suggested that I take the whole piece. "*D'accord,*" I agreed, though I had forgotten how many pounds are in a kilo (2.2) and feared it would be exorbitant. When he weighed the meat, he announced: "Five euros," which is surprisingly little anywhere, and especially in a shop where sea salt cost eight euros. "*Vous êtes sûr, Monsieur?*" I asked. "*Ah, oui, oui, oui. C'est une promotion,*" he assured me. That night, we dined on a delicious five-euro filet of beef! Nevertheless, from that day on, I ordered my chicken in advance and for a specific time, just before closing hour. They were all delicious.

Each daughter prepared one dinner in our small, well-equipped kitchen during her week, and they each chose pasta. Jen made linguine with green and white asparagus; Sharon purchased fresh handmade pasta with homemade pesto from the pasta shop up our street. On our final night, Ali incorporated what was left of our produce in her spaghetti al la vodka, with garlic, cherry tomatoes, basil, and the last drops of vodka.

At markets, I also sampled two typical, new-for-me Niçoise dishes: socca—the traditional chickpea-crusted, pizza-shaped pie made simply with chickpea flour, olive oil, water, and salt—for which I waited in a line in Saint-Tropez. A man baked it in a portable pizza-like oven and his wife sliced and served the entire circle! I tried my first square of *pissaladière*, a popular puff pastry topped with olives and caramelized onions, made in a rectangular sheet pan and served in cafés and boulangeries. Both were interesting but not to my taste.

My spa assignment for *AsiaSpa* magazine was to feature the most luxurious seven spas on the Riviera, so I researched and contacted each in advance, and arranged dates for my visits and treatments. Six hotels extended lunch invitations and three invited me to stay, so those were our "fancy" meals; for the rest, we walked to a neighboring restaurant or ate somewhere convenient to whatever museum, shop, or beach we visited, or we stayed "home."

RESTAURANT CAP RIVIERA

Cap Riviera was the only exceptional lunch Alison and I had in Juan-les-Pins, and a shopkeeper recommended it: "Lunch there for two reasons: *gastronomie et un bon prix*." (Good food at a good price.) She could have also said that it was beautiful, well-located on the beachfront, with a wonderful view! We only ordered starters, which with bread, wine, and a shared dessert was a delicious and satisfying midday meal. My *millefeuille* appetizer separated layers of crab and lobster salad with round tortilla rings instead of the traditional puff pastry. It was topped with a large lobster claw and with citrus segments surrounding the lower circle. Alison's lobster salad was served stuffed within two emptied lobster shells and arrived with tail and claw intact and topped with swirls of homemade mayonnaise.

I write mostly about food, but each daughter visited at least one quaint village, had at least one luxe hotel experience, enjoyed at least one museum—whether it was the Picasso or Léger or Fondation Maeght—and saw marvelous gardens, including those at Villa Ephrussi de Rothschild, where Jen and I spent hours. Those three weeks, each with a daughter one on one, were the best times I ever spent alone with each of them.

chez moi: ROTISSERIE CHICKEN

To achieve his warm, oh-so-crispy, spit-roasted chickens, Monsieur le Boucher dresses them with just a rub of olive oil, salt, pepper, and herbes de Provence, then roasts the *bio* (organic) free-range birds on skewers. Once back home, I bought a new spit for my rotisserie, which I hadn't used since Bob passed ten years earlier. I had some success seasoning the chicken as M. le Boucher did, but it took time to perfect the technique of tying the chickens properly, so that they would rotate and cook evenly.

Cannes

The joie de vivre spirit thrives in Cannes, where La Croisette—the famous broad seafront boulevard—lures le beau monde, the jet-set, the celebrity glitterati, the international elite, the moneyed folks, and their entourages, to grand palace hotels and the adjacent fashionable boutiques. The coastal city also attracts wannabes, Cinderellas, wish-I-were-Julia-Robertses, and more down-to-earth visitors like me.

The cosmopolitan center showcases extraordinary architecture and a gorgeous seafront promenade. The landscape adds palm trees, flowers, greenery, and the beach. Walking along La Croisette, visitors pass art deco villas and palace hotels, and the contemporary Palais des Festivals et des Congrès (where the Cannes Film Festival takes place and tourists queue to take pictures on the red-carpet-covered steps), en route to the old port and the adjacent sloping hillsides in the old town with their quaint pedestrian streets.

I've visited the resort town, now and again, since the early 1990s. After spending four (three-week) stays there in the last six years, I can truly say that it's my happy place.

LE NÔTRE

In 2019, Val and I rented a nicely decorated two-bedroom apartment from VRBO, and had a wonderful three-week stay, though it wasn't perfect. The building had a door to the street, no elevator, one large and one teeny bedroom, and one toilet that never flushed. It didn't matter. We felt lucky to spend time in this idyllic city and decided to return to a nicer place. During our last week, we scouted the streets on a mission to find exactly the perfect location for 2020.

We found Le Nôtre (a pseudonym) on VRBO, considered the location perfect, and sent a deposit for May 2020. Sadly, it was canceled and Covid persisted through spring 2021. In 2022, my family vacationed in Tuscany. Val and I eventually returned in April 2023, in 2024, and again in 2025, always for three weeks before the film festival in mid-May (when the prices soar).

The glass-door entry to Le Nôtre is on a side street, and a second set of doors, which I appreciate, opens to an airy lobby that views an interior garden and leads to the elevators. Our apartment has two bedrooms, each with an en-suite shower and sink, but only one WC. The well-equipped kitchen has a washing machine and opens to one of three terraces; one has a sea view. The location is ideal, on one of many connecting streets midway between the major avenues: the glamorous La Croisette on the shorefront and rue d'Antibes, the shopping street, and footsteps from a myriad of cafés, galleries, and one-of-a-kind mom-and-pop shops with ever-changing window decorations.

The first morning, we set out for the market only knowing that the food stores were on the far side of rue d'Antibes. I asked for directions to Marché Gambetta from a woman with a shopping cart, whom I assumed was a local; she stopped in her tracks and graciously escorted us a block farther to the market. How lovely! The daily market occupies a parking lot where stalls sell produce, cheese, and bread, along with some plants, clothes, straw hats, and shoes. The small specialty food shops—a boucherie with rotisserie chickens; a boulangerie for baguettes; a fish store; and a cheese shop with artisanal preserves—face the market, which is also diagonally across from Monoprix, where we buy staples. The nearby café-lined pedestrian street leads to Galeries Lafayette, the SCNF gare railway station, and the old city.

We share a relaxed routine in Cannes and either make morning coffee at home or go to a patisserie, where we sit on the terrace sipping a cappuccino and eating a croissant. If we're walking or visiting someplace, we lunch where it's convenient; when at home, we eat on the terrace. And we go out for dinner every night, which is not my choice but Val's, who'd rather go to a palace hotel to people watch over a drink, and share a pizza and a glass of Prosecco on the high stools outside La Bohème, than stay inside.

Our daily walks often lead to La Croisette, where Val checks out every shop, from Balenciaga to Chanel and Louis Vuitton. Then, we cross the boulevard to the verdant seaside park and buy a crêpe or an ice cream at a beach shack to eat at a seafront table or bench. If we need or want something, we head to rue d'Antibes, where there are pharmacies, Gant, Sephora, H&M, and Zara, among others. The side streets are lined with mom-and-pop shops, and the ones closest to the gare are frequented by folks who live and work there, ride the minibus, shop at the market, and spend their lunch hour at a café or on a bench. As temporary "locals," we get to shop among them and, occasionally, get to interact with a few shoppers as well as vendors.

One favorite weekend activity is the *brocante*, where vendors sell tempting "previously loved" items, including designer purses and scarves. I go in and out of shops and rarely buy anything, but when I get to the flea market, I get carried away. I can't explain what happened to my self-discipline in 2019, but I had to buy a second suit-case for the trip home. On that flight, customs agents in both France and at JFK opened both bags, which I found very stressful, even though they showed little interest in my "used" clothes or packaged herbes de Provence, scented soaps, and cotton handkerchiefs.

We usually take a day trip or two from Cannes: to Antibes; the Bonnard Museum in Le Cannet, just a fifteen-minute drive away; to Saint-Paul-de-Vence; and, once, to Mougins, for a photography exhibition commemorating Picasso's death fifty years earlier. We've also taken the ferry to overnight in Saint-Tropez and the train to Beaulieu, Monaco, and Ventimiglia, Italy, for the Friday market.

And though we don't usually stay in the grand hotels, we often go to them for drinks and occasionally for an exceptional meal.

HÔTEL MARTINEZ

The Martinez is one of the places we visit whenever we're in Cannes, though I've never stayed there—in fact, I missed the opportunity to lodge in the iconic hotel in 1993, when I was offered a media rate that I considered beyond my budget. I wasn't very savvy about high-season hotel prices then, and made the mistake of saying, essentially, "Thanks, but no thanks." Instead, I ended up paying almost as much for an ordinary, ugly, poorly located commercial hotel. My bad.

Having missed the boat on the "stay," I made sure to lunch at La Plage du Martinez, which turned out to be a memorable and exhila-rating experience, about which I wrote:

"A snazzy maître d' led us to a white-cloth-topped table on the narrow pier jutting into the sea and handed us large menus, which we studied in between furtive glances at the beautiful people around us. A sommelier poured wine; food arrived under a silver cloche. It's the kind of lunch considered Côte d'Azur casual."

Val and I fondly remembered that lunch, and when we returned, twenty-five years later, we decided to go back to La Plage du Martinez on the seafront side of La Croisette. This time we sat on the patio in the shade of a large umbrella near the sand, in front of three teenage girls who were sunbathing, face down and topless, and who never looked up from their phones during our entire meal. At adjacent tables, diners were dressed in business attire—dresses and high heels, or jackets and ties—or in their resort-chic uniforms of white pants and designer T- shirts. Some wore beachwear, like the woman who we watched get up from her lounge chair on the sand, throw a see-through cover-up over her bikini, and step into flip-flops before being seated at the table next to us.

The meal was as lovely as the setting. My spa-style selections started with a gazpacho. The waiter brought the bowl, half filled with thinly sliced raw vegetables, including red onion, tomato, cucumber, peppers, and greens, and poured the chilled tomato broth into it from a carafe. The whole grilled fish was simply and perfectly prepared, with a bit of olive oil and lemon. For dessert, I chose my favorite berries, *fruits rouges*, a medley of strawberries, raspberries, and red currants. Val ordered an oh-so-haute steak frites—filet mignon and fries—that looked terrific.

When I got up to check out the pier, I passed a tent-like cabana set up like a spa suite, which was promoting the spa. Children and their parents gathered beyond the dining tables at the end of the pier and were trying on snorkeling gear and readying to board water-sport boats.

A week or so later, when I saw posters advertising the Festival D'art Pyrotechnique, a fireworks event, I immediately made a reservation to watch from the Beach-Plage restaurant at Hôtel Martinez.

THE CANNES FIREWORKS COMPETITION

The *Festival D'art Pyrotechnique* is an international battle in the sky, a competition held at four-year intervals among top fireworks companies from various countries. The fireworks are set off over the Mediterranean Sea from a floating arena "made up of five barges, one bay, and an entire sky!" according to its organizers.

The evening of the event, Val and I walked the few short blocks from our apartment to La Croisette and could feel the excitement. A parade of motorcyclists chugged up and down the side streets, and supercars clogged hotel entrance drives unable to leave because the waterfront boulevard was limited to pedestrians only.

Car watching ranks as high as people watching here, and the proliferation of luxury and vintage cars—even on a night when the street was closed—is a sure sign of extravagance. These exceptional vehicles are as ubiquitous here as yellow cabs in New York City, and there's a general positive energy among the crowds who stop, admire, and photograph them. Valets routinely park them strategically at the hotels' front doors, to get the most *wow* reaction and *sans doute* (bigger tips). Most of these luxury, classic, and vintage cars are supplied by specialty rental car dealers, but those with foreign license plates are likely to be privately owned and transported here.

With no vehicles allowed on La Croisette, musicians had set up their bands, a lady was selling balloons to children, and vendors were selling snacks, all in the street. Young couples sat entwined on the half-walls facing the beach, with their feet hanging over the sides, while older residents took their usual places on benches lining the far side of the sidewalk.

At precisely 22 h. (10:00 p.m.), Val and I descended the stairs to the Beach-Plage Martinez and checked in at the host desk. Dinner guests occupied the tables, but we had reserved "Champagne and Pastries" and were ushered to chaise lounges at the edge of the stretch of sand and noted that there wasn't a human on the beach we faced. Our chaises were perfectly positioned to see the magic in the sky. The waiter poured the bubbly from a bottle in an adjacent bucket and brought the platter of patisseries, an assortment of delicate dessert *mignardises* (two of each): macaroons, cookies, and petits fours, including two small squares of seven-layer cake.

The 2019 Festival D'art Pyrotechnique was an amazing spectacle, even for a fan who used to see a great show from my own backyard and saw spectacular fireworks once from atop the World Trade Center and once from a tall building in Paris. I reclined on a chaise on the beach, almost flat, and looked up to the sky. Superb! And I was proud to learn that Rozzi Famous Fireworks, an American company, won a Prix Spécial du Jury for its display.

That August, I had a spa treatment there, in their former, sprawling top-floor facility. When we returned to Cannes in 2023 and 2024, we stopped into the elegant Martinez for drinks before dinner next door, on the terrace facing the sea at Le Vesuvio, where I love their linguine and clams. And in 2024, I had the chance to experience the newly redone l'Oasis du Martinez spa, which is reached via a curved, glass-walled corridor overlooking the garden pool deck. It's quite the swank destination spa!

Writing about those extraordinary Martinez experiences reminded me to share the heart-wrenching story about Emmanuel Martinez, the hotelier-creator, which I learned about in *Riviera Dreaming*.

un peu plus: HOTELIER EMMANUEL MARTINEZ

Eminent hotelier Emmanuel Martinez, an Italian noble of Spanish descent, was asked to build the sprawling Hôtel Martinez, an art deco palace in Cannes, constructed with high columns, grand reception rooms, and a centerpiece staircase that spirals up through the building. The swank venue opened on February 20, 1929, just months prior to the stock market crash, which seriously affected business throughout the Depression. During World War II and the German occupation—a time when some locals were deported to concentration camps—M. Martinez was wrongfully accused of collaboration. The hotel became off-limits, nobody dared be seen there, and the hotelier lost everything. He died in 1973, one year before he was finally vindicated. The hotel endured, prospered, and lured an exclusive clientele. The prestigious Taittinger family—of champagne and Concorde Hotel fame—acquired it in 1981. Starwood Hotels purchased it in 2005, and in 2013, it became affiliated with Hyatt Hotels. In 2016, when Hyatt added an "upper-upscale" category for hotels in special and historic venues with award-winning restaurants, the Martinez became part of the Unbound Collection by Hyatt.

THE CARLTON CANNES

The recently restored Carlton Cannes, a Regent Hotel, was the first of the Grande Dame hotels to début on La Croisette in 1913. Val and I had our most elegant meal there in 2023. It had just reopened after a costly four-year-plus restoration, with divine, dramatic results. Architect Richard Lavelle retained the iconic twin domes and interior curvilinear staircases and transformed the former parking lot into a 215,000-square-foot landscaped interior garden. It boasts an infinity pool, cabanas, and a light-filled entry to a lower level and Le C Club Fitness & Spa, with its full-size boxing ring and Dr. Burgener facial products.

In the vaulted lobby, French designer Tristan Auer added Venini chandeliers and stripped eight layers of paint off columns to reveal the original marble. We walked through the lobby to lunch at its Riviera Restaurant, on the terrace facing the sea, where cream-colored balustrades separate it from the sidewalk along La Croisette. *Gojus!* In 2024, we returned for a predinner drink and people watching in the lobby.

MAJESTIC BARRIÈRE

Before it was hacked, my Instagram tag was @sipsupstayspa, because those are my favorite activities. Although I've had drinks, meals, and spa services at these over-the-top five-star luxury hotels in Cannes, I have only once stayed at one, the Majestic Barrière. It was with Emma, on the last night of our weeklong Riviera road trip in October 2015. Emma, who has a remarkable memory, recalled every place name that she'd ever heard from her mother's conversations about her annual business trips to Cannes for the advertising festival; she wanted to go wherever Sharon had stayed, eaten, entertained clients, or shopped. She especially wanted to see the Palais des Festivals where Sharon had once accepted the Palme d'Or for one of her clients, a director of commercials. Because her mom talked about The Majestic, where she's stayed, Emma was thrilled to be there.

That afternoon, when I drove there in a downpour from the lovely, historic little Hôtel Belles Rives, in nearby Juan-les-Pins, it was far too windy to explore the Croisette on foot. We spent time before dinner in our recently redecorated seafront room and viewed the palais across the boulevard through our rain-swept French doors. Our final night's meal was marvelous, with the best antipasto platter, grilled vegetables, and wonderfully sweet langoustines. The following morning, though it was still raining, we ventured outside to cross the side street to Longchamp, where Emma chose a red purse for her twentieth-birthday gift before we headed to the airport.

LE MASCHOU

Le Maschou, which opened in 1963, is a popular restaurant and our favorite. It's located in Le Suquet, the former fishing village in Vieille Ville, the old town near the Old Port, which is also home to the fifteenth-century Gothic-style cathedral, The Church of Nôtre-Dame-d'Espérance; the medieval castle of the monks of Lérins, with its square tower; and Marché Forville, the largest of the city's two daily markets. Le Maschou is one of many mini restaurants that line rue St. Antoine, the sharply sloped, Roman-era path that also houses individually owned, touristy shops. The restaurant opens for dinner only, and its teeny terraces jut out onto the narrow, pedestrian-only cobblestone street, within touching distance of throngs of passersby. Its simple, straightforward prix fixe menu is as limited as the space: the meal starts with a giant basket of crudités served with aioli and the best fire-grilled bread. Then, guests have a choice of fire-grilled steak, lamb, chicken, or salmon, and a dessert selection.

chez moi: AIOLI

Aioli is like mayonnaise, but it's creamier, thicker, more garlicky, and lemonier. It's ideal for dipping raw crudités or croque-monsieur (grilled ham and cheese) and for serving with fried potatoes, fish, or crab cakes. I follow Chef Daniel Boulud's blender recipe, which combines 1 poached egg, 2 raw yolks, 4 cloves of garlic (germ removed and twice poached), 1 tablespoon Dijon mustard, ½ cup extra virgin olive oil, 1½ cups canola oil, salt, and a pinch of Spanish piment d'Espelette, a Basque paprika. (I thin mine with lemon juice.)

East of Nice

———◆———

OST OF MY VISITS ON THE COAST HAVE TAKEN place west of Nice, in Antibes, Juan-les-Pins, Golfe-Juan, Cannes, and all the way to Saint-Tropez, Marseille, and even Collioure, near the Spanish border. I've also treasured time at equally marvelous venues on the eastern Côte d'Azur, in Beaulieu-sur-Mer, Cap-Ferrat, Èze Village, and Villefranche-sur-Mer, nearer to Monaco and the Italian border.

While writing this, I watched an episode of *Emily in Paris*, which brought back memories of the exquisite Grand-Hôtel du Cap-Ferrat, a Four Seasons Hotel, on an easternmost peninsula along the Riviera, even though the young fashionista was, supposedly, weekending in Saint-Tropez, about seventy miles east.

Inexplicably, Emily traveled from Paris on the ultra-luxe Venice Simplon-Orient-Express to Villefranche-sur-Mer railroad station, which isn't even a typical stop. From the tiny train station to the hotel, it's a flat three-mile drive that takes about ten minutes by car, without traffic. Instead, Emily is seen traveling by car along the scenic twists and turns of one of the three Corniche roads from Monaco that overlook the sea and arriving at an expansive estate-based palace, unlike any hotel within the small port village of Saint-Tropez.

I recently learned that the cast and crew spent two weeks as the sole occupants of the Covid-closed Grand-Hôtel. Wearing masks and keeping safe distances were only two of the problems of the pandemic-era shoot, so I imagine that might have accounted for the scenes that supposedly took place in Saint-Tropez but clearly did not. Even the yachting scenes couldn't be more different. The episode shows small boats—like those docked in the Port de Saint-Jean-Cap-Ferrat marina or on the quiet curve along Villefranche harbor—not the huge mega yachts seen in Saint-Tropez.

While viewers don't really expect geographic accuracy, these scenes were obviously false to anyone who has traveled to either location. Nevertheless, the episode featured gorgeous landscapes, appealing boat-filled harbors, and the magnificent hotel, which made me miss every moment I've spent there.

GRAND-HÔTEL DU CAP-FERRAT

The first time I saw the striking villa at the tip of the peninsula, I drove some distance to go there for dinner, ignoring my "dine-near-bed" mantra for the exclusive opportunity. Even in the late 1990s, I was savvy enough to arrive in daylight and pulled into the drive an hour before my reservation, which gave me ample time to explore the lushly landscaped gardens on the seventeen-acre estate. I followed the trail behind the hotel dining terrace toward the sea, where a path carved through rock and a funicular take you down to the sea. (These days, there's a glass elevator at Club Dauphin that descends from street level to the beach, which I don't think existed then.)

Be assured, dinner was well worth driving in the dark.

The next time I visited the palatial structure was in 2015, and because the hotel had just recently begun its relationship with Four Seasons, I was able to arrange "une visite" (a tour) and scheduled it for the morning after Emma and I arrived in Nice by *Train à Grande Vitesse* (TGV) from Paris. A funny thing happened during that short *visite* as we were viewing guest rooms. My host and I were in the small elevator when a man stepped in and we recognized each other. He was someone I had met and chatted with on the deck of a sightseeing cruise boat in Bariloche, Argentina, exactly a year earlier, while we were both taking pictures of the exotic scenery. What a small world!

In 2018, when Jen and I arrived on the Côte d'Azur, we spent our first two nights at the Grand-Hôtel du Cap-Ferrat before moving into the apartment in Juan-les-Pins. I drove there directly from the airport to research the spa for an article, and we lunched on the terrace. At dinner, Michelin-star-chef Yoric Tièche provided locally sourced wellness menu items for my spa article, and I tasted a memorable bright-green spring pea soup. There were vegan, veggie, and gluten-free options too, and breakfast was equally healthful, with freshly squeezed juice and an acaï bowl bar.

Afterward, I walked across the drive to reach the spa from the outdoor entrance, but I returned to the main building through the unique underground walk, which is lined with celebrity photographs of the famous who have visited. That facial service introduced me to the impressive Pauline Burgener *Haute Couture* concept, a Swiss beauty regimen.

The following year, Val and I decided that we really wanted to dine at the Grand-Hôtel du Cap-Ferrat again, where we hoped that even in high season lunch might be a possibility. So, we arranged for an overnight in Beaulieu-sur-Mer before visiting Monaco and arrived for a midday lunch. As it happened, there was room for us at dinner, so we ended up spending much of the afternoon there.

On our way from lunch to the spa, where we planned to spend some time relaxing, we noticed a large group of sports cars parked in the circular entry drive. Their owners must have been part of a group and dining in a private room, because we didn't see them at lunch. Professional photographers were shooting images of the cars, so we did the same. I took pictures of a bright-orange vehicle with red matte finishes and a convertible with a black crocodile interior. I didn't think to photograph the logos, so when I returned home, I showed my gallery of automotive images to a car collector who identified a Porsche 356 Speedster, a Mercedes-Benz 190 SL Cabrio, a Maserati Gran Turismo, Lamborghini Huracán, Aston Martin, Ferrari 488 GTB, Rolls-Royce Wraith (who knew?), and an Alfa Romeo Giulietta Spider.

At dinner, we were seated on the terrace under the trees. It was before sundown and the ambiance was perfect. I was in heaven; Val, on the other hand, was bothered by no-see-ums. She asked our waiter if we could move inside, not realizing that they don't set up the indoor restaurant for meals on divine summer evenings, because 99.9 percent of guests are delighted to dine outdoors with the glorious view of the gardens.

Nevertheless, the maitre d' moved a heavy, round table to the center of the empty dining room for us and placed it immediately inside and facing the entry, so we could still enjoy the view while being protected from the elements. And he placed a vase of flowers on the table before seating us. Dinner continued flawlessly, as if there had been no complaints, no interruptions. At one point, he brought out a chitarra, a stringed pasta cutter, and rolled the yellow and green pasta into strands and prepared the entire dish *à table*.

Much to our surprise and delight, culinary pleasures weren't the only special gifts of the meal. Our door-facing table placement was directly in the path of any dinner guest headed to the facilities or to the elevators up to their rooms. Because each one was so impeccably and beautifully attired, Val and I enjoyed an impromptu fashion show, with Val quietly providing commentary about each Birkin bag or Louboutin shoe as they passed.

The following day, in Monte Carlo, as we were walking past the Chanel boutique, she noticed the same silky summer dress that we had both admired the previous evening. We went in for a closer look and admired the haute couture workmanship, which I assumed accounted for the 4,000€ price tag.

ROYAL-RIVIERA

The Royal-Riviera is a beautiful five-star, beachfront hotel within a former villa and located in Saint-Jean-Cap-Ferrat, a short distance from Beaulieu and Villefranche. In 2015, Emma and I overnighted in a suite with a large terrace and great views from the Alps and the cliffs at Èze down to Beaulieu harbor and across the bay to Villa Kerylos—which looks like an ancient Greek structure—and the adjacent beach.

We dined magnificently.

Emma had her heart set on sunning on a chaise on her private terrace the following morning, while I couldn't wait to see the interior of the Grand-Hôtel, and I drove off along the two scenically stunning miles through the verdant Cap-Ferrat peninsula. Neither of us had any idea that sunny morning that a car problem would ruin our plans that afternoon, that M. Mercadel, the general manager of the hotel, would rescue us, or that we'd be back at the hotel for a second night.

Jen and I lunched there, poolside overlooking the beach, and I recall that meal as clearly as I recall the young waiter deboning Emma's grilled fish three years earlier. This time they presented the whole fish raw, before grilling it and then filleting it tableside. I ate a series of healthy choices to feature in my spa story for *AsiaSpa* magazine, including marvelous skewered tandoori ginger prawns and Thai, *Niçoise*, Mediterranean, and Greek "Buddha bowl" salads.

HÔTEL SELECT

Once our lunch reservation at Grand-Hôtel du Cap-Ferrat was set in August 2019, Val and I found a two-star hotel nearby, in Beaulieu-sur-Mer. We booked Hôtel Select for one night before our stay in Monte Carlo. It turned out to be the epitome of the "little place next door," a welcoming and well-located hotel just a short walk from the gare and directly facing the market square, flanked by all the surrounding shops and cafés. It was also an easy stroll to the Royal-Riviera, where I went for breakfast.

Èze

When I'm in Beaulieu or Monte Carlo, Èze always comes to mind, because every other person you chat with has just been there, or is about to go. Looking up from the terrace at the Royal-Riviera reminded me of two visits to Èze, a tiny medieval village high on the sharp rocky shards overlooking the Mediterranean.

CHÂTEAU DE LA CHÈVRE D'OR

The first time I ventured there was for lunch at Chèvre d'Or (Golden Goat) with Val, who happened to be in Cannes at the time of my trip in 1996. She was there to babysit her grandson Rouben, while his mom, Lisa, was at a convention. I picked them up and we drove to Èze. Once there, I admired how my friend pushed the heavy stroller up the winding cobblestone path. The toddler was comfortable in a stroller and napped soundly while we sipped wine on the stone-walled terrace overlooking the ramparts.

Inside Chèvre d'Or, we enjoyed an idyllic lunch by the window, where we watched parasailers gliding below us over the Mediterranean. By the time we left, it was raining, and the hour's drive took far longer than expected. Whichever of the three "Corniche" roads I chose was scary. (I remembered that in 1992, Princess Grace lost control of her car on the Moyenne Corniche.) It continued pouring on the A8 Autoroute as cars sped past me. I could see nothing, but as soon as I could see an exit, I pulled off the road and waited for the rain to slacken. Finally, I headed back to Cannes, slowly, in the right lane. We didn't have Blackberry phones at that time, so we couldn't call Val's daughter. We arrived considerably later than expected and Lisa, whom I've known since birth, was understandably worried and upset. I don't remember how I felt—I think I was still shaking—and I had to continue driving to wherever I was staying.

In April 2012, after a week traveling with my colleague Janet to three Groupe Floirat hotels (Normandy, Saint-Jean-de-Luz, and Saint-Tropez), I extended my stay in France for three nights and stayed at Terre Blanche again, and then at Château de la Chèvre d'Or in Èze. My luxe hotel room was within one of the stunningly transformed medieval buildings that line the village's steep, curving paths.

Aside from the marvelous meals, I recall two favorite activities: one was browsing in the unique shops along that main walkway and finding the perfect soft white cotton blouse and skirt, which I still wear; the other took place in Èze village at the Parfumerie Galimard Èze-Village, an atelier where I blended my own perfume with scents that I chose, including cinnamon.

Monaco

---◆◆◆---

M Y FIRST TRIP TO THE RIVIERA IN 1990 STARTED WITH four nights in Monaco, where I had wanted to visit ever since Grace Kelly wed her prince there in 1956. My friend Isabel had been to Monaco and recommended Loew's Monte Carlo, so that's where I booked my room. One of the bikini-clad blondes whom I'd met at the Gottex outlet—who sounded expert to me— advised: "Book the helicopter from Nice to Monte Carlo; it costs the same as a taxi." While not technically in France, Monaco reigns as a superb Riviera destination.

That trip was exceptional because a representative from Heli-Air Monaco met me at the gate (yes, with my name on a sign) and accompanied me to baggage claim and, finally, to their check-in counter. The only other passenger on the seven-minute flight was a smartly dressed woman who explained that she was returning to Monte Carlo after having accompanied a business executive whom she hosted in Monaco. (Was she a business associate? A tourist guide? An escort? I wonder still.) I was so excited, and nervous, that I probably chatted nonstop during the short flight and didn't find out.

In what felt like a New York minute, the helicopter descended like an elevator straight down to the helipad, where a waiting van transported me up the hill to the hotel. Soon, a clerk accompanied me to a large, lovely, and well-appointed room with a balcony that overlooked the Mediterranean Sea, and which turned out to be, by far, the largest and nicest room I stayed in during that two-week trip, and superior to many subsequent accommodations. Nevertheless, well before I developed into the design-savvy traveler that I've become, I instinctively shuddered at the corridor décor, where a large-patterned splatter of multicolored blues and purples on the hallway carpet color clashed with the oversize pattern on the adjacent wallpaper. It all seemed more suitable to Las Vegas, where they use bold patterns to stimulate the senses and encourage gambling, than to Monte Carlo, which I had assumed would be more elegant. (Years later, I experienced the elegance that I'd imagined, at Hôtel de Paris and Hôtel Hermitage.)

The "Cinderella at the ball" sensation persisted as I toured the pristine principality. Every moment enthralled me: walking along the promenade at the port, staring at the huge speedboats and mega yachts, and touring the Prince's palace in the ancient Genoese Grimaldi fortress—plus, certainly, window-shopping. I felt smartly attired at the pool each morning, wearing my new bathing suits, each one with a matching long dress, skirt, or wrap that, I hoped, would conceal my decidedly curvaceous body. Everything went "swimmingly."

The belle époque architecture—with all the domes and decorations—intrigued and excited me then, and still does. At lunchtime, I lingered at a table on the terrace at Café de Paris, ordered a salade Niçoise, and watched tourists meander in front of the imposing buildings: to my left, one continual parade entered the beaux arts casino; across the square, a constant line of guests and wanna-sees walked under the distinctive half-circle *porte cochère* at the entry to Hôtel de Paris.

Each night, I chose something special to wear at dinner, although I hadn't given a thought to making advance reservations (one mistake) or asking the advice of a concierge (another). With no destination in mind, I set out looking for a restaurant. When I peeked in at some fancy places and noticed that they were strangely silent and empty, I assumed it was because I was hours too early. On the other hand, hotel lounges, bars, and cafés were crowded and, occasionally, as I neared one, the room erupted with cheers or boos. I soon discovered that my post–July Fourth vacation clearly coincided with some significant final matches of the 1990 FIFA World Cup in Rome, from June 8 to July 8. Everyone was glued to the TV— even waiters stood staring at screens. I submit that 99.9 percent of *le Monagasque monde entier* (Monaco's entire population) was watching football (soccer).

I continued to feel quite regal in Monaco, until the train trip to Nice with unwieldly luggage brought me down to earth. Instead of feeling like a princess, I felt like Her Highness's lady's maid.

The glamour, beauty, and grandeur that first attracted me to the posh principality in 1990 lures me still, and I've returned multiple times: twice with Bob, with Sharon in 2018, and with Val in 2019 and 2023. It wasn't until that last visit to the sophisticated seaside venue that I learned the origin story of Monte Carlo Société de Bains de Mer (SBM), which owns the hospitality-related entities in Monte Carlo and beyond.

un peu plus: SOCIÉTÉ DE BAINS DE MER (SBM)

In 1863, Charles III, Prince of Monaco, founded SBM to bring money into the predominantly agricultural, then-struggling and near-bankrupt principality. Tycoon François Blanc paid for the privilege of a fifty-year gambling contract, and with royal approval established, transformed Plateau des Spélugues, overlooking the sea from an olive and lemon grove, into Casino Square. Early on, his wife, Marie, suggested creating a wine cellar to better fuel the high rollers; by 1864, they had constructed the legendary Hôtel de Paris, an appropriately luxe hotel, with high arched ceilings, grand chandeliers, and a marble colonnade.

Two years later, a royal decree established a special district for the SBM facilities and called it Monte Carlo, after the prince. Gambling succeeded so well in attracting the wealthy that before long, residential taxes were abolished. SBM added Café de Paris, a brasserie, and lush gardens. By 1879, when the Opéra de Monte Carlo added culture to the venue, Casino Square had become a mecca for the elite. Today, tourism attracts sports car racing, tennis, sailing aficionados, and jet-setters. Monégasque residents are ranked as having the world's highest GDP per capita in 2023.

I have always felt safe walking at night, even alone, because the tiny principality installed street cameras everywhere, long before they were even considered elsewhere. The principality was also ahead of its time with electronic notifications on their public buses. Well before North Americans could see a sign with the arrival time at a bus stop, Monégasques could. I toured the Palais Princier, the Princess Grace Irish Library, and the Cousteau Oceanographic Museum, which the mariner whom I lived with loved. He also loved to dine well.

Eating is a priority in Monte Carlo, and I am particularly partial to Café de Paris, where the people watching is amazing and the salade Nicoise is perfect. Buddha Bar, a swank nightclub, is fun and so is Le Salon Rose, a beautiful restaurant with grand windows and intimate alcoves within the casino, where Val and I went in 2023. We also lunched at Le Grill, on the eighth floor of Hôtel de Paris, where excellent Italian fare and seafood is served amid panoramic views.

LE LOUIS XV-ALAIN DUCASSE À L'HÔTEL DE PARIS

In 1990, Le Louis XV was the emblematic restaurant where Alain Ducasse earned the first-ever three-Michelin-star award for a hotel-based restaurant. Ducasse, who trained with such top French chefs as Michel Guérard, Roger Vergé, and Alain Chapel, was a two-Michelin-star chef at Hôtel Juana, in Juan-les-Pins, in 1986, when Prince Rainier III of Monaco made him an offer to become chef of Le Louis XV at Hôtel de Paris. The proviso? Ducasse had to earn three Michelin stars within four years or be fired. It took only thirty-three months to achieve the feat, and so many stars have followed that Ducasse is the world's most decorated Michelin-star chef.

By the time of the first Mediterranean cruise Bob and I took in 2002, eating at Le Louis XV–Alain Ducasse à l'Hôtel de Paris was high on my bucket list. Ducasse was already my favorite chef, and I had interviewed him in French when he opened a restaurant in New York.

I reserved a table at Louis Quinze (sounds like cans) for the day our ship was scheduled to be in Monaco. There was a storm, so the *Wind Surf* found refuge in the deep harbor nearby in Villefranche. Rain and wind didn't stop us, and we boarded a launch to shore, walked to the station, took the half-hour train to Monaco, and arrived drenched. My most prominent memories reflect the exciting, first-for-me Ducasse details even more than the fine food. I was seated beside a low, one-of-a-kind, hand-stitched needlepoint-tapestry-upholstered stool on which to perch my purse. A waiter pushed a long *chariot* laden with herb-filled pots; another appeared with an impressively grand cheese trolley. Wow!

As for the meal, I recall a coastal menu that glorified local produce—fresh pea soup, artichokes, eggplant, and asparagus, garden vegetables, and three mushroom preparations. This was well before anyone identified as vegetarian or talked about farm-to-table fare. I chose lobster from Brittany and noted that the artfully presented dishes were elevated with truffles, sauce mousseline, the finest Ligurian olive oil, and balsamic vinegar.

Fast forward twenty years. In May 2023, on the first of a three-night stay at Hôtel de Paris, I took the elevator down to the ground floor to meet the restaurant's manager, Claire Sonnet, who had just won the Michelin Service Award 2023, and agreed to be interviewed for a podcast that would accompany my article about the celebrated restaurant. I was a little early, so I sat in the back of the stately lobby staring at the stunning women posing for photographs in front of the sumptuous floral display. I began daydreaming about my first lunch at Le Louis XV at Hôtel de Paris with Bob.

At the arranged time, I walked toward the statue of Louis XV astride his horse, which is positioned near the entry of the restaurant that bears his name, just inside the impressive front doors. When Claire Sonnet appeared, she ushered me into the kitchen where Chef Emmanuel Pilon, who was awarded three Michelin stars in 2023—his first year as head chef—greeted me and invited me into a small, private, glass-walled dining room, where we chatted at a table with a platter of square, ravioli-style pastries. He told me they were *barba-juan*, a traditional Monégasque specialty. Similar delicate, spinach-and-ricotta-stuffed pastries were served as an amuse during dinner, where they were presented on a cushion, like rings at a wedding ceremony.

Val joined me for dinner, and once in the dining room, I recognized the historic setting, with its Versailles-inspired mirrors, gilded walls, tall windows, and Baroque moldings, but the décor had been transformed into an entirely more modern look. The circular ceiling was still painted with cherubs and surrounded by images of the loves of Louis XV's life: Madame Pompadour and Madame du Barry. Designers Patrick Jouin and Sanjit Manku installed four cables and reinterpreted the space by hanging a lighted ring—it shines like a diamond choker—above the seating area. The cloth-covered tables were surrounded by comfy, silky-soft, cream-colored leather chairs and flanked by leather sculptures that resembled abstract horses. Each had a flat shelf for a purse.

The room is refined, luxe, and contemporary, and guests arrive dressed for the special venue, some wearing long gowns. Val and I were impressed with the inventive meal. Just to give an example, the *pâte à pain*, a crispy, paper-thin bread, was a work of art with a zucchini flower pressed into the dough; it was presented vertically, in a gold frame, like the menu. Baby vegetables were displayed on a black stone, like a still life; the deep-fried artichoke arrived with caviar; skinny mandoline-sliced red radishes formed a rose-like round; blue lobster appeared with thick white asparagus. The extra-long, double-decker cheese cart that I recalled from my first lunch there seemed shorter now, and though it seemed easier to push between the tables, it was still stocked with a wide variety of choices and arrived before dessert and the post-dessert display of *mignardises*.

At the end of the meal, when the herb cart arrived, the waiter asked for our choice and she clipped the herbs we requested with silver scissors. She infused them like a tea, and sent them on a tea cart to our room, adding a box of Ducasse chocolates. We hadn't left the dining room empty-handed, either. Upon leaving, every guest was handed a large gift box containing the specialty of pastry chef Sandro Micheli: a sugar-topped panettone.

THERMES MARINS

Along with food, massage ranks high on my much-appreciated list. After eating, my second favorite activity takes place within Thermes Marins, the four-story, stand-alone, 75,000-square-foot spa. The structure has tall window walls that view the panorama: the ship-shaped Yacht Club de Monaco, mega yachts at the port, the Mediterranean, and even the Prince's palace.

Guests at Hôtel de Paris—or Hôtel Hermitage—can wear bathrobes in the corridors to the spa elevator, which descends to another long hallway that passes the historic wine cellar and opens directly into the spa lobby and the grand oval-shaped, indoor, heated seawater pool.

During my first spa session there with Bob, I delightedly soaked in a hydro-tub before my massage facing a large window with a sea view. In contrast, my husband wasn't a fan of massages, and he was so bored on the table that he spent his fifty-minute service staring down through the face caddy trying to design an installation system with a television screen facing upward from the floor. I've looked through the headrest and seen fresh flowers floating in a bowl once or twice, but never imagined a TV.

When I was there with Sharon in 2018, my thalassotherapy treatment started with a twenty-minute soak in a multi-jetted hydrotherapy tub, followed by a grapeseed and sesame seed oil rub and a scrub exfoliation, called *gommage,* with *sel de guérande* (a sea salt from Brittany). After a shower, the aesthetician/masseuse applied moisturizer as if it were a full massage. Sharon described her service: "I was on an air mattress above a tub when they applied the mud, then they warmed the air in the mattress to warm the mud. Afterward, I took a shower and a soak in a jetted hydrotherapy tub session. Loved it!" What to say? Some go to Monte Carlo to gamble or show off their cars or wardrobes. We go to spa!

And in 2023, while I was enjoying a treatment, Val browsed the posh boutiques on her own and she convinced me to return with her to Zara's to look for affordable versions of the designer duds on view in neighboring boutiques. Shoppers at Zara's Monte Carlo are so well-dressed that only the cognoscenti know if the Chanel jacket is genuine—or Zara—or if the clients' purses are real Goyard or faux from the market in Ventimiglia. Not that it matters; they look so stylish they could actually be accurately labeled "beautiful people."

L'HIRONDELLE

I had previously overnighted at Hôtel Hermitage during a train journey on the Venice Simplon-Orient-Express and was really pleased to be staying there with Sharon in 2018, when Thermes Marins was one of the seven spas to research for my spa story in *AsiaSpa* magazine. We wore real clothes and not bathrobes in the elevator, because we had reservations for lunch at the spa restaurant, L'Hirondelle, before our treatments.

L'Hirondelle is very swank and known for its *haute cuisine minceur,* or gastronomic spa cuisine, which incorporates fresh, seasonal, and local *bio* ingredients into nutritious, diet-savvy culinary creations. The menu offers à la carte specialties—including gluten-free and vegan options—and three prix fixe menus: *Le Menu du Marché* (market menu), *Le Menu Wellness* (wellness menu with light gluten-free dishes and calorie counts for each), and *Le Menu Veggie* (veggie menu with detoxifying vegetarian options).

Sharon and I met Julia Burg, our host, inside the window-walled dining room adjacent to the pool. Beautifully presented dishes were being served at other white-cloth-topped tables, while I debated about starters: *Panier* (basket) of crudité? Shrimp on a skewer? Poached white asparagus? Salmon tartare? Softly scrambled eggs topped with truffles? I ordered *Taboulé* de quinoa, which arrived shaped like a ring and decorated with individual citrus segments and microgreens.

Our entrées arrived under a silver cloche; my *filet de loup grillé* with ginger (grilled fish, 276 calories) was topped with tiny cherry tomato halves, parsley, and red radicchio slivers and looked as beautiful as it tasted. Desserts were amazing, too, from chocolate mousse to mango mousseline, sorbets, and fresh pineapple or berries. We shared a spectacularly smooth *crème brulée* bourbon vanilla with a crackly crust under a pear sorbet.

Even the cars are impressive in Monte Carlo, and the annual Monaco Grand Prix ranks as the principality's largest and most profitable event. Car gazing is a popular year-round pastime, even when no race is taking place, and I am among those who admire sleek vehicles, even though I can't identify one from another.

As our brief entrée to the *haute monde* would have it, we arrived in May 2023, just as workers were setting up the grandstands and barriers for the big event. Even then, days before the race, exotic automobiles were driving around and around. It reminded me of our previous visit in August 2019, when the evening's entertainment was watching a parade of vehicles from our table on the terrace at Hôtel de Paris.

I recognized some of them, not by brand, of course, but by color, because the day before, when we were in Cap-Ferrat, we saw some of the same cars parked and had photographed them. On this evening, along with those luxury vehicles, there were big, black Mercedes SUVs going round and round, as if they were on the Grand Prix circuit. One of the four young men at the adjacent table loudly announced the cost of every vehicle. He never mentioned the brand, didn't have to; his friends were car cognoscenti.

The allure of Monaco extends beyond people and car watching and the mystery of what language is being spoken by the people standing nearby. But there is one caveat. Many Monégasques who nonchalantly stand by waiting for their dogs to poop, don't pick it up and don't even appear to consider that as an option. They ignore the pooper-scooper law, even with its 100€ fine. It's my perception that they are passively announcing: "These dogs live here and are entitled to poop wherever they want."

I'll continue to keep my eyes on the sidewalk in Monte Carlo, but I'll always joyfully return!

WINE REGIONS

―――――◆◆◆―――――

It's widely known that France is a top wine-producing country, where winemakers have spent centuries cultivating the grapevine. Here, viticulture is steeped in *patrimoine,* which refers to the history of each region and winemaking house. When medieval monks predominated in the industry, winemaking was considered a divine endeavor; since then, it has evolved into an art form through the efforts of multigenerational wine-producing families.

Winemaking is so integral to French culture that families speak of "wine in our blood." That emotional tie to winemaking is apparent to anyone lucky enough to sip wine in a *cave* face-to-face with someone who represents the seventh, twelfth, or seventeenth generation of a wine-producing family.

My informal wine education has taken place at countless sessions with oenologists, *domaine* owners, *chefs du caves* (head winemakers), *vignerons* (winemakers), historians, sommeliers, and knowledgeable guides. I have sampled varieties, vintages, and blends at various vineyards and wineries—mostly in France and, alphabetically, in Israel, Italy, Portugal, and Spain. In the United States, I frequent wineries in California, Connecticut, Virginia, and in New York, where I interviewed the well-known American wine growers Alex and Louisa Hargrave soon after they planted their first vines in 1973, which launched the Long Island wine industry.

I don't pretend to be an oenophile who can identify each region or vineyard or blend, and my familiarity with the nuances of wine vocabulary aside, I'm not comfortable using wine words. I can recognize "acidity," "minerality," or "notes of apple or oak." I taste "floral notes," "earthiness," or "big body." Still, "nice" is the first word that comes to my mind when I taste a particularly pleasing Chassagne-Montrachet or Château Smith Haut Lafitte.

As happy as I am sipping un petit verre blanc, maybe two, I'm cheeriest visiting with passionate vineyard owners, vintners, producers, and pickers, and listening to stories about their challenges and accomplishments. I genuinely appreciate their pride.

The following vignettes reveal joyful memories, mostly of the incredible people I've met in my favorite wine regions.

The Loire Valley

———•◆•———

I N 1976, BOB AND I INTERRUPTED OUR FIRST PACKAGE
tour to Paris together for a thirty-hour overnight indulgence in
the Loire Valley. My lifetime partner relished the idea of driving
outside the city as much as being in it. I had long wished to visit the
castles, towers, and turrets with an alphabet soup of place names—
from Amboise to Azay-le-Rideau, Blois, Chambord, Chenonceau,
Chinon, and Rigny-Ussé, which inspired Charles Perrault's fairy tale
Sleeping Beauty—and had been projecting photographs of them on
a classroom screen each year from a still-favorite picture book, *Les
Châteaux de la Loire que j'aime*.

After a ten-minute quiz every other Friday, I would present
something cultural that I hoped the kids would enjoy. When it
came time to discuss the castles along the Loire, I showed them images and shared some historical tidbits about Catherine de' Medici,
Charles the Dauphin, Francois 1, and Joan of Arc. I liked to talk
about Chenonceau, which has a wing atop an arched bridge that
stretches across the Cher River and is famous as the "Château des
Dames" for its two fabulous rival female owners. Catherine de'
Medici was an Italian noblewoman who married King Henry II of
France and mothered three French kings: Francis II, Charles IX,
and Henry III. Her nemesis was King Henry II's mistress, Diane de
Poitiers, a noblewoman who was a patron of French Renaissance architecture. Another Henri II, king of England, also played a role in a

Loire Valley castle at Chinon. The film *The Lion in Winter* came out, c. 1968, and the story focuses on Henry II's wish to have his youngest son, John, inherit his throne instead of his son Richard the Lionheart, whom his estranged queen, Eleanor of Aquitaine, preferred. I talked to the students about how cold and harsh castle life was in the twelfth century, before central heating and indoor bathrooms, more than I did about the history.

To say that I was thrilled with the chance to drive along a palace-studded riverside drive is an understatement. I was on top of the world to just visit the region and expected it to be magical no matter where we stayed. Be assured, though, I was delighted when Bob was willing to splurge on an overnight at Château d'Artigny.

LOIRE VALLEY ITINERARY, 1976

DAY ONE:

Rent a car in Paris

Drive 2.5 hours to Tours

Lunch at gastronomic Restaurant Charles Barrier

Drive 7 miles to Montbazon

Check into Château d'Artigny

Visit Château de Chenonceau

Dinner and overnight at Château d'Artigny

DAY TWO:

Morning at leisure

Check out at one

Drive along the Loire

Visit Chambord to see the amazing double-spiral staircase

Lunch in any nearby café

Drive to Chartres en route to Paris
Visit Chartres Cathedral
Arrive Paris and drive around before returning the car

We drove from Paris to Tours as planned and lunched beautifully in the former Restaurant Charles Barrier, which at the time was one of France's seventeen three-Michelin-star restaurants. As we headed from the restaurant toward the hotel in Montbazon, we passed a sign in front of a roadside home offering a wine tasting, so we stopped and went inside what likely had been the family garage. Before long, a man stepped out of the house and greeted us, and I learned that he grew the grapes, pressed them, and was the vintner. He offered us a tasting of a wine I had never heard about, Sancerre, and his pleasure at our enjoyment was clear. At that time, I had book knowledge about the famous châteaux in the region but had no clue that the Loire Valley was one of France's important wine regions.

What I remember even more than the taste of the wine was the eye-opening experience of listening to him chat about the production challenges as he poured. Of course, we bought some wine and ordered Sancerre at our meals for the time we were there. I've visited a multitude of vineyards since, but few tastings excited me quite like that first one in a little garage with a DIY vintner.

On that trip, I was also introduced to Vouvray, which is sweeter. Years later, I learned about the other wines produced along the six-hundred-mile length of the Loire. Among the whites are Pouilly-Fumé, the model for Sauvignon Blanc, Chenin Blanc, and Muscadet. Cabernet Franc grapes are used for the reds, Chinon and Bourgueil.

CHÂTEAU D'ARTIGNY

Before it transitioned into a boutique hotel, Château d'Artigny was constructed as the personal retreat for former perfume magnate François Coty, who built the private palace in a style akin to the eighteenth-century Château de Champlâtreux in Épinay, just fifteen minutes from Charles de Gaulle airport in Paris. Our room within the villa had a stunning view of the landscaped estate. This was my first Relais & Châteaux hotel experience, and it was an over-the-top extravagance for us, so I was completely astounded the next morning at the pool to meet parents with three young children who were spending the entire summer there! *Incroyable!* I couldn't imagine such wealth.

Culinary excellence—and *charme*—rank high in the mission of Relais & Châteaux properties, which routinely house the best, often Michelin-starred, chefs. I not only found our dinner menu from Château d'Artigny among my souvenirs, but also a large book of wines that I can't seem to discard even though the prices are listed in French francs. The cover, though faded, is still pretty enough to frame, and the bottom of each of the forty or so pages reads "Service 15% inclus" in small letters. Along with wines from Alsace, Jura, and Beaujolais, there are multiple pages under each heading: Bordeaux Rouges, Bordeaux Blancs, Bourgogne Rouges, Bourgogne Blancs—pages that listed my personal favorites, including Gevrey-Chambertin, Vosne-Romanée, Nuits-Saint-Georges, and one that I've never tasted, Clos Vougeot. Of course, this was a fine-dining restaurant in a posh hotel where prices were high, more than $100 a bottle for many. (In 1976, my research confirms about five French francs, 4.8FF, to the US dollar and the wine bottles were from 500 to 2900 francs.)

That gastronomic multicourse dinner introduced me to the cheese plate, which is traditionally served after the main "plat" as an essential course and usually showcases the finest local specialties. Cheese is such a major component of a gastronomic meal that the waitstaff brings a new plate, clean utensils, and fresh bread before the selections are served in haute style—sometimes on a lavish silver tray or an elongated cheese trolley.

un peu plus: CHEESE

Colette—the noted author, actor, and gastronome—expressed the significance of cheese in these words: "If I had a son in search of a wife, I would say to him: 'Beware of a girl who loves neither wine, nor truffles, nor cheese, nor music.'" Then, there's this famous Charles de Gaulle quote, which hints at the importance of cheese to the nation: "How can anyone govern a country with 246 varieties of cheese?"

(In 2022, France claimed almost one thousand different types; in 2024, I heard a cheese expert interviewed on a David Lebovitz podcast who said there are more than eighteen hundred.)

It's been ages since I visited the Loire Valley, and when I learned that my grandniece, Lyndsey, had her heart set on seeing some castles, we planned a four-day road trip along the Loire for the final days of our trip to Paris in late November 2024. I reserved seats on the sixty-eight-minute *Train à Grande Vitesse* (TGV) from Paris to Saint-Pierre-des-Corps, outside Tours. (We returned directly to Terminal 2 at Charles De Gaulle airport beneath the Sheraton Hotel, where we overnighted before returning to the States.)

My heart was set on returning to Château d'Artigny, fifty years after I stayed there with Bob, because I have such lovely memories. Its beauty was reaffirmed the moment the former Coty mansion came into view at the end of a long, tree-lined allée, which we learned was soon closing for a total renovation. And I wanted to experience the Caudalie vinotherapy spa at Les Sources de Cheverny, the sister property to the Sources de Caudalie, which I had visited in 2007. It also boasts a grand château, though most of the rooms are in wood-sided individual lodges on the beautiful farm, lake, and forest-studded estate.

A colleague recommended two special hotels, so I decided to overnight at each, and arrived by five o'clock, with time to spare before for our pre-dinner spa appointments. At Caudalie Spa at Les Sources de Cheverny, we had an indoor swim and vinotherapy treatments; and we each had a massage at Relais de Chambord, where Lyndsey joyfully soaked in the outdoor barrel-bath-style hot tub facing the exquisite castle. At Fleur de Loire, which views the Château de Blois, I received an exclusive Sisley facial. Later, our gastronomic Thanksgiving dinner in Chef Christopher Hay's two-Michelin-star restaurant featured produce from his local farm, and caviar and fish from the local waters.

Each day between 11:00 a.m. and 4:00 p.m., we went sightseeing along the Loire and on whatever country roads led to our next destination. In Amboise, we viewed Château du Clos Lucé, the large red-brick château where Leonardo da Vinci spent his final years, from 1516 to 1519; in Blois, we browsed shops in the quaint neighborhood near the castle; and, we toured Chambord and Chenonceaux, which were both decorated for the holiday season.

It was not our traditional Thanksgiving holiday *en famille*, but it was a magnificently memorable trip.

chez moi: CHEESE PLATE

Variety is the essence of a cheese platter, because each offering provides new taste discoveries. Items selected will usually represent hard and soft, cow and goat, and, usually, a blue cheese, accompanied by grapes and crackers. Depending upon the type of party and number of guests, select 3, 5, or 7 varieties and serve them on a cheese board, a ceramic cheese platter, or a silver serving tray.

Gascony

———— ◆◆◆ ————

A MANILA FOLDER LABELED FRANCE CAUGHT MY EYE in 2018, as I was filing documents from VRBO for my first apartment rental in Juan-les-Pins. I thought it was empty; instead, I found the original pamphlet promoting Kate Hill's 1996 "Culinary Journey in Gascony." It reminded me of a lovely week in *La France Profonde* (Deep France) in the southwest of the country, where Armagnac production is well-regarded.

The fine brandy is claimed to be the oldest spirit in France, with the first vines planted by the Romans before they left the country in the fourth century. Physical records date Armagnac to 1310. The elegant drink is made by distilling white wines harvested from each of the three AOC (*appellation d'origine contrôlée*) areas of production on the Côtes de Gascogne: Armagnac-Ténarèze, Bas-Armagnac, and Haut-Armagnac.

In addition to Armagnac, there are revered culinary treasures in the region known as "Hidden France." Chicken served as "poule au pot" is one tradition and duck is another. Foie gras, chestnuts, and prunes are so important that each one has its own dedicated culinary museum.

When I arrived in Agen after the drama-tinged train ride from Paris to Bordeaux via TGV, when I lost my computer bag, I met Kate's driver. He dealt with the stationmaster about my lost bag and then we set out through the two-thousand-year-old city, with its eleventh-century cathedral and medieval half-timbered houses. He charmed me with stories about its famous professional rugby team until we reached the little inn where the group was staying.

A Culinary Journey in Gascony

I met the other participants—three couples and another married woman traveling alone—at dinner in our small hotel. It was located near Camont, where the author lives in her canal-side farmhouse and where her kitchen is within a former eighteenth-century *pigeonnier* (a pigeon coop or a dovecote). Outside, cork-lined paths from umpteen empty wine bottles bordered the trail to the canal. The eighty-six-foot Dutch barge that Kate purchased in 1986, the *Julia Hoyt,* was docked behind her house, cooking school, and garden. The barge was constructed in 1872 and moved at a stately four miles per hour along the Canal de Garonne, formerly Canal Latéral á la Garonne, where Captain Kate liked to take her guests for a leisurely cruise and serve them homemade gourmet goodies.

As a sailor's wife and first mate, I often entertained on board our sailboat *With the Wind* and served my guests store-bought, jarred items, such as marinated mushrooms, artichokes, tapenade, and canned baby clams. The fare on our sailboat, while a step up from chips and beer that others served, hardly compared to Kate's elevated artisanal specialties: *"mes olives préferées"* (my favorite olives), which were made into her green olive tapenade, *caviar d'aubergine* (eggplant caviar), *cornichons* (tart baby pickles), *oignons au vinaigre* (pickled onions), and herbed sea salt. *Très chic!*

I was so completely content eating, drinking, and chatting with new acquaintances on the foredeck that day, as the barge passed by a few of the nineteen picture-perfect villages in our host's immediate

"Long Village," between her dock at Sainte-Colombe-en-Bruilhois to the canal's end at Castets-en-Dorthe, that the experience inspired future weeklong barge cruises.

One afternoon, as Kate started preparing a meal to be cooked in her stone fireplace, a few of us gathered around a rustic table outside the kitchen and chopped and diced the farm-fresh vegetables and prepped the necessary mise en place. While working, she described typical Gascon-style fare—*confit de canard* (duck slow-cooked in duck fat), game, and foie gras—and made cooking suggestions that I noted on the pages of my copy of *A Culinary Journey*, which I purchased from her some months earlier when we met in Philadelphia. Kate's recommendations were novel to me twenty-five years ago but are well-integrated in my current cooking protocol. (I've added my thoughts to hers in parentheses.)

> Use an old-fashioned pepper mill for serious prominent flavor.
> Use stainless steel pans with copper bottoms. (I use All-Clad.)
> Wrap cheese in parchment paper to let it breathe.
> Save celery for stock. (I save *everything*.)
> Render (put duck or chicken skin in a pan of water and heat; the water will evaporate and the fat will be left in the pan). Alternatively, buy duck fat (D'Artagnan; dartagnan.com).
> Read M. F. K. Fisher. (Wonderful, much-appreciated advice.)

During our stay, the driver of Kate's brand-new ten-passenger van transported us to the kinds of places that foodies adore: the local *marché*, the village *bric-a-brac* filled with secondhand collectibles (I saved a business card from Menges in Monbalen, ten to fifteen miles outside Agen, for some reason), and a somewhat distant Michelin-starred restaurant.

We accompanied her to buy wine at Les Vignerons de Buzet, the local cooperative winery. Buzet is an AOC wine region adjacent to Bordeaux and located between Marmande and Agen. My notes mention that Kate cooked with Côtes de Buzet, a local red wine made from Merlot, Cabernet Sauvignon, and Cabernet Franc grapes, ideal for cutting through the fat in the rich regional dishes. The helpful staff at the cooperative refilled Kate's wine "tanks" using a plastic tube with a gas-pump-like nozzle, and she explained that the prices are determined by the amount of alcohol in each variety. Surely, the wine cost less than bottled from a retail wine store.

THE PRUNE MUSEUM

One of our excursions included a visit to *Ferme et Musée du Pruneau,* in Lafitte-sur-Lot, a museum located within a plum (*la prune*) grove and dedicated to dried plums (*les pruneaux*) that we know as prunes. Prunes are such a significant Gascon ingredient that they decorate cheese boards and accompany roasts unadorned; they are also served wrapped in bacon, tucked into pies and pastries, and stuffed with all kinds of treasures. We were already aware of the regional importance of pruneaux d'Agen, having previously driven past plum groves. And we surmised that they were a popular ingredient when the finale of our first dinner was a rich and creamy, house-made prune and Armagnac ice cream—the Gascon version of rum raisin. I think prunes suffer from undeserved disrespect in the States, where people mostly think of them as a fiber-rich laxative.

As we arrived, we could see a narrow machine being slowly moved down a path shaking trees on either side of it, and watched the ripened, wrinkled, and sweetened fruit fall loose into a giant net. Inside, the museum displays ancient farm tools and fascinating exhibits, and it houses workers busy making goodies that are sold in the boutique: prunes, prune preserves, and sweets, including gift boxes of *confisserie au pruneau*, candy bonbons containing chocolate-covered or Armagnac-soaked prunes, some filled with prune cream or foie gras. I've seen pictures of the grove when the trees are in blossom and it's gorgeous. In August, they have a Fête de la Prune et du Pruneau, and the site even has a campground where the labyrinth is a geometric pattern that resembles a Greek key, not at all like the circular walking paths that typically enhance spa retreats. The Prune Museum has an online boutique, so I will order some if they have *dénoyauté*, or pitted, prunes.

chez moi: PRUNE-ARMAGNAC ICE CREAM

I buy St. Dalfour deluxe pitted, all-natural giant Agen prunes online, dice them, then marinate them in Armagnac. A few days later, I fold them into slightly softened vanilla bean ice cream.

Poule au Pot

The most noteworthy meal of the week was a traditional Sunday supper that Kate arranged for us at her friends' home. Kate considers her friend Vétou the "finest home cook in Gascony," and she prepared the traditional afternoon-long *poule au pot* (poached chicken) multicourse event, while her husband, Claude Pompèle, amiably hosted the meal and served us his homemade wine. I suspect that he was also responsible for readying the chicken for the cook, as I hint at in this pitch to an editor:

"There were chickens clucking in the yard when we arrived. Once at the table, I realized that one, no doubt, was missing and, most probably, in the kitchen. The *poule au pot* (chicken in the pot) menu is a regional classic inspired by King Henry IV, who supposedly promised something like this in 1598: 'I desire that every laborer in my realm should be able to put a fowl in the pot on Sundays.' The national dish started with a bowl of broth, which Vétou served over vermicelli pasta.

"When we each had consumed half of the delicious broth and vermicelli, Claude picked up a bottle of his homemade wine and introduced an age-old Gascon practice called *le chabrot,* when the host pours—or guests add—a splash of red wine to the final bit of broth. Then, he demonstrated how to drink it, peasant-style, with two elbows on the table and the bowl held with fingertips. The tradition felt even more authentic Chez Pompèle because Claude poured his own homemade wine. Vétou brought out a platter full of chicken pieces, which we passed around the table and topped with her caper-laden red sauce. Dinner also included a delicate onion tart and a green salad, and for dessert she presented polenta cake, a specialty that salutes her half-Italian heritage. Lastly, we had espresso with homemade chocolates."

Kate Hill reflected about Vétou's Caper Sauce in the September 2020 issue of her newsletter, where she wrote: "This is just one part of a whole meal, but the most important part! This simple tomato and caper sauce is often served with the signature Gascon dish poule-au-pot. Twenty-five years ago, I would walk my barge guests up the village road to Claude and Vétou Pompèle's house for a truly homemade French supper. Vétou often made a chicken in the pot on my request, serving the bouillon with vermicelli pasta first, then with a splash of red wine added at the end, followed by the overflowing platter of poached chicken, stuffing, and vegetables. She would serve this bright and tangy sauce alongside, and guests would ask for more, always, and the sauce boat would make the rounds of the table again and again. If there was any left, I would beg to take it back to the boat in an old jam jar, where the crew and I might have it over pasta for a simple family meal. Knowing this, Vétou always made extra, and so do I. Try it over any cooked poultry or fish, over pasta, or even stir it into a pot of soup to enliven the pot."

chez moi: VÉTOU'S CAPER SAUCE

I sauté minced onion or shallot and make a roux with flour and butter or chicken or duck fat. I add two tablespoons of tomato paste, a 4-ounce jar of capers, and simmer the paste, thinning it out with either stock or red wine until the sauce is pourable.

Ducks and Foie Gras

In Gascony, foie gras and duck are ubiquitous and appear on most menus in one way or another: as duck filet, duck confit, duck prosciutto, duck terrine, and magret de canard (a larger breast from a force-fed duck).

During a week in Aquitaine, I noticed a farm where ducks were waddling from their water source on one edge of the grassy field to the corn stall on the far side of the property. The ordeal was specifically designed to strengthen their leg muscles, which were needed to carry the weight of their livers—after being force-fed, these would become oversize and unusually heavy, about one pound to even one and a half pounds. It's no wonder the tough, muscular duck legs are cooked long and slow, in a confit of the duck's own fat.

Le gavage, or force-feeding, dates to when Egyptians handfed their ducks and geese in order to enlarge their livers, and it is legal in France, Hungary, Bulgaria, Spain, and Wallonia (in Belgium). In France, it is widely considered normal and, from what I've observed, as acceptable as collecting *les escargots* (snails) or *grenouilles* (frog's legs)—or truffles, which they hunt with a pig on a leash.

France still supplies two-thirds of the world's supply of foie gras, and the French consider it a super ingredient, found simply sautéed or in a terrine on the best tables in the country; it's the de rigueur menu item at expensive restaurants, where on a gastronomic scale of luxury it ranks with caviar and truffles.

My close-up, firsthand experience watching a farmer force-feed ducks took place twice in Burgundy, some years after visiting Gascony. A few of us stood next to the farmer and witnessed *le gavage* at La Ferme de Misery, a family-owned and operated duck farm that dates from 1850. The farmer informed me that male ducks are brought into a barn at nine weeks old and le gavage is repeated multiple times daily for two weeks and force-fattens them before slaughter. I saw birds wobble directly toward the farmer, who picked each one up, put a long tube in its mouth, squeezed a trigger, and fed it corn. I never heard a quack, saw a tremble, or noticed a complaint. I'm only one onlooker, but to me they seemed to take the episode in stride.

Hand-feeding may be more visually pleasing than the odd-looking long tube, but if the ducks cared they didn't show it. They appeared as calm as the local Long Island ducks who waddle one behind the other from the creek, crossing the street to my neighbors' lawn where they graze on the food strewn there for them.

La Ferme de Misery housed a farmhouse boutique where guests stop for a *visite,* an apéritif, and a tasting of their farm-made products: preserves, honey, jarred confit, and cans of Foie Gras du Canard Entier, which is 100 percent duck liver. Foie gras is a small, light, luxurious gift, and a prime example of "you get what you pay for." Tinned foie gras spans the gamut from the best, pure, artisanal product—a whole block with nothing added beyond salt and pepper—bought directly from a reputable source. On the other hand, pâté de foie gras is not the best option, because it usually includes pork liver or other meats and/or fillers.

Outside of France, there are places where force-feeding is controversial or even considered inhumane. Some who oppose eating foie gras claim that a "fatty" liver is a "diseased" liver. The objections have resulted in force-feeding bans, and it is illegal in several European countries. Israel, where I once visited a kibbutz (a collective farm) that raised geese for the French market, and which was once the world's third-largest producer of goose livers, banned force-feeding in 2003. In Spain, at least one foie gras producer's birds naturally gorge themselves on acorns; as a side note, acorn-fed pigs produce what is widely considered the best cured ham, Jamón Serrano. In 2019, the City Council of New York City voted to ban foie gras produced via force-feeding by 2022, but that city versus state matter is still being disputed in court, probably because the nearby Hudson Valley is a big foie gras producer.

chez moi: SEARED FOIE GRAS AND DUCK BREASTS

The famous Gascon chef André Daguin introduced the food world to Daguin-style breasts, which is how I make them: scored, then seared quickly. I buy them online from d'Artagnan, which Ariane, Daguin's daughter, owns, unless I see duck breasts from Crescent Duck Farm, Long Island's last remaining duck farm. As for foie gras, I buy the frozen *tranches* (slices) from d'Artagnan, and sear one at a time in a cast iron pan, adding sliced apples or pears and/or potato to the fat and garnishing the finished dish with my friend Esther's preserves.

Burgundy

———◆◆———

T HERE ARE REASONS GALORE TO VISIT BURGUNDY. IT takes only ninety-five minutes to get from Paris to Dijon by train, and the historic district in the small capital city boasts half-timbered houses. The Palais des Ducs, the Musée des Beaux-Arts, and the Musée de la Vie Bourguignonne are all worth seeing; traveling around by electric tram is fun, too.

Once outside the city, the region's pastoral beauty, farm-fresh food, great wines, and medieval history captivate visitors. It's an idyllic wine country road trip by car. From Dijon, it's about a thirty-mile drive south on the most exquisite slope-bordered country road, La Route des Grands Crus, through the Côte d'Or to the wine capital of Beaune. This rural ribbon along the Route Nationale 74 (now D122) and its parallel country road, D974, divide lush, vine-studded hillsides with UNESCO World Heritage Site vineyards. The color palette of these wine estates—sunlight-gold, grape-hued burgundy, and vine-green—echo those of the famed geometric-patterned, glaze-tiled roofs that decorate buildings in Beaune and Dijon.

The celebrated UNESCO-listed, twelfth-century Château du Clos de Vougeot is a popular midway destination and reached in less than thirty minutes by car from either Dijon or Beaune. The historic landmark is where well-organized Cistercian monks, who were associated with the eleventh-century Abbey de Citeaux, perfected viticulture. The grapes were grown in plots within many *clos* (walled vineyards) from Côte d'Or to Gevrey-Chambertin, Meursault, and Montrachet. The Confrérie des Chevaliers du Tastevin, the international Fraternity of Knights of the Wine-Tasting Cup, acquired Château du Clos de Vougeot in 1945 to use as their headquarters and as the unique setting for super-spectacular wine dinners.

And from the water, cruising slowly through the countryside on a barge is simply magical.

On Board in Burgundy

Bob and I arrived in Burgundy for our first cruise just weeks after September 11, 2001, when travel came to a halt. The industry was so desperate that an agency representing a French riverboat company invited writers to a promotional luncheon in New York. Our hosts recommended that we put our business cards in a bowl for a raffle. I did and won a five-day riverboat cruise for two on the M/S *Chardonnay.*

We didn't hesitate for a moment about flying and were entirely grateful to be traveling at all. Bob had been ill with severe anemia for a few months earlier that spring and summer, and his local gastroenterologist hospitalized him because he needed blood transfusions. He also told us that he was stymied about how to treat him. Then, just days after 9/11, Bob's brother's best friend, who had contacted a prominent Manhattan gastroenterologist on Bob's behalf, called with serendipitous news. The Mt. Sinai gastroenterologist had an opening the week after the Twin Towers fell, because his out-of-town patients had to cancel long-awaited appointments since no planes were flying. Bob was offered an immediate appointment with the medical team that sustained him for the next eight years.

That good fortune was directly related to other people's tragedy, a fact that has long left me with a weird sense of gratitude and guilt.

With a naïve certainty that Bob's health issue was resolved, we boarded the M/S *Chardonnay* in Dijon that November 2001, along with the other five passengers, and were greeted by a seventeen-member crew. We seven were alone on the fifty-stateroom vessel, and we all dined at one table in the spacious dining room, as the boat glided south on the River Saône to the River Rhône and Lyon.

During the day, as the boat moved silently, "my captain" enjoyed boat-talk with the barge's crew and captain, and I often read inside our stateroom next to open French doors—I think they call it a French balcony—where I could look up from the pages and watch locals fishing or playing *pétanque* on the riverbank not thirty feet away.

It was exciting to stop and dock right in the center of towns, where I would run up the gangplank and explore. The photographer whom I'd married accompanied me to the Nicéphore Niépce museum in Chalon-sur-Saône, where we saw the memorabilia related to the origins of photography. He also went along in the van when a crew member took us on excursions, and, of course, he never missed the chance to discover a new chef.

One gorgeous day, we taxied to lunch in the countryside at the Michelin-starred La Table de Levernois. The beauty everywhere encircled me like an emotional inner tube and raised my spirits after living through towers falling and three thousand deaths.

In the years that followed, Bob and I returned to Burgundy on three European Waterways barges: *l'Art de Vivre*, a six-passenger vessel, and the larger *Belle Epoque* and *L'Impressioniste*, which had six staterooms each. I loved cruising slow and safe (no high winds and threatening seas) and enjoyed my little bubble, savoring meals and scenery while my sociable mate mingled with guests or hung out with the crew and learned the nautical intricacies of maneuvering a big barge through the narrow canal and difficult locks.

I took daily walks or bike rides along the poplar-lined towpath to the next *éclusier* (lockkeeper's cottage). The turtle-slow *péniche* arrived at the cottage so long after me that I enjoyed waiting and chatting with the lockkeeper or his wife. (Are there female lockkeepers? I never met one.) One woman appeared totally relaxed as she puttered in her idyllic little canal-front garden, but she jumped into action to help her husband with the lines (as I always did) the moment the boat approached the lock.

When Bob and I were at home, we had busy careers and mostly spent time together at mealtimes. The stress-free hours together aboard the barge were special, and we sat together admiring the dazzling sun reflect off the water on the thirty-foot-wide canal and listening to still waters lap-lap soothingly at the sides of the vessel, just as happens on sailboats.

Sitting around was not something my husband typically had done in the past, and it was a reflection of his new physical limitations. He was starting to tire easily and didn't jump up and run as he had for the forty previous years of our marriage. He didn't go ashore often, but he did accompany the group when we visited the winery and vineyards in Chablis, which he photographed, and when we toured Vézelay. I'm not all that religious, but I vividly recall that the serenity, beauty, and silence in that twelfth-century Romanesque abbey comforted me.

Each morning, a crew member was tasked with driving to the nearest village for fresh breads and croissants. If he would allow me to tag along in the van, I did, and could barely contain my joy at the sights and smells. No matter how tiny the community, each boulangerie had a tantalizing array of breads, baguettes, and croissants; each patisserie presented an array of tarts, cakes, quiches, sandwiches, and *biscuits* (cookies) of every kind and size. Once, he had to go to the charcuterie, where house-made deli items—terrines, hams, salads, and olives—crowded the display case. Although Bob and I were always overfed, it was hard to resist bringing back a treat for the man who loved every food imaginable.

It was during one of our barge trips, when I was at the market in Auxerre, that I fantasized about staying someplace with a kitchen, where I could either prepare food or serve prepared food. It was fall, and there were so many enticing items that all I could imagine was what I would do with this squash, or how I could serve that cabbage, and what joy it would be to make a risotto with all the types of mushrooms on display.

Auxerre boasts a thirteenth-century Gothic cathedral with stained-glass windows, fine Renaissance-era houses on cobblestone streets, and a popular football (soccer) team. It's the original capital of lower Burgundy, about ninety minutes from either Dijon and Beaune and at the junction of the Canal du Nivernais and the River Yonne. It's known for its wine and timber, but I only recall the market.

Meals on our barge cruises followed a predictable pattern and were served by an impressively well-trained young staff, who always described each wine and each of the cheese varieties in impeccable detail. One person was tasked with folding cloth napkins in a different and always precise style for each meal. Bountiful breakfast buffets included cereals, fruits, and pastries, but usually the chef didn't work at breakfast, and I don't remember any made-to-order dishes. One morning, I asked if I could make individual omelettes for breakfast. Preparing them in the galley kitchen was great fun and they seemed to have been appreciated.

Lunch was also presented buffet style with selections of two or three salads, a country pâté or charcuterie platter, plus hot dishes. Dinner was served restaurant style and showcased some traditional Burgundian dishes, like boeuf bourguignon, Charolais beef, and my favorite, coq au vin. There was always a special dessert.

Best was the abundance of regional wines. I can't speak for every cruise line, but European Waterways offers unlimited premier cru vintages gratis. Before dinner, we sipped fine wines on the decks of barges that moved through narrow canals at four miles per hour, about the same pace that people walk and at eye level with the white Charolais cattle grazing in adjacent fields. We loved every minute.

Whatever the riverboat or barge, they all had vans that accompanied them and someone on staff who was an English-speaking guide and took us on various field trips, including vineyards for tastings. We passed road signs that read like a gastronomic wine list: Aloxe, Chassagne, and Corton. On one day trip in the barge's van, I noticed a familiar wine word *Pouilly* in bold black letters on a rectangular, red-bordered road sign; it signaled the entry to a teeny town. Two seconds later, I spotted the identical word—slashed with a broad, bright-red banner across the place name—indicating the village exit. Then, in a nanosecond, a new sign appeared: *Fuissé*! That was the day I learned that Pouilly-Fuissé, a wine I bought often, was named for different vineyards in adjacent villages.

On a subsequent outing, our guide shared a story about a former British passenger, a marketing manager, who had a passable knowledge of French wine. He was extremely impressed by the distinctive names on the road signs entering or leaving each Burgundian village and credited them to savvy sales skills. He told our guide: "How very clever these French are to name their little villages after such famous wines!"

My most recent barge cruise took place almost ten years later, in April 2013, when I traveled with my friend Susann. From the pristine spot where that vessel was docked, on the Ouche, a tributary of the Saône that flows through little towns and connects with the Canal de Bourgogne, we could view the stony façade of Abbaye de la Bussière-sur-Ouche. That country-house destination hotel (a Relais & Châteaux affiliate) was so close that we walked there for a dinner in its park-like garden.

Why Burgundy?

This is a question friends asked in 2018, before my eighth visit there. I told them about the beauty of the landscape—with miles of vineyards and countless picturesque pastures studded with the region's distinctive white Charolais cattle—the traditional foods, my favorite white Burgundy wines, and a sixteenth-century château. I told them about some memorable Michelin-starred meals at Maison Lameloise, where Jacques Lameloise reigned, and at L'Espérance, where Marc Meneau, who passed in 2020, was the renowned chef. But I never hinted at the strong emotional attachment that I feel about a region where I have spent some of my happiest moments.

Bob and I drove rental cars around the region several times, before or after barge cruises, and once en route from Paris to Nice, when we also overnighted at Maison Pic, in Valence, before Anne-Sophie Pic—the daughter and granddaughter of great chefs—earned her third Michelin star in 2007.

On April 7, 2021, long before I started this chapter, I was putting away one of my white cardboard magazine files and looked through another one labeled FRANCE. Inside, I noticed my husband's familiar handwriting on the cover of a small notebook: FRANCE May 13th/June 2002. His photo journal dated and titled every page and numbered and named every picture: Tournus. Solutré. Vergisson. Pierreclos Castle. It was an abbreviated diary of our trip.

Unfortunately, when Superstorm Sandy struck in October 2012 and flooded my waterfront home, it destroyed his slides, which were stored neatly in plastic pages that hung in Pendaflex file folders. Losing those images felt like losing a part of him all over again. So I was thrilled to read the words on page 1, BEAUNE, and saw numbered images of the Hospice and its tricolored, glazed-roof tiles and subsequent pages with titles like Nivernais Canal: "old men playing boules, a fisherman on a riverbank, kids in a park." I saw the scenes in my head, even without the slides. Of course, there were foods mentioned: foie gras, escargots, and lovely cheese trays. One image was labeled: Mustard@Levernois.

That little notebook brought back memories of the times when I was at the wheel driving through Burgundian vineyards, and my photographer sat, as always, with camera in hand focusing on the sights. Whenever the light was "just right" as it reflected off the grape leaves, his enthusiasm was contagious: "Stop here!" he'd command and jump out of the car. It may not be how other couples find their happiness, but we loved those moments.

When I muse about Burgundy, I realize that I should reveal one of its special pleasures: sipping a Kir, a splash of cassis (black current) liqueur in white Aligoté, or a not-so-great Chardonnay. The server who poured my first Kir told me about the local hero for whom the twentieth-century apéritif invention is named.

un peu plus: KIR

Canon Félix Kir (January 22, 1876–April 26, 1968), had an impressive career as the local Catholic priest. During World War II, he became a French Resistance hero and received the esteemed *Légion d'Honneur* in 1945, for helping five thousand prisoners escape the German Occupation. As deputy *maire* (mayor) of Dijon, and as a member of the National Assembly, *Monsieur le Maire* hosted innumerable delegations and meet-and-greets at the *Mairie.* Postwar wines were not among the best, because grapevines had been neglected during the war years when most vintners were at the front or imprisoned. M. Kir didn't consider them worthy of his guests' palates, so he blended some tart, tangy crème de cassis liqueur with the underwhelming local Aligoté. He created a pleasantly drinkable—and still popular—cocktail, which the world calls Kir for the man who made lemonade from life's lemons.

chez moi: KIR

The best crème de cassis liqueur comes from Burgundy and is called crème de cassis de Dijon or crème de cassis de Bourgogne. It was served on its own as a nineteenth-century apéritif. To make Kir, add ⅓ ounce (1 part) crème de cassis to 3 ounces (9 parts) aligoté. To make a Kir royale, use the same proportions and add crème de cassis to a bubbly crémant de Bourgogne or champagne; to make a Cardinal, add crème de cassis to a dry red wine in the same proportions.

La Vendange

One of the many reasons to return to Burgundy had nothing to do with barges, cruises, or historical landmarks: it was a bucket list opportunity to participate in *la vendange* (the grape harvest) in 2018. The event starts only when the grapes' sugar levels and juiciness are ideal, ending the stillness of mother nature's grape-growing season some one hundred days after the first blossoms emerge. The exact dates vary from region to region, year to year, and are totally dependent upon the vagaries of weather: heat waves and drought, sunlight, rain, even snow showers.

I crossed my fingers and hoped that the harvest in Burgundy would take place early that September, so I could be a bystander or, hopefully, a participant, before I headed to Champagne in mid-September.

MAISON OLIVIER LEFLAIVE

As soon as the Champagne foray was confirmed, I emailed Olivier Leflaive, a Burgundian vintner whose family of *Grandes Domaines* Leflaive winemakers trace their lineage through seventeen generations, from 1580. After a career in music and managing the family *domaine*, he launched Maison Olivier Leflaive and then started Olivier Leflaive Frères, with his brother, Patrick, in 1985. As *domaine* (wine estate) owner, M. Leflaive grows grapes on about fifty acres; as a *négociant* he buys wines from other estates, and as *vigneron* (winemaker) he is a pioneer in biodynamic viticulture. He is also a hotelier.

I met M. Leflaive ten years earlier, on my first trip to France as a widow in October 2008. The charismatic former musician and dapper vineyard/winery owner hosted lunch for our small group of writers in his recently launched small hotel within a seventeenth-century building facing Place du Monument, the town square in Puligny. Some rode bicycles from where we were staying, Hotel Le Cep, in Beaune, to Puligny and, when we all arrived, M. Leflaive escorted us to the large table on the inner *terrasse* and mentioned that the hotel restaurant was closed that day. He poured a lovely Puligny Montrachet and served platters brimming with fresh breads, sliced charcuterie, local cheese, crudités, fruit, and pastries. We enjoyed a perfect *pique-nique*, and I decided then and there that I hoped to return and stay in this idyllic spot.

In my email to M. Leflaive, I asked about the best dates to experience the harvest at his hotel, which advertised *oenotourisme*, tastings, and harvest visits. Olivier responded with a recommendation to arrive the first days of September to coincide with the end of grape picking, which he expected to be earlier than usual in 2018. He wrote: "It's a critical, busy, intense, but happy period."

I booked a Labor Day flight and two nights at Maison d'Olivier Leflaive. From CDG airport in Paris, I taxied to Gare de Lyon, boarded the TGV to Dijon, and then was driven to Puligny. During the forty-odd-minute drive through the Côte d'Or along Route Nationale 974, I noticed the upper torsos of workers in seas of green on both sides of it. There were lots of small, square white trucks laden with grapes on and off the road; it was obvious that the normally quiet countryside was peppered with harvest activity.

When I checked into the hotel, the desk clerk proclaimed, "Too bad you missed the last day of the harvest." My face fell with disappointment. Had I really arrived a day too late?

I went up to my timber-ceilinged room on the top floor overlooking the tree-lined square and thumbed through the hotel brochure that advertised tastings, wine dinners, and the *vendange* package that had lured me there. I read that during the wine cellar *visite*, Olivier or Patrick describe appellations and the entire winemaking process, starting with the *terroir*—that unique quality of soil, sunlight, and topography of each plot, the essential ingredient that imparts a wine's characteristic taste and flavor—to the cultivation, harvest, fermentation, barrel-aging, and bottling. Like most winemakers, the Leflaive brothers express enormous pride in their individual *terroir* and that of the plots from which they buy grapes, such as Montrachet, which has among the finest. For a hotel with fewer than twenty rooms, it also promoted more than the usual activities, including walking and cycling tours and a vineyard tour.

There was still time before dinner, and I wasn't about to move after the long trip. I opened the book on the night table—*Puligny-Montrachet* by Simon Loftus—and read, "For more than two hundred years, wine lovers have claimed that Montrachet/Puligny-Montrachet produces the greatest dry white wine in the world." Loftus wrote that aristocrats whose families date to the twelfth century own parcels of Montrachet.

On the way to the dining room, as I passed the front desk, the desk clerk declared: "M. Leflaive will meet you at the front desk at 9:30 a.m. tomorrow." OK, I thought. At least he'd tell me about the harvest that I missed.

The dining room, appropriately named Le Montrachet, had white stone walls, a planked wood floor, a coffered ceiling, and modern furnishings, including refrigerated wine cabinets displaying labels that read Olivier Leflaive Puligny-Montrachet Enseignères (the name of one of Leflaive's own plots). Color-coded maps representing each irregularly shaped and individually named *parcelle* decorated walls. The Côte de Beaune map illustrated the vineyards of Chassagne-Montrachet, Puligny-Montrachet, Meursault, and Volnay.

I drank Olivier Leflaive Chassagne-Montrachet 2013 and ate *gougères*, small, cheesy popovers. The bread that arrived in a wooden box was beyond compare, as was the *amuse*: cold *aubergines* with garlic and cucumber and a hazelnut dressing. Dinner continued: cold pea soup and seared tuna with herb topping, a particularly good dish considering how far Burgundy is from the coast.

The following morning as planned, M. Leflaive met me at the front desk and led me to his car. "My workers finished harvesting my fifty acres. Today, we're going to Montrachet, where they are picking grapes that I buy." I couldn't believe my luck—I hadn't missed the harvest entirely. Five minutes later, the negociant parked near two stone gateposts etched with the word Montrachet and supporting a graceful wrought iron piece centered with a family crest. *On est arrivé!* (We arrived.)

M. Leflaive warmly greeted his longtime colleagues—three generations of family who own the prestigious Montrachet plots—and introduced me to the matriarch, Mme. Beaucaron, two of her nieces and their husbands, and a grandniece, Aude, a charming young English-speaking woman. My affable host appeared to be doing—or solidifying—some relationship-building, an undertaking that seemed particularly natural.

One sister shared that the family château is empty and only the eldest still lives in the region. The rest of the family members reside in Paris and Normandy, but they all return to help with the harvest, from daybreak until the last grape is picked. "We're up at dawn to be at the vineyard," she said. I noticed that they scrupulously, albeit discreetly, oversaw everything happening at the harvest, which is the most important commercial venture for domaine owners of grands crus vines, because it determines most of the year's sales and profits.

un peu plus: BURGUNDY WINES

Burgundy vineyards are worth a fortune. In 2021, ten wine estates were valued at more than one million euros per hectare (2.471 acres) and one, a Bourgogne Grand Cru, was estimated at almost eight million euros per hectare. The Montrachet estate is tiny, only eight hectares (twenty acres), which encompass half the vineyards in Chassagne (called Le Montrachet) and half in Puligny (called Montrachet). It is the second most valuable wine estate in Burgundy, after Vosne Romanée, and was estimated at one hundred million euros in 2015.

I had no idea about finances in 2018 but was enthralled at being a fly on the wall watching the open-air scene. *Madame* was seated on a chair near a couple of bureaucratic-type brokers, who were positioned facing an open ledger at a small folding table facing rows of vines. I noticed that each page had multiple columns topped with the name and weight of each porter as he or she appeared carrying an empty *hotte,* the basket worn on the porter's back in the fields.

Behind them, on the side of the narrow dirt road (D113) that runs between the Grand Cru vineyard and the less valuable Bâtard Montrachet plots, there was a line of open-back mini-trucks and four-wheel vehicles waiting to be loaded with grapes. Overhead, *douane* (customs) officials in low-flying helicopters checked that the number of laborers in the fields matched the number of official work permits (specific numbers of workers are permitted for each *parcelle* and maps with the names and information are widely available, even online).

I watched as the *vendangeurs* (grape pickers) with pruners in hand, clipped their way through the long *allées* between the vines;

they carefully hand-cut each cluster and gently placed them, bunch by bunch, into a wide-mouthed bucket. Then, they emptied the buckets into a gray rectangular plastic basket until it weighed approximately ten kilos (about twenty-two pounds). When two gray baskets were topped, porters carried them to the front table, where they stepped on the scale. That's when the brokers determined the increase in their weight with filled baskets.

After being weighed, the porters turned around and another worker carried the cases to one of the nearby trucks waiting to transport the grapes to a *cuverie*; there, another crew of workers tended the sorting tables and loaded grapes into vats in which they were immediately pressed. Olivier, who noticed my fascination with the procedure, explained: "When they get to one thousand kilos they stop."

As I surveyed the scene, I noticed that some gray plastic containers were labeled Domaine Louis Latour, a well-known negociant; others were labeled Louis Jadot, another familiar importer. They and other negociants who bought Montrachet grapes were probably also on the scene waiting for the pickers to start in their prescribed rows, although I had no idea how to identify them.

When it was Olivier's turn to harvest, I noticed that he carefully checked that the vendangeurs picked all—and only—the grapes reserved for him. Likewise, as he was watching for the twenty *porteurs* to finish picking his twenty rows, the vineyard owners appeared equally intent that the correct rows of grapes were harvested by the proper buyer.

There was plenty of time to chit-chat that morning, and Aude was particularly forthcoming about explaining the process to me. Each harvest can last two weeks, with long, backbreaking days, because premier cru and grand cru wines demand hand-harvesting, which is arduous, meticulous, and delicate work. Workers start with breakfast and are in the fields at 7:30 a.m.; they stop for a *casse-croute* snack with coffee or wine at 9:00 a.m. Lunch at the winery is from noon to 1:30 p.m.; then they spend the afternoon in the fields until the task is done, usually before 5:30 p.m.

She told me that the little stone building in the middle of the vineyard is called a *cabotte* and is used for refuge from sun and rain. She also shared that she was about to start an art world career in Manhattan. She was so lovely that we kept in touch and met again at an art show in Paris in 2021.

Although many wine lovers consider the *vendange* a romantic uber-celebration, for those who work in the wine industry—agents, coop-cellars, estate owners, grape pickers, importers, journalists, négociants, restaurateurs, sommeliers, vintners, and wine merchants—the harvest is a sobering (pun intended) commercial activity. The harvest requires hiring thousands of seasonal workers, because each standard 750-milliliter bottle includes approximately 220 grapes or about one kilogram (2.2 pounds).

Olivier Leflaive Frères hired 102 workers in 2018 for a harvest that lasted two full weeks. French law requires that most workers be European Union residents, so it's more difficult these days for Americans to participate in the convivial work, though many find spots at small vineyards. Most of Leflaive's crew came from Poland and Hungary, though I also met two students from the UK and a couple of women from Spain. They lauded the strict French laws governing pay, accommodations, and meals, because the best working conditions are assured.

After the workers reached their quota at Montrachet, Olivier said goodbye to his colleagues, headed for the office, and dropped me off at his winery for a tour of the *cave*.

When I returned from that *visite*, he was standing with a group of hired hands next to the open back of his now-filled-to-the-brim Volkswagen Tiguan and appeared to be involved in a casual awards ceremony.

"Who has returned for the second year?" the domaine owner asked, sounding much like a camp counselor at the last lunch of the season. "Who for three?" As hands were raised, people moved forward. He checked their names on a list and presented each with a gift. I recognized some of the logo-emblazoned gift shop souvenirs: Olivier Leflaive corkscrews, polo shirts, or tees—which he made sure were properly sized for each person—and gift boxes of distinctive blue and white Olivier Leflaive china. In 2008, I bought two similar plates and love that there's an OLIVIER LEFLAIVE cork in the center and a blue-striped ring around the edges that spells out the names of forty-eight Burgundy wines, from Aloxe to Volnay.

Gifts became more memorable and more personal according to the number of harvests worked, as he greeted those who had worked for six, seven, or even ten years by name and handed each of them an additional gift, a book about Burgundy. Only returnees attended this gathering, and it ended when he invited all of them back for the following harvest season.

Afterward, everyone went into the winery for lunch. It was prepared in a professional kitchen staffed by one full-time chef plus another hired for the harvest. The people I spoke to appreciate eating well during the long, arduous days of grape-picking, and at the one lunch that I was at, it was obvious they were well-fed: workers were seated at tables laden with salads, sides, and breads, as our host, M. Leflaive, personally passed a hefty platter of sliced pork to his staff.

Walking back from the winery to the hotel, the central square looked so pretty that I decided to sit on a bench and admire it. I greeted a woman who joined me, who told me that she was born in Puligny and was one of fewer than four hundred full-time residents. At some point in the conversation, I disclosed my age. (Admittedly, I wondered if I was older or younger.) She never shared hers, but when I got up and said, "Au revoir, Madame," she replied: "*Madame, vous ne faites pas vôtre age!*" (Madame, you don't look your age!) I still wonder.

Back in my room, I had ample time before the evening's gala to read a few more pages of *Puligny-Montrachet,* and I noticed this: "The Montrachet vineyard, owned by la famille Beaucaron/Guillaume, is so well-known and respected that French troops saluted as they marched by the low stone wall by the parcel." Those troops probably marched by during the French revolution or some long-ago conflict, but it sure confirms the respect that the French have for wine in general and Montrachet in particular. I was gobsmacked to realize that I had met family descendants that morning!

La Paulée

That evening, my first end-of-harvest feast, called *paulée,* was more exhilarating than I could have imagined. The full Leflaive winemaking team was gathered inside the *cave* for the gala celebration: they included the vigneron, estate owners, more than one hundred vendangeurs, as well as musicians and guests galore. To my surprise, Olivier Leflaive placed me at the head of one of more than a dozen long tables under white tents lined up between the enormous wine vats, this one reserved—so the sign read—for La Famille Leflaive. "You! Sit there!" he commanded, as he pointed to the far end. I sat as directed with a choice position between the owners of the Montrachet vineyard, who were seated on either side of me.

At the table, Olivier's adult daughter, who operates La Maison d'Olivier Leflaive, a second daughter, and Olivier's young son were at the other end, in the center of the action, along with Patrick, who was hospitably table hopping, and his wife, who was serving platters of food. Wine flowed generously. The enthusiastic camaraderie was palpable.

At one point, Olivier interrupted the gaiety and hollered above the talking, drinking, and eating. He announced the final morning's agenda, speaking partly in English: "Tomorrow, la paulée breakfast will be served between nine and eleven a.m. From nine to twelve *midi*, clean dormitory!" He bellowed: "No clean, no money . . . please . . . *mes amis*. After I check the dormitory is clean, then you get the money, the paper, and the presents. No lunch, I want you to be out-out." Everyone laughed. They were ready to head home.

Between more singing and dancing to a DJ, Olivier stepped to the microphone to distribute prizes: "*Mesdames, messieurs . . .*" It was a major event, and each award had its particular Oscar-like background music; I recognized theme songs from *The Godfather* and *Rocky*. Golden and silver prizes were awarded to the president of this, the technical director of that, the *oenologiste*, and the vineyard manager. With so many cheers and shouts from an inebriated crowd who'd been guzzling past vintages with gusto, I could hardly hear much less understand what they were saying. I caught an occasional word like "Jean" or an expression such as "Ladies First," but have no idea who merited the many prizes. The festivities continued long after the formalities ended, but I said my adieus.

Recently, I listened to my recorded notes and heard the vendangeurs chant: "La la lalala lalala la . . . Bravo!" Then applause. The thirty-second soundtrack captured the energy and conviviality of the evening and brought back memories of this ancient and exciting Burgundian tradition. Similar festive finales to the vendange are duplicated, to greater or lesser extents, at other wineries throughout the region and at public harvest events that pay tribute to Bacchus, the god of wine, and Saint Vincent, the patron saint of winemakers.

Whenever I notice Olivier Leflaive wine on restaurant lists, as I have in many cities, I order a bottle, take a picture of the label, and smile. *Pourquoi pas?* (Why not?)

Beaune: The Wine Capital of Burgundy

The vendange may have been my priority that visit to Burgundy, but I also wanted to return to Beaune, where I had twice toured the famous Hospices de Beaune, the hospital founded in 1443. It is a mecca for art- and architecture-loving tourists who especially admire its multicolored, glazed-tile roof and where *Les Trois Glorieuses*, the uber-prestigious three-day annual charity wine auction, takes place on the third weekend of November, when wealthy collectors bid on rare vintages.

I enjoy strolling through the wonderful local market in Beaune, and on that particularly lovely September morning, stopped in a few mom-and-pop shops that sell regional specialties—cassis, anise-flavored Flavigny candies, and honey spice cake—and continued walking to La Moutarderie Fallot, where I had a reservation for an English-speaking tour.

LA MOUTARDERIE FALLOT

This last independent, family-run mustard mill in Burgundy opened in 1840, and the present-day mustard business was founded by Edmond Fallot in 1928. It is currently operated by his grandson, Marc Désarménien, whom I met along with an American couple who own a small chain of gourmet food shops. The three of us were shopping in the boutique after our English-language *visite*. We were trying to choose among an array of mustard varieties—stone-ground mustards and honey and balsamic vinegar mustards or gingerbread-, cassis-, basil-, and tarragon-flavored mustards—when M. Désarménien entered.

He explained that Fallot is the region's only private, nonindustrial mustard producer. "Our independent, family-owned mustard production is the only one that uses one hundred percent French mustard seed from the region." He was being modest. The fact is, the third-generation director of this oldest Dijon mustard company in France spearheaded the local cultivation of mustard seeds. (It may surprise you to know that Maille and Amora Dijon mustards use seeds predominantly grown in Canada for their French or Dijon mustard.)

During my few days in Beaune, I also participated in a winery tour that had started earlier that morning, at the train station in Dijon, where they picked up four day-trippers from Paris. I joined the group in Beaune, just before they had free time for lunch and a walk around the wine capital. After lunch, we climbed into the van and spent a lovely afternoon touring two privately owned wineries and enjoying tastings at each. En route back to the hotel, we passed—but couldn't enter—the legendary Romanée-Conti vineyards.

chez moi: VINAIGRETTE À LA MOUTARDE FALLOT

No matter the cost of the extra virgin olive oil, the fancy wine vinegar, or the Fallot mustard, this vinaigrette is much better, healthier, and less expensive than the unhealthy, sugar- and preservative-laden, ridiculously priced, horrible-tasting bottled alternatives. I prefer a three-to-one ratio of extra virgin olive oil and wine vinegar to which I add garlic and Fallot's grainy Dijon mustard with seeds.

LE CEP

I've visited Beaune many times, because the wine capital is a stop on barge cruises, and have stayed at Le Cep on three occasions. The boutique hotel is affiliated with Relais & Châteaux, and the owner, Jean-Claude Bernard, is the epitome of an attentive host. Guests feel like "regulars" on their second visit and by the third feel like friends.

The hotel is a village-like complex. Bob and I had a room within the original main building during our first road trip from Paris to Nice in 2004, and I stayed there again in 2008. In 2018, my most recent visit, my room was in one of the beautifully decorated small buildings that date to the sixteenth and seventeenth centuries and are adjacent to the hotel's pristine fourteenth-century courtyard, where breakfast is served when the weather is pleasant. The innkeeper/owner pays such careful attention to every detail of hospitality that he attends Paris Design Week Maison&Objet to buy antiques and collectibles. He's constantly adding to, updating, and decorating Le Cep with his personal finds.

In 2018, we met for a glass of wine in his recently launched Caveau Saint-Félix, an authentic wine *cave* reached from the courtyard. M. Bernard introduced me to his sommelier, who served a wonderful wine from his vast collection of regional vintages. That evening, I dined for the third time at the Michelin-starred hotel restaurant, Loiseau des Vignes, owned by Groupe Loiseau. The restaurant specializes in regional Burgundian cuisine, and the staff specializes in making everyone comfortable, which is especially appreciated when the lady (moi) is dining alone.

That stopover was also a chance to see and experience the owner's newly opened Spa Marie de Bourgogne, where I spent some time in the outdoor sauna, in a building that resembles a large wine barrel, before receiving a massage.

CHÂTEAU DE POMMARD

Another highlight of my Burgundy visit was the day I spent at Château de Pommard, the largest *monopole clos* of Burgundy, with its twenty-hectare (fifty acre) vineyard Clos Marey-Monge. (*Monopole* refers to a designated wine-growing region controlled by one winery, and *clos* is a walled vineyard.) Longtime wine lovers from California, Michael and Julie Carabello-Baum, purchased the eighteenth-century wine estate in 2014. They grow pinot noir on seven different micro-climates inside Clos Marey-Monge, operate the winery, and offer oeno-tourists an array of appealing adventures: tasting experiences inside the château with access to French-style gardens, vintage car rides on the wine route, and ballooning. They also offer a WSET course at different levels for serious oenophiles. This Wine & Spirits Education Trust diploma is the traditional prerequisite for Master of Wine students.

I participated in their open-to-the-public "harvest" visit, during which my biggest thrill was clipping grape clumps at Clos Marey-Monge, efforts that were memorialized in a photograph of me, pruners in hand. It surprised me how over-the-top happy that made me, because when Bob and I bought the house where I still live in 1979, there were more than twenty grapevines taking up most of the backyard. I gave away most of them to my friend Esther, who still makes Concord grape preserves from their fruit. I tended the half-dozen that I saved for some years and pruned them, protected them from birds with netting, and even made my own grape preserves a few times until the evergreens behind them shaded them into submission.

Yet at Pommard, the physical act of clipping in that historic eighteenth-century vineyard was entirely special and exciting. The program included lunch, which also turned out to be far more fun than expected. Michael, who emerged like a proud papa presenting his domaine, was a genuinely delighted and delightful host. On that day, he personally barbecued various meats and served them to us individually.

Whether Michael's hospitality was typical or not, I can't say, but it was a special event.

Saulieu

During my solo week in Burgundy in 2018, I left Beaune by car for the hourlong drive through the lovely rural countryside from Beaune to Saulieu, prepared to spend the next three days at the famed five-star Relais Bernard Loiseau before heading to Paris. En route, I chatted with the driver, who shared that she was born in the famed Hospice de Beaune and that she had plans for a forthcoming motorcycle trip with friends from San Francisco to Los Angeles. It sounded like a great adventure, and I admired her courage to even attempt it.

RELAIS BERNARD LOISEAU

The Relais Bernard Loiseau is a destination restaurant and a very well-regarded thirty-two-room country inn. It's about two and a half hours south-southeast of Paris and about an hour west of Dijon. The illustrious chef Bernard Loiseau earned his third Michelin star here in 1991 and kept it for twenty-five years. As a chef and popular television personality, he was among the most well-known people in all of France, and I had wanted to experience his cuisine since before our first cruises in the region in the early 2000s. Sadly, the restaurant's namesake chef died suddenly and surprisingly by suicide at the age of fifty-two, in February 2003.

Hours after I arrived and settled into a room with a view of her garden, I met his widow, the always attentive *aubergiste* (innkeeper) Dominique Loiseau. Trained as a biochemist, the former professor was a well-known health writer when she met her future husband. By the time I met her, she had served as the vice president of Relais & Châteaux organizations, was a *Légion d'Honneur* recipient, and the head of Le Groupe Bernard Loiseau, which owns several restaurants, including the one where I've eaten a few times in Beaune. I soon found out—not from the host herself—that Dominique was scheduled to be featured on a popular French television program to acknowledge her role as a top female entrepreneur.

The first evening, Madame Loiseau, Fabrice Rosset, who was head of Champagne Deutz at the time, and I posed on the hotel's famous interior staircase. Later, alone, I savored an epicurean dinner prepared by the two-Michelin-star executive chef Patrick Bertron, who served traditional *le style Loiseau specialités*, including sautéed foie gras and *jambonettes* of frog's legs in a garlicky parsley jus. Chef Bertron had been at Bernard Loiseau's side for twenty of the forty-one years he worked in the Burgundian kitchen, and he only recently moved on from the famous kitchen where he spent most of his adult years.

I also ate at the less formal *santé-plaisir* (healthy-pleasure) restaurant at Villa Loiseau des Sens, the newly built wood-clad, four-story, 16,000-square-foot spa that opened in 2017. Along with a new indoor pool and hydrotherapy playground (with aqua bikes, showers, and jets), a Moroccan hammam (steam room), an ice fountain, a multi-jetted shower, and a windowed sauna with a view of the interior garden, there's a spa suite on the top floor outfitted with a fireplace, whirlpool tub, a huge bed, and two treatment *cabines*.

Madame Loiseau, who believes that the nectar of Burgundian black currants has incomparable aromatic, cosmetic, and nutritional qualities, curated the spa's signature treatments. Cassis, the vitamin-rich antioxidant, is incorporated in the service I received, "*Secrets de Cassis®* by Dominique Loiseau" and was followed by a sip of Kir—made with cassis and young white wine—which is the apéritif of choice in the treatment *cabine*. Dominique also personally designed and tends the adjacent exquisite garden that guests walk through and see from their rooms, the spa, and dining rooms.

un peu plus: BERNARD LOISEAU UPDATE

I saw Dominique Loiseau and Chef Patrick Bertron again at a special dinner at Restaurant Daniel, in Manhattan, on September 14, 2023. That evening, Chef Daniel Boulud hosted a tribute dinner to celebrate the legacy of his friend Bernard Loiseau, twenty years after the famed three-Michelin-star chef died. Francophiles, gastronomes, and oenophiles flocked there to celebrate his life, recount personal memories, recall menus, and share pictures of their gastronomic experiences in Saulieu. For me, it was an opportunity to reconnect with Madame Loiseau and meet her daughter Bérangère. That evening, Chef Bertron prepared *specialités* from Relais Bernard Loiseau, starting with bite-size hors d'oeuvres: Gougères Feuilletée au Comté, a cheesy puff pastry; Sphère d'Escargot à La Bourguignonne, a snail encased in an edible shell; and Chips de Ris et Bille d'Époisses à la Menthe, a cow's milk *époisse* cheese atop a rice cracker.

chez moi: POTATO LEEK SOUP FAÇON BERNARD LOISEAU

Bernard Loiseau is said to have loved childhood dishes that accentuated "pure, original flavors," and limited "fats and sugar as much as possible." I make a similar potato-leek soup and start by cooking quartered potatoes in salted water. Meanwhile, I sauté thinly sliced leeks in butter and extra virgin olive oil and then simmer them in chicken broth. When cooked, I purée the potatoes, thinning them with more chicken broth, and add that combination to the pot of leeks. I serve it often in winter, as he did, with bacon bits on top.

Champagne

W HEN I VISITED CHAMPAGNE AND BURGUNDY IN September 2008, I didn't know which destination excited me more: the chance to discover the noted Champagne region or the opportunity to return to Burgundy. What was certain was that it would be my first time in France as a widow. It was also a rare occasion to socialize with a few other writers with whom I'd be traveling.

VEUVE CLICQUOT

Our first stop after Paris was Reims, the historic wine-centric capital of the region that's reached via high-speed TGV from Paris in forty-six minutes. After meeting for dinner and an overnight at Hotel de la Paix, we set out the following morning for our first *visite* to a *maison de Champagne:* Maison Veuve Clicquot. (Happily, for visitors, it's within walking distance of two other notable *maisons*: Ruinart and Taittinger, where World War II troops occupied the cellars.)

At Maison Veuve Clicquot, we toured soaring, cathedral-tall medieval chalk quarries, called *les crayères*, dozens of stairs below ground level. *Les caves,* the underground wine cellars, are cool (51°F), earthy, and humid tunnels. At Veuve Clicquot, thousands of bottles of wine are stored on the V-shaped riddling racks, in rows of twelve bottles across, ten bottles high, that Veuve Clicquot herself had invented.

I could translate the word "veuve" to widow, but even though I'd seen the name on its distinctive golden label, I never considered its real meaning. On that day, just a few months after I experienced Bob's death, the word took on a more personal connotation, and I related to the story about French aristocrat Barbe-Nicole Ponsardin.

She was only twenty-seven when her husband died in 1805, at a time when French women were not allowed to work or have their own bank accounts. The Napoleonic Code of 1804 prohibited married women from owning businesses without the consent of their husbands or fathers. Widows, however, were exempt from this rule, which allowed Barbe-Nicole Clicquot-Ponsardin to manage her late husband's champagne company and become the first woman to own a champagne house. According to the film *The Widow Clicquot*, she was summoned to court because she operated the business as an unmarried woman, and she cited the Napoleonic Code to keep it. Barbe-Nicole took full control of the *maison*, and just one year later, in 1806, used a circuitous route to defy the Napoleonic blockade and ship her wines to Russia and beyond.

In 1810, La Veuve was also the first to produce a vintage champagne using grapes from one year. By 1814, she established her wine in the royal courts of Russia and Europe. Then, in 1816, she invented the riddling rack by cutting a kitchen table in half and adding lots of little holes. The V-shaped structure holds the bottles by their necks at a 45-degree upright angle and is rotated 90 degrees each day. This technique, which is still used today, collects the yeast sediments and clarifies the wine, as can be seen on a tour of Maison Veuve Clicquot today, where thousands of bottles of wine are stored this way. According to the maison: "Ever since she invented it, we have used this exact same method for our champagne. Though machines can now do it more quickly, we still keep that savoir-faire in the House by using it for our special bottles like Cuvee Grande Dame and for our big three-liter bottles."

Veuve Clicquot created one of the most prestigious and long-lasting labels in the world, and part of her workday was spent communicating with international clients. It's said she sent and received more than seven thousand letters. In 1818 she produced a rosé. The color alone signified her brand, and more than two hundred years later, the legacy of the *Grande Dame de la Champagne* is undeniable. (I've seen her mustard-colored bottles dominate liquor store windows, including one on Ninth Avenue at Twenty-Third Street in Manhattan.)

"Her life was such an achievement," says Isabelle Pierre, a historian specializing in the house of Veuve Clicquot. "The most fascinating thing about her for me, as a historian and a woman, is the way in which she twisted all the rules of the time by saying: 'Yes, I am a woman, but I'm going to run this company without a husband.'" By the time she died in 1866, she had invested in more than forty hectares. Today, Veuve owns almost four hundred hectares and produces several million bottles a year.

Barbe-Nicole Ponsardin, aka Madame Clicquot, aka Veuve Clicquot, has been my hero among champagne widows—including les veuves Pommery and Bollinger—since that first September 2008 morning. I am a commoner; she was an aristocrat. I was nearly seventy when my husband died, she wasn't even thirty. I lived during an era of Women's Liberation; she faced her future with great legal barriers and personal challenges. Although we had little in common, this world-famous icon's spirit inspired my determination to thrive alone.

DOMAINE LES CRAYÈRES

After a tasting in the *cave*, we lunched in elegant style just a short drive away, at Le Parc restaurant at Domaine Les Crayères, a Relais & Châteaux affiliate housed within a well-appointed mansion surrounded by a verdant park. Award-winning chef Philippe Mille reigned there and boasted multiple awards: two Michelin stars, Bocuse Europe and Bocuse d'Or, Meilleur Ouvrier de France, and Grand Chef Relais et Châteaux. The formal, three-course set lunch was lovely, but I'd prefer to return for an à la carte "snack" in the exquisite bar La Rotonde, where I'd order foie gras on country bread or the smoked salmon.

En route to Burgundy, we stopped at Champagne Drappier in Urville, where, in the 1960s, Charles de Gaulle personally purchased bottles en route to his country home in Colombey-les-Deux-Églises, where he served them at private receptions. He often chose a cuvée rich in pinot noir (80 percent) that was renamed in homage to him: Charles de Gaulle Cuvée.

When I arrived back in the States after that trip, tears started flowing as I was pulling my wheelie bag through the International Arrivals Terminal at JFK, and they continued during the interminable line through passport control (this was years before I had a Global Entry pass). I realized exactly why I was crying: it was the sudden, excruciating awareness that the decades of repeated happy moments at Arrivals—where Bob had always been "all ears eager" to hear about my adventures—had ended.

That arrival ritual had been one of the constants in our relationship. I usually traveled to the terminal on my own when leaving for a trip, but when I returned to the US and exited the "no entry" doors into a lobby crowded with waiting family members and drivers carrying name signs, his golden waves—long-ago lightened and relaxed from his youthful tight red curls—were visible above the masses.

He'd grin, I'd beam. Never again.

The Champagne Committee

Ten years after my first visit to Champagne, the Washington, D.C., office of the Champagne Committee invited me to join a group of wine writers there. The serendipitous case of "who you know" resulted from a lunch with a colleague's British contact, who was visiting New York to make connections with travel agents and travel writers. "What are you working on?" she asked while we were waiting for our food to arrive. I told her that I was researching an assignment about the grape harvest in France. She mentioned that she had colleagues at the Champagne Committee whom she would contact on my behalf. She did. They sent me information—and, months later, an invitation appeared via email.

As soon as the dates were confirmed, I arranged a flight to France that arrived two weeks before our meet-up in Reims and organized a solo itinerary: eight nights in Burgundy, four in Paris, and an overnight at the Royal Champagne Hotel & Spa, the newest chic hotel in the region.

ROYAL CHAMPAGNE HOTEL & SPA

Boston financier Mark Nunnelly and his wife, Denise Dupré, constructed the Royal Champagne Hotel & Spa within, and attached to, a historic nineteenth-century *relais de poste*, a country inn in Champillon, which had originally served as a coach stop where royals could freshen up thirteen miles before reaching Reims. Napoleon, who was a great fan of the Champagne region and its wines, had life-long friends there—the Moët-Chandon family—and frequented the inn en route to visit Reims. It is said that the only time he did not stop in Champagne was on his way to Waterloo!

The new owners refurbished the original *relais* that dates to Napoleonic times and added a newly constructed contemporary, wood-and-stone, multilevel hotel, which is oriented to take advantage of its rural vineyard views. In fact, most of the sweeping, semicircular modernist space that contains the lobby, restaurants, terraces, spa, swimming pools, and all forty-nine hotel rooms boasts floor-to-ceiling windows and private terraces overlooking centuries-old Möet & Chandon vineyards, listed as a UNESCO World Heritage Site. They are so vast they seemingly stretch miles to Épernay.

I was excited to experience the pristine and oh-so-very-perfect place that had opened just weeks earlier in mid-July 2018. I arrived via TGV from Paris to Épernay, from which a charming driver, Thomas Delord, taxied me to the hotel.

The new hoteliers brought in a general manager with top contacts, who subsequently hired the spa director from the Trianon hotel in Versailles and Karim Loqrifi, the former *chef concierge* and Clefs d'Or member at the Negresco Hotel in Nice. Karim enticed the two-Michelin-star chef Jean-Denis Rieubland of Le Chantecler Negresco, who was MOF (Best Cook France, 2007), to join him there.

Karim came out to the taxi and welcomed me, as he did all arrivals, and behaved as if he remembered me from my visit to Le Negresco five years earlier. He greeted all who entered the front door as warmly, whether they were hotel guests, locals, or tourists looking for a drink or a meal with a view. He directed them all up the stairs across from his desk and to the bar, terrace, and restaurants.

The elegantly modern interior was created by Paris-based designer Sybille de Margerie, of the Taittinger family, whose work I had previously admired at the Mandarin Oriental Paris (and later at the Hôtel de Paris Saint-Tropez). She is known to showcase a sense of place in her décor. The local viticulture industry of which her family is very much a part is reflected with a burgundy-rose palette and recurring vine-leaf patterns, which appear on printed fabrics, a spa lounge wall, and bathroom tiles. Even the chandeliers resemble delicate grapes or bubbles!

An important aspect of that sense of place is Napoleonic history, which is emphasized with the horse-and-rider logo throughout the property, including on a large mural on the bistro wall depicting Napoleon and his troops on horseback. She also references the military leader under the gold-leaf-studded dining room ceiling at Le Royal restaurant, where four curved panels display portraits of the women who shared his life.

And bees . . . yes bees! At his coronation as emperor, the ruler wore a coat embroidered with fifteen hundred golden bees; Josephine's ermine-lined coronation robe had bees of gilt wire attached and, at the Battle of Waterloo, his cape was fastened by bee coat clasps. This symbol of the Napoleonic era is incorporated into the décor. They may appear elsewhere, but in the lady's lounge, Sybille de Margerie's custom-designed whimsical 3D golden metallic bees adorn the floor tiles and mirrors.

By the time I checked in, it was late afternoon and I was starving. At Le Bar Bellevue, I ordered a coupe and foie gras du Gers served with chutney. After that late lunch, Chef Jean-Denis Rieubland introduced me to some of the brigade at the Relais & Châteaux affiliate, where they use local and regional *les beaux produits* (perfect products). I enjoyed many later that evening at dinner, when the waiter, Florent, impeccably served me artfully presented dishes. The main course was *suprème de volaille*, chicken in champagne sauce. Since that visit, Le Royal, the gastronomic restaurant, earned its own Michelin star. When I came back to the region in 2021 with Val, we had a memorable dinner there.

I had previously booked a massage for 5:00 p.m., which is the perfect hour to relax after busy daytime activities and gives me ample time afterward to prepare for a European dinner reservation at 8:00 p.m. or later. The only downside of my dinner-hour spa appointments is that I miss socializing on a bar stool at apéro hour. My very amiable mate always claimed, "That's the best time of day to meet people!" It's the time when I prefer to be alone.

I could have spent five hours—or five days—at the sprawling 16,000-square-foot Biologique Recherche spa. While most spa facilities are decidedly and purposefully dim, here the light-filled walkway from the entry to the private *cabines* offers the expansive vineyard view through window walls separating the indoor and outdoor temperature-controlled pools.

Each of the nine treatment rooms has its own changing room and shower. The fitness area includes a yoga studio, and the wet area encompasses a mosaic-tiled hammam, a eucalyptus-infused sauna, and a hot tub. Individualized treatments are the hallmark of the spa menu, and facials and massages, even couple's services, are customized according to guests' wants and needs. *Assemblages* combine a facial and massage or a massage and a "treatment bubble," which is a little goodie like a back or foot massage, makeup application, or manicure. For the ultimate in pampering, guests can book the *Coeur de Vigne* (Heart of Wine) set of services, a personalized ten-hour package to be used throughout the stay.

The following day, I enjoyed a healthy brunch: *saumon fumé* and shrimp and *fruits rouges,* which are usually only red berries but here were raspberries and figs stuffed into a crown of strawberry halves. I wish I could have spent multiple nights there instead of an overnight, because I might have had time to see more wineries, take a hot-air balloon ride, or retreat to the spa.

I recommend that every visitor to the region stop by, if only for a beer, soda, or a coupe on the terrace, no matter where else they dine or sleep. It's worth the drive.

Champagne Tour

The first evening of this part of my trip in 2018, three wine journalists, a photographer, and our escort from Washington, D.C., met for dinner in Reims with our hosts from the Comité Champagne, the local trade association, which arranged our itinerary. Afterward, we returned to a modest commercial and quite comfortable hotel next to the railroad station.

The following morning, we were driven to the Maison de Champagne in Reims, where we were ushered into a classroom for what I call "Champagne 101." Our instructor, an oenologist, started our session with the most basic fact: "A sparkling wine cannot legally be called champagne if it is not produced in Champagne, from grapes grown in Champagne." Copycats who falsely call their product champagne, he explained, have a negative economic impact on families and the entire region.

During a seminar filled with many facts about the product, the oenologist dipped a stick in a small cylinder partly filled with wine, and our test was to determine its age by the smell. I did fine. However, among wine experts with apparent limitless knowledge, some can identify the *parcelle* of land where the grapes were grown and a few can identify the percentage of pinot noir or chardonnay in the blend, or whether some Meunier grape juice is included in the *assemblage*.

We spent five enjoyable days touring and tasting, with *visites* to *grandes maisons*—including Taittinger and Dom Perignon—and small producers, usually multigenerational, family-run wineries where the owners toured us through their vineyards and *caves*. A few introduced their wines in their tasting rooms; one young couple invited us into their living room, past where the family's rubber boots were lined up at the door and where their kids and dogs were playing.

Whether in English or French, the vintners used wine vocabulary and talked about *assemblage*, the blending of varieties of grapes; *cuvée*, the juices from the first pressing achieved via gravity to avoid pumping; *vintage*, the season's yield; and, most proudly, about their specific and particular *terroir*.

Winemakers pay attention and adapt to each terroir. Its significance was exemplified at a tasting that took place at a small producer, Champagne Penet-Chardonnet. Alexandre Penet, a young winemaker, was lucky to have inherited grand cru (the top designation) vineyards that have been family-owned for four hundred years—in Penet, which belonged to his dad's family, and in Chardonnet, which was part of his mom's family's vineyards and only a short distance away. He offered us wines to taste that were produced from the same variety of grape but from the two different terroirs. Even I recognized the difference!

We were equally impressed by other vignerons. At Lacourte-Godbillon, an organic vineyard in Écueil, Geraldine Lacourte introduced the wines her husband, Richard Desvignes, makes. At Champagne Bruno Michel, which is certified organic, Pauline is both the namesake of her dad's Cuvée Pauline and the current vigneron. At Champagne Philipponnat, vigneron Charles Philip-ponnat produces Clos des Goisses from grapes grown in a walled vineyard nearly one hundred years old and stored in cellars dating from the eighteenth century. The list goes on . . . and if you start each day with a tasting, as we did, and continue to drink sparkling wines at lunch and during midafternoon, which we also did, it's best not to be the driver!

One lunch was on a vineyard-edged terrace at Château de Sacy, a twelve-room country inn in a renovated Napoleonic manse, c. 1850, where I chose dorade tartare (sliced Mediterranean fish), *filet of saumon*, and a *poire aux épices* (a spiced, poached, pecan-topped pear).

Reims

During each of my trips to the region, in 2008, 2018, and 2021, we spent one day sightseeing in the historic centre-ville Reims, which was 80 percent destroyed during World War I. The city's famed thirteenth-century Nôtre-Dame Cathédrale, with its imposing Gothic spires and stained-glass windows, is the first and most important must-see.

The cathedral, a UNESCO World Heritage Site, dates from 1211. It was built on the square where the previous cathedral had been and where twenty-five kings had been crowned from 816 until it was destroyed by fire in 1210.

The cathedral was the tallest building in the city during World War I and was a target for daily bombing between 1914 and 1918. In 2018, a centennial photography show illustrated an entire universe of life that took place in the chalk cellars under the cathedral, moving scenes of children who went to school at desks within the vast underground tunnels and of invalids in hospitals located there.

After the war, international leaders, including President Roosevelt, witnessed the damage firsthand and spread the word about the destruction. Restoration of the sacred site was originally funded by the Rockefellers, with support from the Carnegies, Fords, and many other philanthropists. The reconstruction featured a fireproof structure and used as much of the original stone as possible; it reopened in 1939. Subsequently, Marc Chagall designed its magnificent, modern, biblically themed stained-glass windows. Nearby, the art deco–style Carnegie Library, which the pacifist philanthropist helped the city build as its first postwar construction in 1928, is another notable and inspiring place to visit.

The walkable historic center has lots of landmarks, including Place Royale. A statue of Louis XV dressed as a Roman emperor, c. 1819, stands in the middle of an eighteenth-century square surrounded by lovely buildings with arcades, columns, and balustrades. The current statue was erected on the site of an earlier one of King Louis XV (who funded it), which was melted down to make cannons during the French Revolution. The square itself is on the site of a Roman forum. Another beautiful spot is the baroque-style Subé Fountain, placed at the end of the pedestrian allée. Its centerpiece is a tall column on which a winged angel stands, poised on one foot atop a laurel-leaf crown. Despite the extensive bombing during World War I, the column survived intact. The fountain was finally restored to water-flowing perfection in 2016.

Other sights in the city are accessible by taxi: Porte de Mars, a third-century AD Roman ruin, which was the largest arch of its era, and the eleventh-century Romanesque Basilique Saint-Remi. On my second trip in 2018, during Rosh Hashanah, one of the Jewish High Holidays, I revisited the Reims Synagogue, which was consecrated in 1879. It has a tall gate along the street and is fronted by grand blue doors. The memorial plaque lists far too many names of those who perished during World War II.

One afternoon in 2018, we stopped in a boutique that specializes in Biscuit rose de Reims, a local pink cookie that has its origins in 1690, when someone supposedly left some dough in a hot bread oven after the bread was removed, creating this biscotti-type cookie.

Perhaps the most fun was a cooking class at Chef Éric Geoffroy's *atelier culinaire* in Reims, called Au Piano des Chefs, where the chef hosts events and offers private and group classes. That's where we cooked our own dinner. His atelier is a storefront directly across the street from a side entrance to the famous Reims cathedral. Inside his atelier, there's a wall of shelves lined with local and regional products and cooking paraphernalia facing a large, efficient prepping, cooking, and dining space. Chef Geoffrey was a good-humored teacher who taught our group of four (a fifth colleague took pictures) how to make paté choux (puff pastry) for our gougères, the wonderful cheesy puff pastry. Afterward, he walked around the large rectangular table where we were trying to mimic his techniques, and he watched and helped us use the pastry bag with a tip to make the teeny swirls on the baking sheet.

Next, we made a simple squash soup, which the chef prepared by roasting butternut squash quarters and using an immersion blender to purée the soft insides of the vegetable. Before starting the main dish, we steamed individual meringues in round metal molds. Finally, we flambée-broiled fish with a blowtorch and checked the temperature with an instant-read thermometer. Of course, his presentation was a fancy one. We were each given a pastry brush to decorate our dishes with *encre de seiche* (black squid ink) from a jar. (I do not like squid ink and didn't touch it, but I have used the technique to get that chef-designer look, substituting pesto or cranberry relish for the ink!) We toasted the event with the three bottles we had brought, champagnes by Copinet, Mailly, and Jacquesson, and ate what we prepared!

The TGV ride from Paris takes less than an hour, making Reims a perfect day trip—or overnight getaway—from Paris. The city is an excellent home base for visitors to the region who aren't driving, because it's easy to take tours or taxis, or rent a car to drive the forty-mile Route Touristique that leads to top-quality small producers and Épernay, the champagne capital.

chez moi: GOUGÈRES

I try to follow Alain Ducasse's recipe. I preheat the oven to 400°F, and boil ½ cup water and ½ cup milk with 1 stick unsalted butter and salt in a saucepan. He adds a cup of flour and continuously stirs until the dough comes off the sides of the pan. Then he beats in 4 eggs, one at a time, until the dough is smooth and shiny before adding 4 ounces of grated Gruyère, and some pepper and grated nutmeg. I spoon what he pipes onto a baking sheet lined with parchment paper, top with more grated cheese, and bake for 20 minutes. They freeze well and are as convenient to impress company as they are to "nosh" on with a friend.

The Louis Vuitton Moët Hennessy Experience

For our final tasting of that 2018 tour, we were driven to Abbeye d'Hautvillers, the famous abbey where the Benedictine monk Deus Optimus Maximus (D.O.M.) Pierre Perignon is buried. The cellar master, born in 1638, entered the abbey in 1668 and prayed seven times a day. (Perhaps he prayed to improve the reputation of Champagne wines; at that time wines from Bordeaux and Burgundy were favored by the French.) He invented a press that made clear wine from dark grapes and reintroduced corks in the bottle, but when he failed to eliminate the bubbles that formed during fermentation, he announced: "Come quick, I am drinking the stars!" History reveals that this monk is forever credited with creating the process that produces the essential bubbles and which the world knows as "méthode champenoise."

Our private Dom Perignon tasting took place behind the church at a long cloth-covered table erected in the gravel courtyard that overlooks the *clos*. After the formally dressed sommelier poured the last of the three Dom Perignon vintages, the wine writer who kept a log of each bottle we drank announced that we had sampled sixty different wines that week.

Jessica Miller, a stylish woman speaking English with an American accent, then introduced herself as a representative of Moët Hennessy, which she explained is part of the prestigious Louis Vuitton Moët Hennessy brand. (The French call it by its initials, LVMH, and pronounce it so quickly that it sounds like: *elle vay emm ashe*.) She had made the day trip between Paris and Reims expressly to invite us all back to the Champagne region the following week when LVMH would be hosting wine experiences at Dom Perignon, Krug, Moët & Chandon, Ruinart, and Veuve Clicquot. The events were each part of a preview of the luxury group's fourth *Journées Particulières*, which are free, open-to-the-public *visites*, organized tours, and behind-the-scenes sensory experiences. Since 2011, LVMH has hosted these opportunities, giving guests access to see wine estates, meet winemakers, and enjoy entrée to haute LVMH ateliers, such as Dior, Fendi, Guerlain, Hermès, and Sephora. Our specific invitation would preview the October 12 to 14, 2018, event in the Champagne region, which was just one of among seventy-seven exceptional venues that year featuring fifty-six brands in fourteen countries, from Argentina to Australia, France, Germany, New Zealand, and the United States.

Jessica barely finished inviting us before I responded: "I'd love to join you if I can change my flight home from Paris." And I did. Unexpectedly, she also arranged for my long weekend stay in Paris, starting with a car service at the gare, which delivered me to Hotel Bel Ami, and ending with a car service late afternoon on Monday, when I was driven back to the gare to meet Jessica—who was with some Paris-based press—for the hour-long TGV train to Reims.

At dinner the first night of the LVMH trip, I met a few more media professionals: an editor of a men's magazine, a staff writer on a culture beat, a prominent interior design journalist, a television host, a Chinese-language radio personality, three oh-so-elegant female influencers, plus one male model dressed in a trim jacket and pointed wing-tip shoes. (The influencers in the group—no matter what else was happening—spent the majority of their time primping, posing, and posting selfies!)

HÔTEL DU MARC

Our first gala evening was at Hôtel du Marc, the former home of Barbe-Nicole Ponsardin (the Veuve Clicquot). Constructed in 1840, the mansion served as Madame Clicquot's home. Later, it was the family home of Édouard Werlé, her hand-picked successor. Despite its name, the mansion is not a public hotel in the American usage of the word; it is a private residence so exclusive that its five newly designed guest rooms are reserved for family, close friends, dignitaries, and important industry professionals. Jessica and her LVMH colleague spent the night there, but in less appealing attic rooms!

After LVMH acquired the Veuve Clicquot brand in 1986, it funded a four-year total restoration of the villa, which repaired World War II damage, including facades pockmarked by shrapnel. By 2007, the decoration of the formal nineteenth-century neoclassical mansion was completed. Restored were such typically ornate architectural features as a mansard roof and a grand marble-floored entry with a sweeping staircase up to the salon, dining room, and library.

The interior décor is contemporary and eclectic, some say avant-garde, and showcases mirrors, unique pieces of furniture, interesting accessories, and an array of Veuve Clicquot–brand memorabilia, including a life-size stuffed ostrich in the living room on which a fine leather saddle sits. I was told the ostrich is named Nicole, for you-know-who (Barbe-Nicole Ponsardin).

We sixteen guests were sipping champagne in the salon when the French doors opened and two uniformed, white-gloved servers stood at either side of the opening and announced "*Madame est Servie,*" just as had been done nightly during Madame Clicquot's lifetime. They led us inside the dark, wood-paneled dining room to our seats around a long table set with flower-filled glass orbs and under an enormous, lustrous chandelier. While one waiter dramatically decanted and served wine, two more served the entrée and the plat. Later, they presented cheese from a *chariot* and decadent desserts under glass domes. After dinner, we were escorted to the bar. We walked past a large portrait of Madame covered with bubbles to a contemporary space backed by a refrigerated wall stocked with Veuve Clicquot. It was an amazing evening.

RUINART

The following morning, we toured the public Veuve Clicquot *caves* and continued to Ruinart, where we gathered for lunch in a private dining room with a window wall adjacent to a garden. Once assembled at an all-white table, the curtains were drawn, the lights were dimmed electronically, and a magical, animated cartoon was projected from the ceiling onto our plates and even the tablecloth. The amazing theatrical performance illustrated the Ruinart story, from its start in the silk-trading business, for which they had an ongoing distribution network that was perfectly suited for the eventual wines they produced from 1729 to the present day.

Lunch was nice, too: oysters, turbot, *pintade* (guinea fowl), cheese, and pears—plus each of the four courses was paired with vintage Ruinart wines! (I spoke with the manager at Ruinart, who told me that he welcomes one and all to experience this unique event.)

MOËT & CHANDON

The following noon—after another gala dinner—we were feted by Moët & Chandon, the Champagne region's largest landowner, with twenty-five-hundred acres, and biggest producer with thirty million bottles annually. I was lucky to have been seated next to Benoit Gouez, chef du cave at Moët & Chandon, Winemaker of the Year 2013, and the person responsible for the annual production, though his impressive titles in no way interfered with his charm.

Winemaker Gouez politely tapped on his glass between courses, as is the custom at wine-centric feasts, where the host, winemaker, or sommelier explains each wine's complexities. In this particular setting, he explained that for this meal, the menu was determined by the wines rather than the other way around. And he described the terroir and the wines he had selected for us to drink: Grand Vintages

2009, 2002, and 2009 (a rosé). The chef paired those wine choices with bouillabaisse, lamb chops, and raspberry soufflés.

After the grand finale, M. Gouez—along with six toque-topped chefs, the entire kitchen brigade, plus the three servers who presented the gastronomic indulgence—posed for a picture.

When it was time for the group to board the van and head to the train, Jessica leaned over and whispered, "I thought you'd be more comfortable in a car." She directed me to the limo that she hired, courtesy of LVMH, to drive me from Épernay to CDG Paris, which was muchly, muchly appreciated.

P.S. A couple years later, after I learned that Jessica had moved to New York, I invited her to lunch. At the restaurant, when I noticed Ruinart on the wine list, I ordered a bottle to toast the wonderful few days together in Champagne.

un peu plus: FUN FACTS, CHAMPAGNE EDITION

During the two-hour drive back to Paris, I shared some recently learned history with the driver:

- Louis XV was the first to make it legal to transport champagne in bottles, which is how the royals learned to love it.
- During the French Revolution, the *citoyens* established a new calendar, called the Republican calendar, in which September 22 to October 21 was the first month of the year and named Vendémiaire to honor the vendange.
- M. Krug, a winemaker in Germany, whose great-grandson still runs the family business, inherited one hectare of vineyards from his boss in Germany and sold it to buy his first land in Champagne, where he established the maison in 1843.

MANOIR HENRI GIRAUD, AŸ

In 2021, when Val and I decided to spend three nights outside of Paris, I recommended Reims as the ideal destination. Our original plan was to stay at the centrally located and affordable Hotel de la Paix in Reims and do a day trip to wineries; instead, we ended up staying in the countryside and doing a day trip to Reims. Here's the story.

In January 2020, I met Rowena and Mark in the Priority Lounge at JFK, which is a perk for Chase Sapphire Reserve Card holders. We were all waiting for a flight to Barcelona, where I invited them on a walking tour and lunch with my colleague George, whom I had met on the Route Napoléon in 2004. Subsequently, during the pandemic, Rowena invited me to her weekly French class on Zoom. Almost two years later, when I mentioned plans to visit Champagne, Rowena encouraged me to make an appointment to visit her friend Claude at Champagne Henri Giraud, which I did.

Turns out that their friend, Claude Giraud, is the domaine owner of Champagne Henri Giraud, and he had just established a country inn, Manoir Henri Giraud, which opened in June 2020, smack in the middle of the pandemic. Subsequently, Claude invited me to stay at his new inn, which we did much to our delight.

Claude is the twelfth generation of an Aÿ vine-tending family dating to 1625, and his prestigious Giraud maison complex in Aÿ is one of only seventeen grand cru wine villages in the region. His wine emphasizes an *esprit sain* (a healthy spirit) and is called Triple Zero, because it is produced with zero herbicides, zero insecticides, and zero pesticides. In 2018, Henri Giraud became the first Champagne House, and the first estate in the world, to promise total transparency about its wine: via a QR code on the back label, customers have access to a full analysis of the wine, which is carried out by an independent laboratory.

For years, Claude Giraud harbored the idea of expanding the family wellness vision by creating a true *art de vivre* experience based on the concept of "healthy mind, healthy body." When he stepped down as winemaker, he devoted some of his creative energies to developing an intimate hotel, enlisting his good friend, the eminent architect Gerard Batalla, to execute the reimagined five-star, five-room, art-filled country escape.

A taxi transported Val and I the seventeen miles from Reims to Manoir Henri Giraud, an imposing three-story, stone-fronted nineteenth-century traditional manor house, with large windows (some of them arched) that the architect reconfigured with a modern, wood-faced, window-walled addition.

We walked through the garden to enter the reception area in the new addition with its high stone walls, and where the kitchen area is centered by a U-shaped tasting table. Steps at the far end of the room lead to a wine-walled boutique with a barrel-topped tasting table and a door to a private staircase. At the top of those stairs, Chambre 2, a spacious suite, houses a kitchenette and a bedroom with a sitting area and doors that open to a balcony overlooking the garden and neighboring vineyards. The sleeping area has a gorgeous gilded dome above the bed and a painting of a ridgeline behind it, and the rest of the room is furnished with a desk, a dining table, and a couple of blue upholstered armchairs. The spacious bathroom features a decorative floor-to-ceiling blue *Starry Night* wall, a standalone tub in front of a big picture window, a private toilet, a shower, and artisanal wooden *objets*—tub tray, towel rack, and toilet paper stand—custom crafted locally from used Argonne oak barrels.

un peu plus: THE ARGONNE FOREST

The word "Argonne" may be familiar to history buffs who recall that the Battle of the Argonne Forest was a turning point in World War I: it was the final offensive that forced the Germans to agree to the Armistice. At Maison Henri Giraud, Argonne refers to the specific kind of oak selected from the Argonne Forest, which the winemaker uses for wine barrels and which gives the wine a superior taste. In the manoir, reused Argonne oak is used for multiple practical and decorative objects. And one of the spa activities includes a walk in the forest for a *shinrin-yoku* (forest bathing) ritual, a wellness practice based upon the Japanese walk-in-the-forest tradition to connect with nature.

The afternoon Val and I arrived, we strolled from the manor to the center of Aÿ, a short walk, where we wanted to see the René Lalique statue, because the famous glass artist was a native son. It stands in front of the hôtel de ville and close to the boulangerie, boucherie, and *tratteur* (prepared foods store), where we bought food for our pique-nique supper in our room.

After a room-service breakfast, we walked down to the impressive spa and wellness center, with its two treatment rooms and a hammam. The blue-mosaic-tiled heated swimming pool is sided by hand-charred wood that was gilded, Japanese style, on-site, and incorporated into the décor. The pool is illuminated by a front-facing window wall and views of a fountain with its gilded centerpiece, an egg-shaped amphora, in the gated entry garden.

We hung our bathrobes on a sculptural coat stand that resembled a minimalist tree, also made of the same oak, and entered the couple's *cabine*. We each climbed onto a heated massage table for the signature service called *Crajothérapie*, which starts with a warmed mud wrap using local clay, known for its restorative, softening, and soothing properties. Afterward, we giggled trying to get our less-than-flexible selves into a double-size hydrotherapy tub for a bubbly bath, where I stayed to soak during her body massage before it was my turn to receive a wonderful massage.

The private winery visit we experienced is available to any visitor by appointment: We toured the cellars and had a wine tasting at a table constructed out of one long piece of Argonne Forest oak.

We also opted for a private seven-course Table Experience paired with Champagne Henri Giraud wines, which is also available to anyone who books it. Ebby, the manor's chef, cooked his custom-curated seasonal dishes in front of us, then served them paired with seven extraordinary house selections. And he showed us how to open a bottle without losing a drop of wine, claiming that it's an easy technique: "Six twists to remove the wire; then turn the bottle, not the cork!" Voilà! First, he poured a fruity Homage au Pinot Noir—a 100 percent chardonnay cuvée made in oak with 50 percent reserve wines—served with a roasted spiced pumpkin and a purple potato chip, made from blue-violet-colored *vitelotte* potatoes.

He suggested that his gratin of creamed *haricots blanc* (a white bean puree) made with pistachio oil paired nicely with the citrus notes of a highly iodized Blanc de Craie, and the minerality of MV16 contrasted with the richness of a chestnut foie gras crème brulée. Next, he poured a fruity Esprit Nature—which is pinot noir—to go with grilled scallops smoked in Argonne-oak sawdust from the cooperage. Then, a Dame-Jane, a rosé with tastes of strawberry and ginger, enhanced a rich brie with bacon.

The wine I liked best was Aÿ Rouge Grand Cru 2018, which he served with a locally sourced Magret duck breast. Ebby grilled the sous vide duck in front of us and served it with potatoes mashed with rosemary-infused butter. For dessert, he poured a glass of Ratafia Champenois Solera S90-16, which is a grape juice that has its alcoholic fermentation blocked by adding 17 percent fine champenoise. He served this with thinly sliced caramelized apples in local honey and topped with an artisanal ice cream flavored with Madagascar vanilla. It was quite the meal, and after all that wine, I was grateful for the short walk to bed.

The day we taxied to Reims, we started at La Maison Pommery, with its grand brick-trimmed doors that are typical of the region. Inside, the huge art-filled visitor center attracts 130,000 guests annually. After visiting the winery, we lunched amid whimsical décor in their restaurant, Le Réfectoire, and called a second taxi to take us to central Reims where we spent the afternoon sightseeing.

Épernay:
The Wine Capital of Champagne

The beautiful, walkable regional wine capital, Épernay, where opulent nineteenth-century mansions line the Avenue de Champagne, is only five miles from Aÿ and fourteen miles from Reims. It's claimed to be the world's richest street because it is located atop more than sixty miles of cellars and millions of valuable bottles. In 2018, when I attended the LVMH lunch at Moët & Chandon, I didn't tour the city; on this day, in 2021, we walked the avenue and visited Champagne de Vonage, a smaller, lesser-known winery, which was founded by a Swiss family in 1837.

At the visitor center, we ate cheese, charcuterie, and grilled vegetables served with baguettes in the lobby café. They served de Vonage Princes, told us that de Vonage was the first to launch a Blanc de Noirs, made with dark grapes, and showed us the Louis XV–decorated villa and one of the four guest suites.

Whether you stay in Reims and tour the wine region, or stay in or near Épernay and tour Reims, a day, overnight, or weekend trip to Champagne is worth your while.

Bordeaux, Biarritz, and Beyond

———◆◆◆———

T HE ILLUSTRIOUS AMERICAN OENOPHILE THOMAS Jefferson—who tried in vain for success as a vintner—endured weeks on a transatlantic crossing in May 1787, plus many days on horseback, on a mission to sniff, swirl, and sip La Tour de Ségur, a premier cru by Château Latour. Our third president was but one of the countless admirers of the world-class wines produced in the Bordeaux region, which is primarily known for its red merlot, cabernet sauvignon, and cabernet franc grapes. In the fourteenth and fifteenth centuries, Bordeaux wines were pale, and by the 1700s the British named them claret, which meant clear.

In today's world, it takes only two hours on the fast TGV train from Paris to reach Bordeaux, three hundred miles away, on the southwest Atlantic Coast. I was on one of those trains in 2006. By 2007, when I finally had the chance to stay in Bordeaux, the city was on its way to being ranked, as it is today, as France's second favorite city after Paris. One reason is that it boasts the second highest number of listed historic monuments, at 350.

Religious sanctuaries there include an abbey, a basilica, and multiple churches, plus there are gorgeous squares, glorious gardens, and a long pedestrian shopping street, rue Sainte-Catherine, with well-known shops, including Galleries Lafayette, Zara, and H&M. The place name, Bor d'eaux, refers to its position bordering the left and right banks of the Gironde, an estuary that tempers the climate and shapes its vintages. The unique and varied composition of the soil and its terroir influences these outstanding wines produced from an assemblage of thirteen authorized grape varieties used in the appellation.

Wine connoisseurs flock to more than fifteen hundred Bordeaux wineries these days, including such renowned labels as Haut-Brion, Lafite-Rothschild, Mouton Rothschild, and Pétrus. Visitors tour the distinctive regions of Medoc, Saint-Émilion, and Sauternes, and many join private guided visits and tastings at some of the best wineries: Château d'Yquem, Château Pavie, Château Pape Clément, and Château Smith Haut Lafitte. Wine-curious tourists also learn about the world of wine in La Cité du Vin, an architecturally exciting ten-story exhibition and tasting venue.

According to literature about Bordeaux (from the French Atlantic Coast site), "In the eighteenth century, Bordeaux was transformed from a medieval town with a tangle of filthy narrow lanes surrounded by swamp" into a "well-planned city of wide boulevards, harmonious streets, magnificent buildings, gardens, and busy quays." The port city made wealthy by the wine trade, boasts villas with glorious pale limestone facades decorated with distinctive wrought iron balconies and monuments adorned with stone masks, which are called *mascarons* in French, from the Italian word *mascherone*.

In Old Town Bordeaux—which is spread out on a curve along the western side of the River Garonne—there are more than five thousand eighteenth-century houses, among which many were restored in the 1980s and 1990s and are integral to the UNESCO listing as a World Heritage Site, which was awarded in 2007.

Early in the twenty-first century, the local government transformed the dark, dirty abandoned warehouses along the river and created pedestrian walkways; they even added high-tech transportation. In 2003, the city launched the smooth, silent Tramway de Bordeaux, which covers almost 50 miles with 133 tram stops, many in the exact places that I wanted to visit just a few years later.

While I was there, I noticed a cruise ship, one of the ones that ply the Atlantic from the UK to Biarritz and Bilbao, Spain. Nearby, along the riverfront, on the quay of Garonne in front of the Place de la Bourse, children joyfully frolicked in the Miroir d'eau (Water Mirror), the world's largest reflecting pool, which was designed by landscape artist Michel Corajoud and alternates a mirror effect and an artificial misting on a gigantic slab of granite. It was installed in 2006 and covers 37,100 square feet.

There's so much to see in Bordeaux: the Musée des Arts Decoratifs et du Design de Bordeaux (MADD), with interior displays of an eighteenth-century bourgeois mansion, and La Cité du Vin, a wine-centric cultural center that opened in 2016. If I were to return, I'd love to stay at The InterContinental Bordeaux–Le Grand (it was closed and being refurbished when I was there in 2007) in a room facing the Place de la Comédie and the Grand Théâtre de Bordeaux, which opened in 1780 and where the National Opera and National Ballet perform.

During my 2007 sojourn, I got to see the replica of the Caves of Lascaux, about a two-hour drive outside the city. Visitors are no longer permitted to see the original caves, with their ochre, red, and black animal drawings, because human breath destroys the fragile prehistoric cave art.

I also went twenty-five miles east of Bordeaux, a thirty-five-minute train trip, to the most alluring French village, Saint-Émilion, one of the oldest wine-producing regions in the world. It's known for its merlot, cabernet franc, and bold Médoc wines, which are blended with cabernet sauvignon. That day, I walked through a vineyard at the edge of town, toured the partly subterranean, twelfth-century Monolithic church, lunched in high style at the Hostellerie de Plaisance, and browsed in tiny boutiques along a steep cobblestone street.

LES SOURCES DE CAUDALIE

In September 2007, I extended my stopover in Bordeaux to experience another bucket-list spa destination: Les Sources de Caudalie, the world's first dedicated vinotherapy spa. By that time, I already had a keen interest in vinotherapy, a therapy that incorporates the vitamin-enriched antioxidant properties of grape skins and pips, and I had featured the first-person treatments that I had experienced at former Caudalie outposts in New York City, Paris, and Sonoma, California. Naturally, I was eager to try grape-based treatments at their "source."

At breakfast the morning before my departure, a rude young woman at the next table was loudly—and repeatedly—demanding that the innkeeper tell her driver to wait until she finished breakfast. The previous afternoon, I walked away from reception because she was berating the innkeepers. Knowing that she could go on and on, I wasn't about to let her verbal abusiveness put a damper on a day that I expected (rightly) to be incredible. I left my hot cup of coffee on the table, rushed out of the lovely Hôtel Bord'eaux dining room, and waited for my taxi outside.

The driver reached the vineyard estate in Martillac, about ten miles away, in less than thirty minutes. It's in the Graves wine region, a subregion of Bordeaux, located on the left bank of the Garonne River, the side closest to the Atlantic Ocean. The wellness compound occupies one part of the sculpture-studded Château Smith

Haut Lafitte wine estate vineyards, where owners Florence and Daniel Cathiard, former French national ski team champions, live in the original château built by George Smith in 1739. After their impressive athletic careers, the entrepreneurial couple expanded the family grocery store chain, Genty-Cathiard, into one of France's top-ten distribution businesses, and launched GO Sport sporting goods stores. Their friend, the famous French skier and wine enthusiast Jean-Claude Killy, introduced them to Bordeaux.

I arrived too early to check into my room, so I deposited my luggage at reception and set out to explore the beauty of the pastoral property before lunch, making a mental note of it all: impeccable grounds, manicured hedges, a horse-drawn plow, a *potager* (kitchen garden), and a little farm with chickens that supplies fresh eggs.

This open-to-the-public portion of the resort includes the spa pavilion, a window-walled restaurant, and various timbered lodgings that have been charmingly converted to serve as country-chic hotel rooms. From the outside, they reminded me of Marie Antoinette's Le Hameau at Versailles, except these buildings welcomed down-to-earth spa-goers, not just royalty. The construction repurposed building materials gleaned from local abandoned farmhouses, including beams from one barn claimed to have come from a local Rothschild estate—a detail that indicated that the owners were dedicated to sustainability before it was a trend. My room was decorated with one accent color: a deep, purple-tinged, Bordeaux-wine red.

At lunch, a well-turned-out crowd filled the dining room in the rustic La Table du Lavoir. They looked to me to be prosperous wine merchants, vintners, domaine owners, and culinarians who, I assumed, were meeting for business lunches. In addition, there was a leisure clientele, probably visitors to the region like me, and local regulars. Although the members of the country gentry were not formally dressed, their clothes were tasteful—tweed or cashmere blazers and soft-soled shoes—and even the jean-clad teenagers were wearing soft leather jackets. I noticed this because the ambiance was far more cosmopolitan than at most destination spas, where in-house spa-goers typically lunch in workout gear and rarely dine with the sophisticated public.

The menu featured fabulous regional ingredients that the former chef, Franck Salein, sourced locally: Aquitaine honey, Arachon oysters, Bazas beef, Blayais asparagus, Médoc mushrooms, Pauilliac lamb, and so on through the alphabet. He featured a full range of local items, including caviar, cheese, duck, fish, foie gras, lobster, and pigeon. I valued the Asian touches in that lunch: the fat white asparagus was flavored with ginger and the red tuna fillet was served with wasabi and rice cake swirls.

After a lengthy meal, I arrived at the spa facility where, instead of a dressing room with individual lockers, they had an unusual storage system for everyone's clothes. Each arrival approached an open window within the dressing room, where a matron handed the client a bathrobe on a numbered hanger with an attached basket. Then, after donning a bathing suit and bathrobe, the client returned the hanger with the basket now filled with clothes, and watched the matron hang it high on a moving machine (it resembled the one at my dry cleaners). With time to spare before my scheduled treatment, I headed to the natural spring-fed thermal indoor pool and lounged under the high ceiling feeling like a happy camper and looking forward to trying a body treatment that used antioxidant-rich grape seeds and skins.

My barrel bath came first: it was a simple long soak in a wine-barrel-shaped hot tub appropriately placed in front of a large picture window overlooking rows of grapevines. As the service came to an end, an attendant offered me a glass of red wine, a welcome amenity that I remembered from former Caudalie treatments. Next came the Cabernet Crush, an exfoliating treatment using textured—but not coarse—grape seeds mixed with local Gironde honey. That was followed by the Premier Cru Treatment, which moisturizes the skin and includes an antiaging *masque* and massage with a rich premier cru cream.

The most memorable moments took place the following day, during my rendezvous with Florence Cathiard, who invited me to visit her at her home in the grand château, which I reached via a lovely stroll on sculpture-lined paths that cut through the vineyard. Mme. Cathiard shared the origin story of vinotherapy.

un peu plus: HISTORY OF CAUDALIE

During the 1993 harvest season, the Cathiards' daughter Mathilde was walking the Smith Haut Lafitte wine estate with her husband, Bertrand Thomas, when they met Professeur Joseph Vercauteren, an eminent professor and noteworthy director of the pharmaceutical faculty in Bordeaux. Professor Vercauteren, who noticed a pile of discarded grape seeds and grape skins, informed the couple that the grape pips contained antioxidant-rich polyphenols. *"Savez-vous que vous jetez des trésors?"* ("Do you know that you are throwing away treasures?") He explained that the powerful effects of polyphenols in promoting blood circulation and against aging were far too valuable to discard. The entrepreneurial pioneers embarked in further scientific research and, in 1995, founded the vinotherapy industry. Caudalie Vinothérapie uses the grape skins and seeds for numerous beautifying and antiaging products, including face masks and toners, body scrubs, and hand/foot services.

The Cathiards' second daughter, Alice, and her hotelier husband, Jerome Tourbier, own and operate Les Sources de Caudalie, which they launched in 1999 and have continually improved through the years. Since my visit in 2007, the hotel has expanded into its own little six-house hamlet, with sixty-two rooms and suites, which were entirely redecorated in a more contemporary, still elegant style between 2022 and 2023. (One exclusive getaway less than a mile from the hotel complex is a historic private retreat with nine rooms and two suites.)

The fabulous meals there showcase one-Michelin-star-chef Franck Salein's preparations. The chef, who met me at their wine bar, Le French Paradox, for a before-dinner apéro, chose a (quite memorable) white Smith Haut Lafitte for me from the bar's fifteen-thousand-bottle cellar, which features the region's best choices. It was quite the treat for me to taste my first Château Smith Haut Lafitte, which was classified in 1842. Here's what I read about it: "The Smith Haut Lafitte 2001 red has a reputation as the 'Gravest of the Graves,' consistently earning high praise from experts and laymen alike."

I asked Chef Salein about some specific ingredients that I had remembered from lunch, and he expanded upon the richness of the region and his warm relationship with the owners of the local purveyors. He also gave me a copy of his cookbook, *Flavours Bordeaux*.

Later that evening, at the super-chic La Grand'Vigne restaurant, I ordered the five-hundred-calorie spa cuisine prix fixe menu, a gastronomic three-course meal. Haute spa cuisine has always intrigued me, as a spa-goer and foodie, because it's astonishing how satisfying some low-fat, low-calorie meals are. Chefs accomplish miracles with their talent, creativity, wonderful products, and, *sans doute*, the staff to do all the prep work—the time-consuming expert cutting, chopping, and dicing that the French call mise en place. Chef Salein, who overcame his own weight issues, diligently learned how to prepare what he calls a "hypercalorific" way of cooking. He presented exquisite vegetables, smallish but satisfying servings of beef, and a sweet white-grape sorbet with low-cal, delicious ladyfingers. I am confident that if there were helpers in my kitchen to prep vegetables for such artfully healthy meals I'd be slimmer!

Chef Salein departed the hotel since that 2007 visit and is currently senior corporate executive chef for Seabourn Cruise Lines. The current chef, Nicolas Masse, was awarded two Michelin stars at the restaurant La Grand'Vigne.

un peu plus: SPA CUISINE AT CAUDALIE

This quote is from the *New York Times* article "Bordeaux's Culinary Stars" by Ed Alcock. It appeared on April 20, 2008, some months after my trip. Note the cost of the 2008 meal! "What does roughly 500 calories get you? Three very flavorful, oddly satisfying courses, such as a cheese-like scallop mousse rolled in emerald ribbons of zucchini, served with sweet dehydrated beet chips and beet purée (115 delicious calories); four rosy slices of beef surrounded by tiny vegetables and a sauce that was nearly identical to the puréed vegetable soup my sick fiancé ordered from room service (265 meaty calories); and a zingy passion fruit dessert served with white-grape sorbet and lady fingers (120 unstingy calories). Three of these courses range from 69 to 86 euros."

On the train back to Paris, I opened the cookbook and read Chef Salein's inscription:

To Irvina
It's always a pleasure to meet people who like to share a conversation about food.
  Un plaisir en cache un autre . . .
  Ravi de vous avoir rencontre.
  (One pleasure hides another . . .
  Delighted to have met you.)
19.9.07
Franck Salein

The cookbook features thirty-six recipes, full-page bios of the many local producers from whom he sources ingredients, and a culinary philosophy that relates to my own. Here are two quotes that express his personal taste:

"Gastronomy is the choice of products. In the kitchen, it is only a question of putting things together, cooking, and presentation."

"My principle is that a chef should make ingredients nobler through his techniques and not try to deconstruct them."

During my all-too-short overnight stay, I cherished moments in the spa, in restaurants, at the *tonnerie*—where they make wine barrels—and at a tasting in the gala-reception-ready *cave*, where they pour delicious wines and offer English- and French-speaking tours daily.

chez moi: FRANCK SALEIN'S TOMATO CONFIT

Several Salein recipes start with the preparation of tomato confit, which he serves with grilled scallops, roasted lamb loin, beef onglet (hanger steak), and roasted asparagus spears. He adds it to salads and frittatas, and as an hors d'oeuvre it tops bruschetta, crostini, or a large crouton. For a puff pastry tart, he adds fresh basil, and for relish, he adds red wine vinegar, capers, olives, and fresh herbs. I follow his basic recipe and skin and remove seeds from four tomatoes, quarter them, place them on a parchment-lined baking sheet, and toss with salt, pepper, olive oil, thyme, garlic, bay leaves, and other available herbs. Soft tomatoes fall apart, so I use firm ones and roast the confit for four hours at 200°F.

Biarritz

Bob had a business trip to Biarritz sometime in the late 1990s, and I organized an itinerary around it that focused on my dream destination list, starting with Hotel du Palais in Biarritz. When we arrived at the Biarritz train station, we immediately walked to Budget, with all our paperwork handy, including our confirmation and driving licenses ready to show.

That didn't seem to matter when we confronted the first—and only—truly discourteous, imperious, and rude French individual that I've ever met. She was beyond unhelpful and typified the negative generalization of a pompous bureaucrat. I imagine she was miserable with her lot in life, because she had no cause to be nasty to us. Once we were in the car and driving through the elegant seaside city to Hôtel du Palais, those few unpleasant minutes were forgotten.

HÔTEL DU PALAIS

We arrived at the palace, a notable brick-red-and-beige belle époque mansion with a mansard roof, which Napoleon III built c. 1854 as a token of affection for his wife, Empress Eugénie. She was a Spanish royal from Granada, who had vacationed in the Basque seafront as a child and loved it so much that they set up their summer Imperial Court in the palace. In 1893, two decades after the end of the Second Empire, the building became a hotel.

I barely entered before realizing how right my spa colleague and good friend, Bernard Burt, had been; he had stayed there and told me that I'd love the hotel. The interior was sumptuous, with crystal chandeliers hanging from high ceilings, a grand staircase, marble floors and mantels, oversize windows and massive doors, and gilded ceilings and window frames.

Our grand suite was at the top of the curved staircase, which I loved walking up and down. The apartment—it was far grander than a suite—included a gracious foyer, a large living room, and a window-walled, semicircular dining room that faced the sea and opened out to a vast semicircular terrace above La Rotonde Restaurant. I was told that foreign royalty and their security team were ensconced in the apartment above ours. Their apartment was "safer" than ours because it didn't have a terrace, where someone with bad intentions might scale a wall, enter, and cause harm. We had no such fears.

I was captivated by all the historic Second Empire details in the public spaces: original gold leaf, splendid marbles, and antique furnishings. I simply did not want to leave such a magical place and asked the longtime general manager, Jean-Louis Leimbacher, who has since retired, if we could extend our reservation. When he agreed, we shortened our hotel reservation in the nearby Basque seaside resort town, Saint-Jean-de-Luz.

When I returned to stay in Saint-Jean-de-Luz in 2012, I made it a priority to schedule a facial at the Hotel du Palais's new five-floor spa. I left a message with M. Leimbacher that I would love to say hello and planned to be at the bar at 6:00 p.m. Lady Luck appeared in the guise of the elegant recipient of "The Best Hotel Manager in Europe," and during an apéro together, I commented on all the workers who were gilding mirrors, door and window frames, and the ceiling. M. Leimbacher told me that the city owns the historic property and reinvests all profits for hotel maintenance and preservation.

P.S. When people ask me, "What is your favorite hotel in the world?" I never pause before answering Hôtel du Palais Biarritz, because of its décor, service, location . . . everything! Today, it's managed by Unbound Collection by Hyatt and is one of thirty-one five-star hotels whose status has been elevated to "palace" distinction.

LES PRÉS D'EUGÉNIE

Bob and I departed from the luxe and formal ambiance of Biarritz and headed east through the pristine rural countryside between the Landes and Béarn regions of France. Within ninety minutes, we arrived in Eugénie-les-Bains, named for the empress, who granted her patronage to the small spa town in 1861. From then on, it became the place to be seen and where guests "take the waters." We drove into Les Prés d'Eugénie, a rustic and charming resort that is equally as classy and memorable as the seaside hotel, though with a provincial vibe.

Les Prés d'Eugénie, the famous spa hotel, is a forty-acre resort complex developed by Michel and Christine Guérard, a couple who seemed to be born into the hospitality industry. Chef Michel Guerard comes from the world of great French chefs and his haute cuisine minceur had been on my wish list forever. He is acknowledged for having revolutionized Gascon fare, is considered the father of "nouvelle cuisine," and claimed to have invented "cuisine minceur." His spa cuisine is served at La Table des Prés d'Eugénie, which has held its three Michelin stars for the past forty years. "The point of slimming cuisine is that it is delicious," Mr. Guérard told the European Food website in 2017. "You don't feel like you're making a sacrifice. Moreover, you eat what you need. You are not starved." Sadly, this great chef died at age ninety-one on August 19, 2024, just two years after losing his wife.

I had heard that his wife's family had long been involved in the Soleil Thermale chain of spas and about her talent and expertise in the wellness community. Christine Guérard's father had purchased the property in Eugénie-les-Bains about ten years before the couple took over its stewardship. The estate feels more like a pastoral farm village than a resort, with charming lodgings, an aquatic spa facility with a medical staff (doctors, dietitians, and physiotherapists), and a swimming pool and tennis courts. En route, the walkways pass kitchen gardens, where *bio* produce is grown for use in their restaurants.

Madame Guérard's inimitable taste and her affection for mid-nineteenth-century country antiques is apparent throughout and reflected in the ambiance and décor. I fell in love with the French Provençal design in our little cottage—complete with toile fabric and wallpaper—and her signature collectibles, which included a bevy of old stoves that decorate the covered walkways.

Two hot springs supply the mineral waters used for short- or long-term thermal cures that take place in a neoclassical building called The Great Baths and at La Ferme Thermale Spa, which is housed in a more rustic eighteenth-century building. I spent much of the morning in the spa, enjoying the steam bath, a massage, and the mineral-rich heated waters that are thought to help digestive and urinary disorders and regulate the metabolism. (Hotter waters are recommended for rheumatism and osteoarthritis.)

We had a lovely lunch at the rustic La Ferme aux Grives, where they serve hearty farm fare from the Landes region, which is known for its chickens, ducks, and foie gras. But later that afternoon, I developed a rare and truly horrible headache. Though I managed to get out of bed and walk to our long-awaited reservation at La Table des Prés d'Eugénie, I was barely able to appreciate the dinner I had so longed to experience.

What I read about a meal there published in *France Today* in 2010, gives a better sense of that haute spa cuisine menu than I can remember: ". . . the oreiller moelleux de mousserons et de morilles aux asperges, an ambrosial pasta pillow filled with duxelles of five varieties of mushrooms and a truffle purée; an amazing floating island of truffled iced pea soup; and a warm strawberry tart with a feather-light lemon mousse. A recent discovery: just-opened oysters *à la perle*, with a ginger, coriander, and green-coffee-laced foam magnifying the ocean-fresh flavor of the best oysters I've ever tasted."

Except for the rental agent and that headache, Bob and I had the best time traveling and dining together on the trip. We traveled like a well-executed team: he usually drove long distances from here to there and, when we arrived where he wanted to take pictures, I took over the wheel so he could easily jump out of the car to shoot. It's nice to relish that idyllic region and the good times we shared there.

Lyon: Auvergne-Rhône-Alpes

————— •◆• —————

THE TWO-THOUSAND-YEAR-OLD CAPITAL OF THE Rhône department in the Auvergne-Rhône-Alpes region is Lyon, the third-largest French city, after Paris and Marseille. *Vieux Lyon*, the Old City, was settled in Roman times, where the Saône and the Rhône rivers meet. The Rhône Valley wine region borders the river for 125 miles from Vienne to Avignon; as an Appellation d'Origine Contrôlée (AOC), it is the country's second-largest producer after Bordeaux and its most familiar beverage is Châteauneuf-du-Pape, from southern Rhône. Lyon itself is best known for its full-bodied red wines, such as Côtes du Rhône, Hermitage, and Saint-Joseph, made from Gamay and Pinot noir grapes, and for the popular Beaujolais Nouveau, which is released each year on the third Thursday of November and produced in the Beaujolais region, less than an hour's drive north of Lyon.

The city has a remarkable history, with revolutions and two world wars, but it is best known as the gastronomic capital of France.

That was what influenced me to stop in Lyon during my train journey from Nice to Paris in 1990. I longed to taste preparations by its two greatest chefs, Paul Bocuse and Alain Chapel. Murphy's Law prevailed: "Anything that can go wrong will go wrong." I missed both gastronomic temples on that trip.

Sadly, a week earlier, while I was touring the Riviera, Chef Chapel, then fifty-two years old, died suddenly of a stroke on July 10, 1990. His status is still so revered that when recently asked about his best meal ever, a gourmand acquaintance responded: "It took place decades ago at a restaurant outside Lyon. The chef was Alain Chapel."

The evening that I arrived in the city, I checked into the hotel later than expected. When I asked for a taxi to Restaurant Bocuse, the concierge told me that the Auberge du Pont de Collonges, its original name, would be closed by the time I could get there because it was too far away. He recommended the nearby Restaurant Pierre Orsi.

RESTAURANT PIERRE ORSI

"Desolé, Madame. La cuisine est fermée, le chef est parti." Surprisingly, Madame didn't send me away, but instead welcomed me warmly, explaining that the kitchen was closed and that the chef had left. En route to a table, she assured me that she'd find something that would please me. "*Pas de problème,*" she said.

I wondered if the desk clerk had called her, because Madame, who had never seen me before, treated me like a favored regular. She was so hospitable—and so chic—that I suspected that she might be "family" and not some hired host. (An internet search confirmed that the personable *patronne* who greeted me was Geneviève Orsi, Maître de Maison of the Relais Gourmand affiliated with Relais & Châteaux, which—after nearly fifty years of culinary excellence—permanently closed in 2023.)

Madame disappeared into the kitchen and returned with items from *la garde manger,* the station where salades, hors d'œuvres, appetizers, canapés, pâtés, and terrines are prepared. With a glass of wine, perfect bread, and sweet butter, I was already satisfied before the arrival of *une tranche de paté* (a slice of paté) with little salad greens. Then, she brought a cheese selection followed by some *confisseries*, the tiny sweets that follow formal desserts.

As I time-travel back to that idyllic late supper thirty years ago, it's still the perfect meal, and far lighter than the dinner I had yearned for at Restaurant Bocuse. I still can't fathom how I missed that opportunity. Was the train late? Did I misjudge the timing from the train to the hotel to the restaurant? Should I have taxied to the restaurant (with luggage) before going to the hotel? I don't know.

The Silk City

Lyon was awarded the title *Lyon-Patrimoine Mondiale*, a UNESCO World Heritage Site, in December 1998, to honor the city's heritage, history, architecture, art, culture, traditions, industry, and food. The French Tourist Office invited some travel writers to experience events there and included me.

The trip started with a Stateside mini drama on a rare morning when Bob was available to drive me to the airport. I offered to carry my bag out to the car, a task he usually handled, but it never dawned on me to lift it into the back of the van. I left it on the ground, assuming Bob would see it and take care of it. I returned inside, and by the time we were ready to leave, I had completely forgotten to ask about the bag, which he hadn't noticed.

After an easy forty-minute drive to JFK, I kissed Bob goodbye, stepped onto the curb, and opened the empty trunk. There was not enough time for him to drive home and back, so while trying to calm my hysteria about the prospective cost of buying a week's worth of "stuff" at retail prices, I made a desperate call to a neighbor.

Her husband was willing to pick up the suitcase from my driveway and bring it to the airport and, luckily for me, arrived just before they announced the flight. Crisis averted!

In Lyon, I admired lovely rose-colored Renaissance buildings, the Romanesque and Byzantine architecture at the Basilique Nôtre-Dame de Fourvière, and Gothic architecture at the Cathédrale Saint-Jean Baptiste. A visitor needn't know the names of architectural styles to appreciate the appeal of the very old juxtaposed with the up-to-the-minute.

A case in point happened while touring a *traboule* in a Renaissance-era building, where I felt like a fly on the wall at a fashion shoot for *Vogue*, watching a contemporary scene set in the vestige of centuries past. We were walking through one of the city's four hundred pastel-colored interior covered passageways, where some date to the fourth century, when a trendy young woman dressed to the nines in a miniskirt and stiletto heels rushed by under the vaulted ceiling. Was this fashionista hurrying home? Was she late for a business appointment? Was she rushing to meet a lover?

Touring those traboules, I learned about the deep roots of the city's silk industry and its intrinsic role in the city's *patrimoine*. Traboules showcase Middle Age and Renaissance architecture as they wind through buildings in the Croix-Rousse neighborhood down Fourvière Hill to the Saône River.

Originally, *canuts* (silk workers) used the remarkable interior passageways to transport fabrics from workshops down to riverside dealers to avoid the dirty streets and bad weather. (Guides, walking tours, and DIY directions help visitors see the forty trabules open to the public. The route I wanted to see started at the green door at 54 rue Saint-Jean, identified as "La Longue Traboule," and crosses five courtyards and four buildings.)

Louis XI chose the city to become the center of a silk-weaving industry in 1466, because it was on the river route to the Mediterranean; the city has reigned as the world's preeminent center of silk manufacturing ever since. In 1535, Francis I granted a royal charter to two Italian silk merchants, who built a school to teach young girls how to weave silk; by 1620, there were more than ten thousand silk looms. The industry prospered until the French Revolution began in 1789, when revolutionaries destroyed looms and production dropped 90 percent. It survived the Napoleonic era, in the early 1800s, but failed during the Canut revolt in the 1830s. Workers used those passageways to sneak into the city center and take over the town. A century later, during World War II, the French Resistance used the same secret corridors to evade the Nazis.

Among the city's public events to celebrate the *Patrimoine* was an unforgettable Hermès pop-up exhibit, "Hermès Scarf Printing 101." Watching the creation of scarf art was fascinating, with its complex craftsmanship during various stages, and it enticed me to buy my first Hermès scarf. I remembered wanting, and not buying, the Giverny scarf years earlier, and I decided that it would be a perfect pre-sixtieth birthday present to myself. I mused about the expense briefly, then purchased *Jungle Love*—a pale-aqua square with a leopard motif—which I still pack often.

un peu plus: HERMÈS

In 1937, Hermès restored the silk tradition by introducing its luxurious sought-after scarves. At first, the raw silk came from China, was spun into yarn, woven into fabric, and individually screen-printed from a woodblock design by Robert Dumas, a family member. Now the silk comes from mulberry moth cocoons in Brazil, and even today, it takes eighteen months to make one scarf. Hermès designers spend months creating a design for the two collections each season. Sometimes they spend six months choosing the colors from a cache of seventy-five thousand different shades. The next and most time-consuming process, silk printing, called *méthode lyonnaise,* takes 750 hours. While most manufacturers use eight to ten colors in a silk scarf, the typical thirty-six-inch-square Hermès scarf has twenty-seven colors, with some having more than forty. Each color uses a separate engraving screen and fills in certain spaces on the stretched silk, like a paint-by-numbers canvas. Here, however, the designs are complicated with only teeny spaces allotted for each color. Until 1937, scarves were printed on one side. Now, with an innovative procedure, they are printed on both sides. Even the scarves' edges are the result of painstaking activity, as each is hand-rolled and hand-stitched. An expert seamstress can complete only seven scarves in a day! If you are checking to see if a scarf is fake, look at the edges.

My favorite Lyon museum is Le Musée des Tissus (The Textile and Fabric Museum) near Place Bellefour in centre-ville, dedicated to the local silk and textile industry. Opened in 1864, it is located within one of two six-story manses from the eighteenth and nineteenth centuries that have been transformed into house museums. The one next door is Le Musée des Arts Decoratifs (the Fine Arts Museum).

That trip I went to my first Christmas market in France, and the artisanal crafts and edible pleasures, sold by vendors in cabana-size wooden huts, delighted me. Among the abundance of candied fruit and mulled wine, I discovered silky, rich, delicious *aligot,* which are oh-so-cheesy mashed potatoes.

chez moi: ALIGOT LYONNAISE

In Lyon, this outrageously rich, fondue-like mashed, cheesy, creamy whipped potato dish is made with two pounds of Tomme cheese, two sticks of butter, and 1½ cups heavy cream. In my calorie-conscious kitchen, I boil and mash 4 pounds of peeled Yukon Gold potatoes, substitute whole milk or half-and-half for cream, add 1 stick or less of butter, and salt and pepper. I beat in about 8 ounces grated Gruyère and mozzarella until smooth. (The potatoes can be stored in an airtight container in the fridge before adding cheese and reheated over boiling water in a bain marie.) It's good, not Lyon Christmas market good, but rich enough for me and my guests.

PAUL BOCUSE

In the world of gastronomy, Paul Bocuse, whose chef-studded family dates to 1765, earned innumerable accolades, awards, and titles. He won the distinguished Meilleur Ouvrier de France (MOF = best chef) award in 1961 and retained his three Michelin stars, without interruption, from 1965 until 2020, two years *after* his death!

Dining at Restaurant Bocuse in 1998 was the highlight of that December trip and the next, in 2001, when Bob and I had dinner there the night our riverboat cruise from Dijon debarked in Lyon. Although we were bursting at the seams from the multitude of on-board meals and a few onshore epicurean lunches, we couldn't wait for our gastronomic grand finale at Restaurant Bocuse!

The first time I saw the large neon letters—Paul Bocuse—perched atop the boldly painted pistachio-colored building with deep raspberry murals and brightly painted shutters, I thought it looked like Vegas. The ground-floor courtyard façade showcases culinary-themed trompe l'oeil murals, some featuring recognizable chefs with whom Bocuse has worked, others with obvious product placements. In one, Bocuse waves to arriving guests; in another, he appears in a large portrait inside the former family home.

I wasn't yet familiar enough with the city to know that murals are intrinsic to Lyon's cultural heritage and thought it belonged at Walt Disney World, where his son, Jérôme Bocuse, manages *Les Chefs de France* brasserie in Epcot's French Pavilion.

The restaurant's interior was remarkable, too. I recall painted and gilded ceilings, arched doorways, curtained windows, patterned wallpaper and floors, and lighted chandeliers. It was a busy, formal, ornate, and somewhat over-the-top backdrop for tables with white tablecloths and tall leather chairs, but it felt *"comme il faut,"* (as it should be) for this traditional old-world, elevated cuisine. Current images posted on the restaurant website and in YouTube clips illustrate rooms with a far more refined décor, with gorgeous millwork, pale ceilings, serene grays, and creamy white walls tastefully displaying framed photographs and objets d'art.

One classic Bocuse dish impressed me on both occasions, *soupe aux truffes Élysée,* with its golden-dome crust rising many inches above the individually decorated, ovenproof soup tureen, which is a replica of the one served to the *président de la République.* The magic is created in a super-hot oven, which steams the soup and puffs up layers of traditional French paté feuilletée into a buttery bubble.

un peu plus: CRAIG CLAIBORNE

The late food editor and critic for the *New York Times,* Craig Claiborne, wrote about Bocuse's 1975 visit to his Long Island home: "When Paul Bocuse, who is almost indisputably the most famous chef in the world, made his presence known in our kitchen, he had in his satchel a kilogram of Stygian black truffles valued at slightly more than $200. He would combine these with cubes of truffled fois gras, a hastily made but rich and full-bodied chicken consommé, and a topping of butter-layered puff pastry. This soup would be placed in the oven at 2:15 p.m. and 20 minutes later, 16 guests would sit down to dine on the soup from dishes marked '*Palais de l'Elysée, 25 Février 1975, soupe aux truffes V.G.E. Paul Bocuse.*'" The bowls commemorated the soup he prepared for Valéry Giscard d'Estaing, France's president, when he awarded Bocuse with France's Legion of Honor.

The "mythical" Monsieur Paul worked the room and charmed guests at both dinners; he was attired in his spiffy chef's jacket, with a Paul Bocuse signature monogram and the distinctive blue and red piping around the mandarin collar, which is exclusive to only those who earn MOF stature. His tall, white-starched toque extended his 5 feet, 11 inches and, from my seated vantage point, "Monsieur Paul" appeared like a jolly, towering giant. He was a very nice one who, on my second visit, acted as if he remembered me—a honed-to-perfection talent that some in the hospitality business manage to attain—and amiably invited us to tour his copper-pot-decorated kitchen. He even gave me time to mingle with the group of intent chefs busily working at individual stations around the huge square stove.

The following day, I noticed some of the city's 150 whimsical murals and the most famous: La Fresque des Lyonnais or Mural of the Lyonnais, an eight-thousand-square-foot award-winning trompe l'oeil opus painted on a windowless seven-story corner building. The work showcases thirty prominent "who's who" in the city: Laurent

Mourguet, the puppeteer-creator of Guignol; the Lumière Brothers, who created the first motion picture camera and cinematography; author Antoine de Saint-Exupéry with his curly-haired goldilocks, the Little Prince; and, *bien sur*, super-chef Paul Bocuse.

Seeing them, I realized that the Bocuse murals are intrinsic to a true sense of place: Lyon.

Three years passed before I met M. Paul for the third time, on this occasion it was in the countryside, at Laffrey, outside Grenoble, in September 2004, when Bocuse hosted a magnificent *pique-nique* for the *Association Amie de l'Automobile Ancienne de Grenoble* (Antique Automobile Club of Grenoble), on the last day of the Rallye de l'Empéreur. He served glasses of a white Apremont 2002 from Savoie, and delicacies, including his renowned game *paté en croute*. The always imposing emperor of gastronomy was even more prominent in the broad, black Napoleonic hat he was wearing. He greeted us warmly and explained, "My great-great-great-grandfather served in Napoleon's honor guard."

By the time I saw him there in his Napoleonic salute, he was at the peak of the culinary world and named "Cook of the Century, 2004" by Gault & Millau, "Chef of the Century, 2011," by the Culinary Institute of America, and his name was associated with the International Gastronomic Competition, established in 1987, called Bocuse d'Or, the classic French restaurant at the CIA, the Institut Paul Bocuse hospitality school, and the marketplace Les Halles de Lyon Paul Bocuse. In popular culture, his large personality is claimed to have inspired the role of chef Auguste Gusteau in the movie *Ratatouille*.

Bocuse's macho reputation is almost as familiar as his talents, and well-recorded. According to Craig Claiborne, when Bocuse was asked: "Why have there been so few women chefs throughout history?" he replied: "Women lack the instincts for great cooking. It follows in the same sense that there are so few great women archi-tects and orchestra leaders. Women who become chefs are limited in their accomplishments."

Colleagues took notice of his sexism in real time. One expressed surprise by the comment; another excused it, like this: "he said it to enhance his heavily macho and high-profile sex image." The ever-diplomatic Eric Ripert—the famed three-Michelin-star French chef/restaurateur at Le Bernardin in Manhattan—referred discreetly to his reputation as a "bon vivant," when speaking about Bocuse in a May 2021 podcast.

Considering his age—Bocuse was born in 1926—and occupa-tion in a male-dominated vocation, this sexist opinion would be understandably typical were it not for the fact that his own illustri-ous career started in the kitchen of the single most prestigious female chef of the twentieth century, La Mère Brazier. Here's how Bocuse acknowledged his youthful experience working for Mère Brazier during an interview with a reporter at Associated Press: "There was rigor, you had to wake up early and milk the cows, feed the pigs, do the laundry, and cook . . . It was a tough school of hard knocks."

In a 1970s interview, he famously claimed that he would "rather have a woman in his bed than behind the stove in his restaurant." Naturally, the remark garnered media attention. And news reports decades later commented that his wife and a few long-term lovers at-tended his funeral in 2018. That scene implied that he liked women personally, if not professionally, and they him.

So why had he dissed the very idea of female chefs? He may simply have been a provocateur who sought publicity for chefs in general, and himself in particular. He is justly credited for using his media savvy to elevate the position of "chef" from a behind-the-scenes laborer to a front-of-the-camera celebrity.

chez moi: PAUL BOCUSE-INSPIRED SOUPE AUX TRUFFES ELYSÉE

The original Bocuse-inspired *Soupe aux Truffles Élysée* recipe is a colossally extravagant dish, with vermouth in the broth, thinly sliced truffles, and diced foie gras, all of which is covered with puff pastry and sealed with an egg yolk wash. The pastry puffs in 20 minutes in a 450°F oven. Home cooks can substitute less costly mushrooms for truffles or chicken liver instead of foie gras, and can even use prepared stock and Dufour or Pepperidge Farm frozen puff pastry.

LES MÈRES LYONNAISES

It sounds counterintuitive, but the silk industry is inextricably linked to Lyon's reputation as the gastronomic capital of France for a simple reason. After the 1830 Canut uprising and the collapse of the silk industry, the once prosperous bourgeois dealers could no longer afford to pay their home cooks. Several jobless women who needed to earn a living founded small convivial and casual eateries called bouchons, which became the signature down-to-earth restaurants where common folks in Lyon were served lusty, bold, earthy, often pork-centric dishes on wooden tables, often in the chef's home.

Les Mères Lyonnaises shopped the morning markets, prepared the midday meals, and operated their bouchons. They founded Lyon gastronomy and became the face and the backbone of the city's culinary history. In these individual shrines to pigs, a worker might savor a smoky pork sausage with pistachios served on a dollop of mashed potatoes with a cream sauce.

Mère Fillioux, aka Françoise Fayolle, was the first superstar Mères Lyonnaises, known for poaching chicken inside a pig's bladder, sous-vide style, to preserve the succulent juices inside the bird. Her distinguished name still appears on the Bocuse menu, where the classic dish is one of the restaurant's most popular and served tableside with a flourish: *Volaille de Bresse en Vessie à la mère Fillioux* (chicken in a pork bladder in the style of Mère Fillioux).

Mère Brazier, aka Eugénie Brazier, started her career in the all-female kitchen of Mère Fillioux and began welcoming diners to her own place in 1921. A dozen years later, she was the first female chef anointed by the Michelin guide. She held three stars for twenty-eight years at La Mère Brazier restaurant, and for twenty of those, she held six stars for her two restaurants, where General de Gaulle and Marlene Dietrich were fans. Until Alain Ducasse surpassed her, she was the most decorated chef in the world. As mentioned, Paul Bocuse started his exalted career in her extraordinary kitchen.

Mme Brazier's most famous creation was *gratinée Lyonnaise*, cheese-topped French onion soup. Her signature dish, quenelles, are still a popular Lyon tradition, called *mousseline de brochet* served with lobster meat and an absinthe-touched sauce. (To make quenelles, flaked white fish, often pike, is creamed, usually bound with an egg and some breadcrumbs, formed to resemble an egg-shaped ball, and poached.) In 2008, Restaurant Mère Brazier was purchased by Meilleur Ouvrier de France Mathieu Viannay, who received the first of his two Michelin stars in 2004 and still had two stars in 2023.

La Mère Bourgeois, aka Marie Bourgeois, ran a restaurant north of Lyon where she held three Michelin stars until she died in 1937. She created the most typical bouchon item: *pâté chaud en croute* (a loaf of ground meats, including duck liver, wrapped in a crust).

I tasted Paul Bocuse's rendition of *pâté en croute* at our *pique-nique* in 2004. An authentic version is on the menu at Alain Ducasse's restaurant Aux Lyonnais in Paris. On my last day in Paris, in May 2024, I rushed past la Mère Brazier Epicerie Comptoir on rue Boissy d'Anglais, near the Madeleine, and I hope to taste it there when I next return. (In Manhattan, it's always available at Bar Boulud, which is owned by Lyon-born Michelin-star chef Daniel Boulud.)

Other fabulous Mères Lyonnaises included Mère Guy, Mère Poupon, Mère Léa, and La Grande Marcelle and Mère Blanc, who founded the Blanc legacy and whose grandson is three-Michelin-star chef Georges Blanc.

Vonnas

Back to our 2001 post-riverboat cruise. Even after a culinary triumph chez Bocuse, Bob and I were ever eager to experience the next great chef's talents. We awoke in Lyon the following morning, picked up a rental vehicle, and set out on a culinary car trip through the countryside and back to Dijon. Truth be told, we spent more time à table than in the automobile. It was my kind of road trip!

Our first stop was in Vonnas, just forty miles from Lyon and, in those days, very much in the countryside. I was enthusiastic about a gastronomic meal at the three-Michelin-starred Restaurant Georges Blanc. Fortuitously, I was on assignment for an article to be illustrated by Bob Lew Photography, and we were both as excited by the prospect of that "work" opportunity as for the subsequent dinner and overnight at Georges Blanc Parc & Spa, a Relais & Châteaux affiliate.

We arrived hours early. Wandering around the flower-bedecked village of Vonnas, an enchanting storybook-style community, reminded me of Williamsburg, Virginia, the "town-museum" where

John D. Rockefeller Jr. established the Colonial Williamsburg Foundation and restored the eighteenth-century appeal of the second colonial capital. The Rockefellers kept a home there, they provided jobs and generated a tourist economy, but never lived or worked there.

Au contraire, Blanc family chefs date to 1872, and their first inn opened in Vonnas in the late nineteenth century. The first Blanc couple's son, Adolph, and his wife, Elisa Gervais Blanc, took over the inn in 1902 and renamed it La Mère Blanc. As one of the famous Mères Lyonnaises, she won her first Michelin star in 1929 and her second in 1931, and was identified as "nothing less than the finest cook in the world." Her son Jean married Paulette, who took over in 1934, establishing a specialité that is still on the menu: *cuisses de grenouilles* (frog's legs in rich butter and garlic sauce). Their son, Georges, was born in 1943.

GEORGES BLANC

He was top of his class at École Hotelière in Thonon-les-Bains in 1962. He worked with top chefs before starting in his mom's kitchen, where he became head of the house by age twenty-five. This fourth-generation Blanc family chef/innkeeper earned his prestigious reputation as a finalist in the Meilleur Ouvrier de France, 1976; as an affiliate with Relais & Châteaux, also in the 1970s; as Gault et Millau "Cook of the Year"; and as a three-Michelin-star chef in 1981 and as one of Les Grandes Tables du Monde. Blanc is so much more than simply a "Chef Patron" that it didn't surprise me to read that he's called the "King of Vonnas."

Having lived and worked in Vonnas for generations, the Blancs established their gastronomic reputation, invested in their community, and accumulated their real estate, enterprise by enterprise. I once read that Georges Blanc bought every building facing Place du

Marché, ". . . so that no ill-suited, multinational chain store could spoil the charm of the square."

As we meandered that early afternoon, we had plenty of time to browse through the town, which, even then, felt like a mini-empire: two hotels, a bakery, gourmet store, and eateries for various budgets, including the restaurant L'Ancienne Auberge, which replicates the 1900-era Blanc-family restaurant. I recall appealing items for sale in the gift shop and many with a distinctive chicken motif—there were chickens everywhere.

Until that day, I didn't realize that Vonnas is a chicken collector's mecca because of George Blanc's relationship to the "best-in-the-world" white chickens with red combs and blue feet that are raised nearby in the small village of Bresse. For decades, Georges Blanc served as chairman of the local poultry trade organization, the Bresse Poultry Interprofessional Committee, and is credited with establishing the prestigious *appellation d'origine controlee* (AOC) for *poulet de Bresse* or *volaille de Bresse*. The status assures Protected Designation of Origin under EU and UK law, and requires that the special birds eat only regional maize corn, spend most of the day outdoors, be protected at night, and be served with the distinctive square AOC clip attached to the blue foot.

When we arrived at Restaurant Georges Blanc before dinner service, we noticed chicken statues in the low-ceilinged dining room; later, we saw them decorating the china dishes. Madame Blanc greeted us amiably and led us into the kitchen, where each member of the brigade was intensely focused on a task at hand. She introduced Georges and their two sons, Alexandre and Frédéric. I chatted while Bob set up his portable stands, the heavy set of lights and filters, all of which he carried when we traveled in the pre-digital era, and took pictures of the brigade at their stations, of food, the family, and the restaurant.

At the table, chicken dominated the menu, with the signature dish *poulet de Bresse* with morels and a cream sauce. In this preparation, the wonderfully moist chicken breast is served with a very rich foie gras and a champagne- and morel-enhanced cream sauce. I loved it.

Bob ordered the frog's legs and suggested that I dunk fresh bread into the delicious garlicky butter. Here's how an anonymous food writer described them: "Frog's legs, purple basil, celeriac, saffron. Gorgeous moist and succulent frog's leg morsels served in a crispy pastry case with a stunning and very elegant lemon and basil sauce." Dinner was a detail-perfect culinary delight at a grand traditional restaurant in the French countryside.

Today, Village Blanc occupies more than twelve acres in Vonnas, where the Blancs own restaurants, hotels with reception facilities, a spa that won the World Luxury Spa Award, a cinema, a museum, and a multitude of boutiques. Maison Blanc houses a gift boutique, bakery, gourmet shop, and wine *cave* at the gastronomic restaurant with thousands of appellations, appropriate for a family that has collected the best wines for decades. (These days, Georges Blanc grows chardonnay grapes in his own Mâconnais vineyard in the southern part of Burgundy.) And while many chefs operate outposts internationally, Chef Blanc stays close to home: within Village Blanc, in Vonnas, in the nearby region, and in Lyon, where Le Splendid-Chez Nos Mères (at our mothers' homes) serves mid-priced regional dishes that were originally created by les Mères Lyonnaises, whom he salutes in the mural-tradition that is particular to Lyon. The large black-and-white portraits of these female pioneers decorate the wall like frescoes.

chez moi: BRESSE-STYLE CHICKEN

The Georges Blanc tribute to the La Mère Blanc recipe was published online by allmychefs.com. My version is simplified for the stovetop. Cut, season, and sauté in butter, a 4-plus-pound chicken cut into eight pieces (save the breasts for last, so they don't overcook). Add 1 chopped onion, 10 mushrooms, and a chopped garlic clove. Dust with flour and moisten with a cup of white wine, then reduce while scraping the pan. Incorporate crème fraiche, sour cream, or strained plain yogurt, stir, and simmer for 25 to 30 minutes, until the chicken is cooked. Transfer to a plate and top with sauce and chopped parsley.

A Day Trip to Lyon

In April 2013, after musing about a road trip on the Riviera for years, my friend Susann and I visited Paris, spent a few days on a Burgundy barge cruise, and scheduled a train trip, first to Marseille and then to Nice. Susann suggested stopping in Lyon, where she had never visited, and I agreed. Just before the other barge passengers returned to Paris by van, we were dropped off in Dijon for the ninety-minute ride to Lyon, where we checked our luggage at the station and climbed into a waiting taxi. I asked the driver to take us to Vieux Lyon, where we were confident that we'd find a nice bouchon for lunch on one of its ancient cobblestone streets.

From the cab, I spotted the street sign for rue Antoine de Saint-Exupéry and asked the driver to stop. I was a fan of the author, having read and reread *The Little Prince* repeatedly from ninth grade through graduate school. I knew that he was born in Lyon and had recognized his image on a mural there, but I had never seen the statue unveiled in 2000 to celebrate his one-hundredth birthday. There it was. Lyonnais sculptor Christiane Guillaubey depicted the writer seated in his aviator costume with Le Petit Prince standing behind him atop a white marble column. It is special.

From there we walked along the riverside quai to the Grande synagogue de Lyon, the mid-nineteenth-century Byzantine structure facing the Saône River. Alas, it was locked, so we paid our respects outside the building, where in June 1944, just months before Lyon was liberated that September, Nazis had launched hand grenades inside, arresting everyone and sending them to prison camps.

We continued across the Saône on the Passerelle Saint-Georges, a footbridge famous for love-inspired padlocks hanging from its steel wires, passed the Église Saint-Georges de Lyon, admired the Renaissance-era architecture, and continued toward the ancient Cathedral of Saint-Jean (1180–1480). It was an enticing stroll with scenery that juxtaposed ancient with "living memory" and "just-yesterday" history, which is one of the reasons I keep traveling.

RESTAURANT DANIEL ET DENISE

It was well past 1:00 p.m. and we were hungry when we spotted Daniel et Denise. The stone façade looked appealing, with arched windows half-covered with lacy white curtains, and by that hour early diners had already left and we were welcomed to a table. The host led us to a cheery farmhouse-chic dining room, where the large horizontal mirror hung below a narrow shelf lined with white pottery and reflected light from the window. The décor, with straight-back wooden chairs at tables topped with red-and-white-checked tablecloths, felt brighter than the dark Grandma's-kitchen-type bouchons that I remembered.

Two aspects of the menu interested me: an entire page dedicated to a list of the artisanal producers and a section labeled OFFAL, noting the bits and pieces of the animal—from shoulder to hoof, nose to brow, kidney to liver, and tripe to brains—that are left after the affluent buy more tender cuts. These ingredients are deftly prepared to provide wholesome, hearty, and low-cost meals for locals in the bouchon tradition. I have no idea what they taste like because, as the French say, "*Ce ne sont pas mes goûts gustatifs*" (it's not my culinary choice).

We sipped a local Côte de Rhône house wine and quelled our appetites with wonderful bread slathered with sweet butter, while wondering what the waiter was delivering when he placed two gratin dishes, a red and a white one, on each table. Ours revealed crisp goose-fat-fried potato rounds and the other, a bubbling cheese-topped pasta, a bouchon-style mac and cheese!

At one point, the waiter was carrying a black cast-iron pan with two sunny-side-up eggs and another dish, which I recognized by its shape: the Lyonnais dish called *quenelle de brochet* à la Lyonnaise. It's a golden mousse-like oval dumpling here prepared with sauce Nantua (a creamy crayfish- or shrimp-flavored béchamel sauce).

The house *specialité* is an award-winning decorated-pastry-crusted *pâté en croute*, prepared by the bouchon's chef, Joseph Viola; in 2009, his terrine was proclaimed the best duck foie gras and sweetbread in the world, and that same year, he won the prestigious title, Meilleur Ouvrier de France (MOF).

The Daniel et Denise menu also offered salade Lyonnaise topped with a poached egg and served with big cuts of bacon lardons, and smoked salmon and salad. But I was in *Bresse* country for the first time in twelve years, so ordered the *volaille de Bresse AOC aux mo-*

rilles, a leg and thigh quarter smothered in a creamy mushroom sauce. Susann had escargots, six snails nested in their special plate and served with a green persillade topping and a pale-green sauce along with the typical snail holder and skinny fork. She also ate "a coarse-grained sausage made with pork, chitterlings, pepper, wine, onions, and seasonings," an emblematic bouchon dish, cooked three different ways: grilled, fried, and gratinated. She loved them.

That day's photos include an image of the cloth napkin monogrammed with the restaurant's logo, Daniel et Denise, in a distinctive font and in red; the two carbo-rich side dishes; and our desserts, my *île flottante,* a ball of meringue floating on a sea of *crème anglaise,* and Susann's house-made tarte tatin, with thinly sliced glazed apple crescents neatly swirled atop a puff pastry round.

It felt serendipitous to have stumbled upon this most wonderful little bouchon, with its traditional farm-to-table fare and professional, caring waitstaff. Along with a listing among the top-ten bouchons in Lyon, there's a mention of a fixed price *formule* lunch and a Michelin 2021 recommendation, The Michelin Plate, which designates a restaurant with quality cooking.

Looking back at other images from that day, I took a picture of a stand advertising crêpes at 2 or 2.5 euros each and of two adorable little girls. They were happily licking their cones in front of a tiny ice cream shop with a sign boasting *fruits de nos regions* (local fruits) labeled *bio,* including a violet-infused fig sorbet. I also photographed two men on stilts—one dressed in white, the other in black—walking precariously on the ancient, narrow cobblestones.

After an ideal six-hour stopover, we boarded a 6:00 p.m. TGV from Lyon for the two-and-a-half-hour trip to Marseille. (From Paris, the TGV takes only two hours each way.) I may not get back to Lyon, but if I ever return, I would try to do the following:

- Stay in the old Saint Jean neighborhood, preferably at the sixteenth-century La Tour Rose, with its ochre-colored staircase tower.
- Begin a visit to the *Longue Traboule* from behind the green door at 54 rue Saint Jean.
- Visit the Halles de Lyon Paul Bocuse food market and restaurant complex near the gare.
- Explore the foodie exhibits at the 43,000-square-foot Cité Internationale de la Gastronomie, within the twelfth-century Hotel-Dieu, a former hospital.

Think of me there, won't you?

mes bonnes idées

———◆•◆———

THE FOLLOWING SUGGESTIONS ARE "IDEAS THAT work" for me when I'm traveling and that I want to share. Often, "stuff" happens when we are away from home, but sometimes we can avoid stressful, inconvenient, or unnecessarily expensive fixes. These tips save me aggravation or money and enhance the overall experience.

Pack Smart

As a "professional" traveler, I typically leave home with a carry-on wheelie bag topped with an atttached, expandable tote with my purse, laptop, medications, and whatever I need for the plane. I roll most items—mainly lightweight—inside packing cubes, including UNIQLO long-sleeve undershirts to layer under a non-bulky sweater. My basic policy is to be comfortable but elegant enough for a nice restaurant: a soft outfit for travel, black pants and dark jeans, cashmere and silky tops, and scarves for color. I try to remember a bathing suit (so many French hotels have indoor pools) and pack a bathrobe and slippers, unless I'm certain that hotels provide these. That said, twice I over shopped on the Riviera to the extent of having to purchase a second bag for the trip home. In 2019, I unpacked each item into like piles and started counting: ten purses, ten pairs of shoes, and way too many tops, pants, scarves, and gifts. Ridiculous. I promised myself, never again!

Language

Greet everyone. In France, people who staff businesses, ateliers, boutiques, restaurants, and even market stalls consider their personal workplace as an extension of their home, where gracious guests are welcomed—rude ones, not so much. Someone who asks, "Where is this?" or "How much is that?" without a preliminary and polite "Bonjour, Madame" may be either ignored or admonished with a chilling rebuke: "Bonjour, Madame." Likewise, it is essential to thank and say goodbye before leaving: "Merci, Madame (or Monsieur)" and "Au revoir, Madame (or Monsieur)."

Here's the short list of "must-say" words and my suggested spelling for the best pronunciation. The nasal "n" is difficult, so ignore it; I use an "h"; for example: on=OH, ion=EEOH; en/an=AH; in=EH.

If you can master the following expressions, with a friendly smile, that's great. Don't fret correct pronunciation because it's courtesy that counts. To hear the correct pronunciation, go to translate. google.com, click the sound icon, listen, and repeat.

10 ESSENTIAL FRENCH WORDS AND PHRASES

Madame (Mme)	mah dahm	madam
Monsieur (M)	muhsyuh	sir
Mademoiselle (Mlle)	mahdmwahzel	miss, young woman
Bonjour	bohjzour	hello
Bonsoir	bohswah	good evening, after 5:00 p.m.
Au Revoir	oh rvwah	say this when leaving
S'il vous plait (svp)	sea voo pleh	please
l'Addition, svp	ladissioh, sea voo pleh	the check, please
Merci	mare sea	thank you
Je voudrais	je voodreh	I would like

Hotels

USE THE *MICHELIN GUIDE*

With my first 1976 *Michelin Guide* (guide.michelin.com) in hand, I studied their rating system: hotels by pointed-roof symbols (five peaks are best); restaurants by crossed forks and spoons plus stars (three maximum). Red print designates a special ambiance, décor, character, or scenery. A little Michelin-man head signifies Bib Gourmand, the "value for money" award. The newer, green stars award sustainability. That 1976 guide is long gone, but my much-used, yellow-highlighted 2004 copy, with entries circled, underlined, checked, and dated—from trips in 2004, 2006, and 2008, after I was widowed—is a veritable souvenir.

LOOK FOR A SAFE HOTEL LOCATION

Paris is a relatively safe city, but crime exists, as it does everywhere. Security is my priority, as it should be for all, especially for vulnerable, older females who are targets. Although security is best at well-located luxury hotels that have cameras and are well-staffed at the front door, on my budget, I have to book at the closest less costly option, where I can still take advantage of the luxe hotel's lobby, bar, and valet.

Here's what I do:

- Search online before choosing flights, if you can be flexible, and avoid dates of major conventions, holidays, or events when prices skyrocket.
- Input: "Top-Ten Luxury Hotels" and check their addresses to find the best neighborhoods/arrondissements. (The last two digits identify the arrondissement; note: Booking.com lists addresses.)

- Search the map for these five-star hotels and write down names of neighboring hotels.
- Check rates, reviews, and distance for each of the two-, three-, or four-star hotels nearby.

RESERVE ROOMS DIRECTLY WITH HOTELS

While major third-party sites are an excellent research tool, and useful if they have a last-day cancellation policy, there's a caveat. My travel agent colleagues have persuaded me that hotels set aside only the worst rooms for those clients, because they must pay them a huge commission. Under normal situations—and providing there's a decent cancellation policy—they recommend booking directly with the hotel and asking for email proof of confirmation and cancellation policies. I still call by phone, because I think the small expense is worth finding out how random staff members respond in English, especially when I make a specific request. I might ask about a room with French doors or if the windows open; if it's an older hotel, I might ask for the newest refurbished room. Sometimes I request a location away from the (noisy) elevator, and I often ask how much more a room with a balcony costs.

CHOOSE AN AIRBNB/VRBO CAREFULLY

These were my three lists for my first rental: Must-Haves, Wanna-Haves, and No-Nos. Your wanna-haves may differ, but consider them carefully before booking:

- Must-Haves: a safe, convenient location; an easy walk to nearby food shops and cafés; two master bedrooms (second bedrooms often offer twins, futons, pull-out couches, bunk beds); a terrace (for claustrophobia); and an elevator (for bad knees).

- WANNA-HAVES: a view; two bathrooms (who doesn't prefer a private bathroom?); in-building parking (which I no longer require, since I don't rent cars anymore).

- No-Nos: *No* steep hillsides, since they hurt my knees; *no* cobblestones, which get slippery, and I've already broken an ankle, an elbow, two wrists, and a shoulder; *no* circular staircases or lofts, especially if the bathroom is on another level.

CALL TO CONFIRM

Calling to confirm will spare you what I experienced on my first Riviera trip—a bidet almost touching the bed—when I didn't call and arrived at dinnertime. "My" room had been given away and I was assigned the only one available. I didn't know enough then to request a nicer room the next day or as soon as one became available, which I do now. Hospitality businesses depend upon confirmations; many require a credit card deposit in advance and charge for no-shows or a cancellations that didn't follow the rules. Once, when I forgot to cancel my third-party booking on time, I had no recourse when I was charged for the entire stay, although the hotel would have charged for two nights. Confirm diligently: record the name of the person you speak to, and the time, date, and confirmation or cancellation numbers.

SPEND THE LAST NIGHT AT THE AIRPORT

Because I get anxious waiting for a taxi to the airport and sitting in traffic en route, I circumvent that stress by spending my last night at an airport hotel. In Paris, I head to Sheraton Paris CDG Airport Hotel (usually after dinner when there's little traffic), where the lobby door opens directly into Terminal 2 and the gate. (In Nice, I'm happy at the Radisson Nice Airport Hotel.)

Restaurants

ORDER A CARAFE OF WATER

Ask for "Un carafe d'eau, s'il vous plaît." That tip, from *Paupers' Paris* by Miles Turner (1976, rev. 1988), has been well worth the book purchase. Bottled water is an unnecessary expense because potable tap water is available everywhere in a carafe, for no charge. I hydrate with water when I stop to people watch and rest between meals, since I can no longer drink coffee all day. As soon as I'm seated, I put a two euro coin on the table before ordering only water and hope the *serveur/serveuse* will feel appreciated.

FINE-DINE AT LUNCH

Typically, lunch costs much less than dinner, and even top restaurants have well priced "business" lunches. Most French restaurants, including luxe Michelin-starred ones, offer attractive fixed price options, which are *bon marché* (a good value), but only if you like one of the choices. (I study the menu online in advance.) One reason the final cost is reduced is the charge for alcohol, because most guests drink less alcohol at midday. For wine drinkers, a carafe or a bottle is the economical choice *if* you plan to consume more than one glass of the same selection.

CONSIDER CHALKBOARD MENUS

The handwritten menus are almost always guaranteed to be freshly prepared. And *le menu du jour*, or *formule*, is a special menu at a fixed price. It's usually a bargain compared to *à la carte*, if you like the dishes—the *entrée* or *plat*—offered.

DINE ALONE STRATEGICALLY

I enjoy traveling alone, except at dinner, when I'd rather chat with someone than read or look at the phone. (I tried a "silent" dinner at a spa once and hated every long minute.)

These techniques comfort me when I dine alone:

- Choose a restaurant where the waiter may give exceptionally good service. If you can, splurge on a gastronomic meal where there are multiple opportunities to interact with the maitre d' and servers, runners, and the waitstaff who bring fresh cutlery for each course.
- Eat at a counter, bar, museum, or food court, where it's easy to converse with strangers.
- Treat a nice, newly met stranger or staff member to a drink, snack, or dinner.
- Invite another solo guest waiting for a table to join you: "If you prefer company at dinner, we could eat together and pay separately."

TIP KNOWINGLY

Service inclus or *service compris* means the tip is included, which is typical. (If it doesn't say, ask.) After the inclusion, many guests also add an extra 10 percent. Note that the VAT (Value Added Tax) must be clearly stated and that the fee has nothing whatsoever to do with a tip.

Getting Around and Sightseeing

CAR RENTALS

- Decide what you need: automatic transmission; air-conditioning; four doors; big trunk; GPS; insurance.
- Choose a rental car that's similar to what you drive, if possible. (Certainly, selecting a car based upon the lowest price backfired on my first solo road trip.)
- Ask for help finding what you need (windshield wipers, defroster, gas panel opener) before leaving the agency lot.
- Check credit card car insurance benefits that may apply in France.
- Confirm the car prior to arrival, even (especially) if a travel agent booked it; if an agent is reachable, he/she might be helpful. It's happened.

TAKE THE HIGH-SPEED TRAIN

In France, dedicated high-speed trains, TGV or *Trains à Grande Vitesse,* reach regional cities faster than getting there by car, and rental car agencies are always at the destination *gare.* Tickets (I use raileurope.com) are for reserved seats and are best made well in advance. At the *gare,* there's good signage and tracks are posted at least 10 minutes in advance. Sometimes, it's a long walk to the numbered railroad cars and, regrettably, there are no porters or carts, and sometimes the elevator or escalator is out of order. Be advised, the complimentary Assist'enGare handicap assistants must be reserved 24 hours in advance.

PRE-PLAN MUSEUM VISITS

- Buy museum passes online to avoid waiting on a queue.
- Schedule your arrival for the opening to avoid busloads of students or tourists. Or arrive ninety minutes before closure (some museums restrict entry during the last hour).
- Plan a sixty-to-seventy-minute visit unless you are with a museum lover, says the teacher who for decades escorted thirty students at a time to New York art museums. (Kids who remember boredom from too many hours in one museum sometimes shun them for life.)
- If you're traveling with others, plan to meet up at a certain time, at a place where it's comfortable to wait, such as the café.

CONSIDER SECURITY PROTOCOLS

Unlike most churches, where an open-door policy prevails, security threats require advance appointments and passport proof of identification to enter synagogues and other religious sites.

CRUISE THE SEINE

Travelers going through multiple time zones usually develop favorite ways to deal with jet lag. When I arrive tired after an overnight flight, I choose an easy, less active day and may ride the hop-on, hop-off bus (I only get off once and taxi back to my hotel). Lately, I've loved post-flight massages, either before lunch, while waiting for a room, or at five o'clock, before dinner.

In Paris, my usual and recommended first-day sightseeing is on a boat cruise on the Seine, which I find a comfortable, convenient way to see many iconic monuments in about an hour. In fact, my

British cousins who took the Eurostar to see me for the day in November joined us for a boat cruise. Then, we walked across the street to lunch at Les Ombres Quai Branly facing the Eiffel Tower. Choices range from large sightseeing boats—*Bateaux Mouches, Bateaux Parisiens,* and *Vedettes de Paris*—to private yacht tours.

Save the Batobus, the hop-on, hop-off tour boat, for a day when you want to visit multiple places—the Louvre, L'Orangerie, Place de la Concorde, Musée d'Orsay, and the Jardin des Plantes.

Postpone the extravagant dinner cruises for when you will be refreshed.

REDUCE TRAVEL STRESS

I noticed while writing these vignettes how often travel stress created personal challenges. My problem is losing things, and I've lost my share: two meaningful rings; two gold chains left in the pockets of spa bathrobes; car keys (room keys are easy, they replace those); a computer; my passport—and, as described, even that rental car! Others react in their own style.

These ideas work for me:

- My first day advice: try to stay awake until bedtime. Experts taught me that it's the best way to stay in circadian rhythm.
- Avoid parking and traffic stress by choosing trains and taxis, when possible, and using fewer car rentals.
- Make photocopies of passport, Global Entry, and credit cards and carry one copy, store one at your hotel, and leave one at home.
- Hand a written destination address or business card to drivers.

- Keep yout hotel business card handy.
- Keep small bills and change handy and separate from big money.
- Store all valuables in the room safe, including passport, jewelry, and money.
- Don't carry a room key with an identifying room number.

PHOTOGRAPH BUSINESS CARDS

Today, practically everyone takes screen shots of tickets, barcodes, VIP information. Back in the day, people collected matchboxes with place names and business cards. I still do and save them. Once home from a trip, I assemble them on a page, date/place name them, and save the pages in an album organized by year. Before a trip, I photocopy what I need to take with me to remind me of places I'd like to return and because asking for a person by name is an entrée, even after the person named is no longer there.

TAXI, TOUR, OR GUIDE

Decide when and whether a guided tour is necessary, warranted, and preferred. Even if you are on a package tour, if you add on personal days to sightsee, you must decide if you want an organized tour, a private guide, or a taxi to take you around. It's a personal decision.

Guides enrich travel experiences with their personalities and because they articulate specialized information, hopefully in a language that's easily understood. On the other hand, I've often heard too much information, "hasta los ojos" (up to my eyeballs). When I know where I want to go—or what I want to see—and am satisfied with visual information, without explanation—I hire a driver for a day or half-day (even in Russia, where I couldn't even read the language). I enjoy reading about places in advance more than standing to listen to endless information at someone else's pace. I prefer a personalized, relaxed, and efficient use of my time, and sometimes it costs less. A caveat: When traveling alone, spending a few hours with a guide or a tour group can be most welcome.

CHECK OUT CURRENT REVIEWS

Restaurants close, great chefs move on or pass away, spas change brands, hotels need to be refurbished. The glowing experience I had may no longer be as glorious. So, it's always a *bonne idee* to check the most current and reliable reviews.

un dernier mot
(a final word)

Spring 2025

When I started writing *Forays in France* during the pandemic, I hoped that my little collection of anecdotes would give readers some pleasure, add some intriguing tidbits of information to their memory banks, and inspire them to travel, especially to France.

At the time, travel was out of the question, and while I wondered if I'd ever be able to travel again, I was optimistic for younger generations. Truth is, we are each just an accident—or a medical test—away from being unfit for travel at any age.

Each trip has been a gift for which I have felt grateful—before, during, and ever since. Years ago, when I traveled monthly or more, acquaintances asked: "Why do you travel so often?"

I answered: "Because I can. My window is open."

In November 2024, when a "Winter Courses at the Sorbonne" email arrived, I took my own advice, seized the opportunity, and registered. Who says you can't go back? Having just returned home after a joyful week and five challenging three-hour sessions in French literature, in a room just footsteps from where my first French classes took place six decades ago, I feel content. How better to complete the circle of forays—and this memoir—than to have returned to the same (now more gentrified) neighborhood? What's more, I attended a marvelous first organ concert in the exquisite, newly restored Nôtre-Dame de Paris.

To be sure, the love affair with France that began at the Sorbonne in 1958 continues.

And I was able to return to Cannes for three weeks in spring 2025.

Quelle chance!

At age eighty-six, the window could close at any moment. Who knows how many more opportunities there will be? So I'm planning to celebrate each future adventure as if it were the last, because it might be.

I am optimistic that you will do the same, at any age.

Bon voyage!
Irvina

Acknowledgments

A heartfelt thanks to all those who inspired, encouraged, and advised this passion project, especially these four favorites, who are alive in my memory.

Bob Lew, the center of my universe for fifty years, who encouraged me to follow my dreams.

Julie Franchi, my high school French teacher, who initiated my love of all things French.

Louise Smith, my art-loving Francophile friend, who inspired my art-centric visits to France.

Bernard Burt, my spa colleague and travel buddy, who shared his contacts and affection.

My wholehearted gratitude to my three daughters, whose incomparable one-on-one company in Juan-les-Pins gave me the best weeks of my life. They each helped me realize this book.

Alison Bloomer designed the book, and advised me about publishing.

Sharon Lew gifted me with StoryWorth, which motivated me to write about my life.

Jen Lew created and maintains my websites and has long encouraged me to write personally about my travels.

Genuine acknowledgments to countless colleagues from every facet of the hospitality industry who generously facilitated my encounters in La Belle France, especially Marion Fourestier at Atout France.

Immeasurable thanks to the long list of chefs, concierges, drivers, guides, hosts, hoteliers, servers, spa therapists, and vintners who enriched each visit and enhanced my life.

Merci mille fois to all the extraordinary folks who "star" in the vignettes, including my cherished travel companions, whose unique interests and insights expanded my own discoveries. And heartfelt appreciation to the many editors who were willing to publish my observations for the past forty years.

I am grateful for the individual efforts of two colleagues who are skilled copy editors, Faye Wolf and Judy Colbert, and the invaluable work of my dedicated editor, Tricia Levi, who edited, organized, and improved the final manuscript.

Mistakes, omissions, repetitions, and spelling inconsistencies are all mine.

About the Author

IRVINA LEW is an author and a freelance food, spa, and travel writer, who taught French for more than thirty years. A five-year stint writing about restaurants and spas for *New York Nightlife*—plus book and media tours to thirty cities—motivated her transition from teacher to full-time writer. Irvina has won awards from the Society of American Travel Writers and Society of Professional Journalists: Press Club of Long Island. The Francophile is a musical theater fan who loves to garden and serve gougères, rotisserie chicken, and stuffed zucchini blossoms at her Long Island home.

www.ingramcontent.com/pod-product-compliance
Lightning Source LLC
Chambersburg PA
CBHW021703120626
46545CB00004B/1381